Nice Job!

The Guide to Cool, Odd, Risky, and Gruesome Ways to Make a Living

By Lookout Media: Jake Brooks, Nicholas Corman, Chuck Kapelke, Jamie Rosen, Sara Smith, and Michelle Sullivan

Ten Speed Press
Berkeley, California

A Kirsty Melville Book

Ten Speed Press
P.O. Box 7123
Berkeley, California 94707
www.tenspeed.com

Distributed in Australia by Simon and Schuster Australia, in Canada by Ten Speed Press Canada, in New Zealand by Southern Publishing Group, in South Africa by Real Books, in Southeast Asia by Berkeley Books, and in the United Kingdom and Europe by Airlift Books.

Design by Catherine Jacobes

Library of Congress Cataloging-in-Publication Data
Rosen, Jamie.
Nice job! : the guide to cool, odd, risky, and gruesome ways to make a living / by Jamie Rosen.
p. cm.
ISBN 1-58008-033-2 (alk.paper)
1. Vocational guidance. 2. Occupations. I. Title.
HF581.R7615 1999 98-56096
331.7'02--dc21 CIP

First printing, 1999
Printed in Canada

1 2 3 4 5 6 7 8 9 10 — 02 01 00 99

If I had only known,
I would have been a locksmith.

—Albert Einstein

I don't want to achieve immortality through my work;
I want to achieve immortality through not dying.

—Woody Allen

No labor, however humble, is dishonoring.

— The Talmud

Contents

ACKNOWLEDGMENTS

MORE THAN TWENTY VERY TALENTED PEOPLE contributed the research and writing that makes Nice Job! more than just a blank diary suitable for jotting down recipes, doodles, and telephone messages. We gratefully acknowledge the efforts of J.P. Anderson, Elizabeth Angell, Alec Appelbaum, Gillian Ashley, Frank Beidler, Lusan Chua, Adam Day, Noah Dauber, Sean Fitzpatrick, Matt Haber, Billy Hulkower, Amelia Kaplan, Andrew Nieland, Doug Rand, Chip Rossetti, Elizabeth Russo, Leeore Schnairsohn, Evan Sicuranza, Kathy Squires, and Lindsey Turrentine. Many of these writers worked together previously at Let's Go Travel Guides while at Harvard University. Take note of their names: Listed above are some of America's best and brightest young writers.

We'd like to especially thank Vanessa Rosen, the book's first intrepid researcher. She stalked beekeepers, perfumers, and hand models, located sperm banks, and hunted down art forgers with aplomb. Without her tireless work at the outset, the book would never have materialized.

Our agent, Alan Kellock, also helped kickstart the book. He jumped on board with alacrity and never lost enthusiasm throughout the two years it took us to get from the concept to the final product. He gave us sound advice, creative suggestions, and kind encouragement throughout the process.

Our editor, Aaron Wehner, overcame the confusion of dealing with multiple authors and went above and beyond the call of duty to whip the manuscript into shape in record time. He proved eminently competent, creative, and a pleasure to work with. We are also grateful to Aaron's colleagues at Ten Speed Press, especially Kirsty Melville, whose vision was absolutely vital.

We would also like to acknowledge a long list of accomplices who helped in one way or another. Stephanie Buchanan scavenged photos, saving the book at the last minute from being one big block of dense text. Catherine Jacobes would

never have let that happen, however. An immensely talented designer, Catherine is responsible for the witty illustrations and superb design and layout. Claire Ellis shouted our name from atop the tallest buildings in Manhattan to get the word out. We also appreciate the inspiration and support of Anne Chisolm, Judy and Avery Corman, Bill Crowley, Wade Fox, Sofie Forsgren, Gerald Gamm, Pat George, Chris Harden, Andrew Kaplan, Sarah MacArthur, D.W. Maze, Laurent Ruseckas, David Stires, and the whole gang at Comet Systems.

We would also like to thank the people whose intangible contributions made the project fun. Norman and Estelle Rosen opened up their home, their refrigerator, and their liquor cabinet for two weekend retreats which thankfully involved no more than one person needing to be bailed out of jail. Judy and Leon Rothenberg provided their dining room table for our editorial meetings.

Finally, we'd like to thank the people with wonderful stories and fascinating jobs who graciously took the time to talk to us. This book is dedicated to their indomitable creative spirit.

Jake Brooks
Nick Corman
Chuck Kapelke
Jamie Rosen
Sara Smith
Michelle Sullivan

PREFACE

No matter how big or soft or warm your bed is, you still have to get out of it.

—GRACE SLICK

WORK, FOR MOST ADULTS, IS A FACT OF LIFE. It's a four-letter word, a necessary evil, something you do to eat, obtain shelter, and meet your car payments. "Work," as Oscar Wilde wrote, "is the refuge of people who have nothing better to do."

A hundred and fifty years ago, in his *Communist Manifesto*, Karl Marx foretold a grim capitalist society where the exploited masses toiled at demeaning jobs as appendages to an inhumane, profit-motivated system. He predicted the marginalization of artisans and craftspeople who plied their trades in the tradition of their parents and their parents' parents. A few decades later, Frederick Taylor, the management guru of his time, helped make Marx's fears a reality by championing what he called scientific management. Using time-motion studies to make workers as fast and efficient as machines, he promoted conditions similar to those Charlie Chaplin was subjected to in *Modern Times*, making workplaces harsh and impersonal. According to Taylor, "one of the very first requirements for a man who is fit to handle pig iron as a regular occupation is that he shall be so stupid and so phlegmatic that he more nearly resembles in his mental make-up the ox than any other type."

It is rare today to find jobs where stupidity and brute strength are prized to such an extent, yet elements of Taylorism survive. For millions of white-collar workers, the Information Age has put a new face on Marx's dystopia: Instead of forging iron and steel, they process words and crunch numbers at PC workstations, helping to make Bill Gates one of the richest men in the world. While less physically strenuous than shoveling pig iron, this kind of work can be just as harsh, impersonal, and unsatisfying. As J. P. Getty noted, "Going to work for a large company is like getting on a train. Are you going sixty miles an hour or is the train going sixty miles an hour and you're just sitting still?"

Nice Job! rejected convention and celebrates the creative ways that independent-minded people have carved out alternative occupations for themselves. It is about smokejumpers who parachute into forest fires and holistic veterinarians who perform chiropractic medicine on elephants; it is about cryonicists who freeze dead people in the belief that doctors of the future will be able to thaw them out and revive them; it is about blimp pilots who glide slowly above the fray, smiling down as people wave up at them wishing that they, too, were floating serenely in the gondola of a blimp.

It is about having fun at work.

We hope you find their stories as inspiring as we do.

* * *

This book arose from a simple, annoying question: "So what are you going to do when you graduate?" It's a question that college seniors hear ad nauseam. One senior's response was to reset his stopwatch and tell the person how long it had been since the last time he was asked the same thing. *Nice Job!*, written by a team of recent college grads, was originally intended as a humorous response to this god-awful question, providing silly, bizarre, interesting—and thoroughly researched—answers for your busybody uncle or neighbor who asks too many questions.

In the course of working on the humor book, we realized that so-called career guidance books on the market today are depressingly vapid. These stale books repackage the same earnest and mind-numbingly banal advice: Don't forget to wear socks to your interview, be sure to show up on time for your first day of work, get a high-tech degree, etc. In our opinion, job-seekers don't need more information on which sectors of the economy will be booming in the twenty-first century or how to study to become a CPA at night or any other such "practical" career advice. We heard the forlorn career shelf crying out for some original thinking.

And so a few former writers and editors from Let's Go Travel Guides got together to write a new kind of career guidebook, one that was fun and useful. We then recruited friends and colleagues to contribute ideas and profiles to this book.

Will you use this book to become an executioner? A sports mascot? A rodeo clown? Probably not. Our mission in writing this book is not to lead you to jobs, but to broaden your perspective, to help you start thinking outside the box, and to inject some creativity and nonconformist thinking into the process of choosing a career path. At the same time, we have undertaken painstaking research to

make it 100 percent possible for you to become, say, a bounty hunter, if that catches your fancy.

The people we've met in the course of our research are, by and large, unusually happy with their off-beat occupations. Most stumbled across their jobs serendipitously, but this book is proof that you don't have to. With the right mindset and some diligence, it is possible to forge an unorthodox career. If you put your mind to it, you, too, can end up delivering $10 million Superprizes with the Publishers Clearing House Prize Patrol, get paid to track down Bigfoot, or make a fortune as a voice-over actor for television commercials. Open your eyes to all the strange and wonderful jobs out there and it will change your perspective permanently. When Dave Raymond went from being an office assistant for the Philadelphia Phillies to the team's mascot, the legendary Phillie Phanatic, he never looked back. "It was like a gift from heaven," he said. "Here I am, just a regular guy working at a job. Then all of a sudden, I'm a mascot. I am the luckiest guy alive."

* * *

We have heard a saying that if you find a job you love, you'll never have to work a day in your life. The authors of this book have been looking far and wide for that magical job. Writing a book about wacky jobs is about the closest any one of us has come so far.

Alec Appelbaum became fascinated with careers on a walk through an experimental sheep herding farm in Old Chatham, New York, during his first year as a reporter. In the intervening years, he has negotiated cake size and shellfish selection as a fund-raiser at an Atlanta nonprofit, lobbied to remove culturally demeaning icons from a sweepstakes promotion for a famous all-news Web site, and interviewed a rebellious Border Patrol agent for a business school project. Appelbaum, a journalist and writer, lives in Manhattan.

Jake Brooks has worked as a bicycle repairman, chef's assistant, travel writer and editor, and CEO of a small publishing company. He once tried desperately to teach multivariable calculus to a population of bored college freshman. He now works at *Outside* magazine—but dreams of giving it all up to be a bicycle courier. Or maybe a mystery shopper. Whatever, as long as he doesn't have to go to law school.

Nicholas Corman grew up, and still resides, in New York City. He has worked in the prominent journalistic capacity of fact checker for a local newspaper, where he

was instructed to ensure that no less than 70 percent of all printed assertions were "basically right"; he has scrubbed dishes in rural Vermont, trekked through Mississippi and Texas conducting research for a travel guide, and filled space as a dashing movie extra. He is currently employed by an Internet start-up company in Silicon Alley.

Sean Fitzpatrick has delivered flowers to Richard Nixon, sold Ferragamos to Imelda Marcos, and faxed scripts to Jim Carrey. He has also been paid to perform interpretive dance, bike across Ireland, ride the subway, and pick vegetables on a New Jersey farm. He currently advises foreign countries how to attract more American tourists.

Billy Hulkower drives an aged cherry red convertible up and down San Vicente Boulevard in Los Angeles. The diagonal direction of the street confuses most Angelenos, and pleases Billy. The street is also near his house, which makes driving it convenient. Mr. Hulkower, presently unemployed, will gratefully accept any job that doesn't require him to leave his apartment. Previous employment has included freelance transcription, tax preparation, ghostwriting, temping, painting, sanding and plastering, puppeteering, heavy metals speculation, sperm donation, second unit film directing, and a brief dismal stint as a local-access televangelist.

Chuck Kapelke has washed clothes with his feet in a Mother Theresa clinic in Calcutta, toiled in the brazier pit of a Dairy Queen in Denver, won lots of stuff on the radio, schlepped pizza, delivered flowers, shelved books in a library, and worked as a travel guide researcher in Central America and India. He currently writes the "Calendar of Events" for *Boston Magazine*.

Andrew Nieland—the less said, the better. A longtime gadabout, mountebank, and effete ne'er-do-well, he's currently employed as a copywriter and enjoys working indoors.

Jamie Rosen has hatched his share of harebrained schemes. As a teenager, he and his sister, Vanessa, teamed up to win radio contests after school. In college, he had a business that briefly involved forwarding an 800-number into his dorm room, making for some confused conversations when his roommates answered the phone. He bankrolled a friend to compete—and win—on *Jeopardy!* He wrote a semi-bogus restaurant guide to get free meals. One day, he and his cousin Steve flew back and forth between New York and Boston on the Pan Am Shuttle nine times in order to get frequent flier miles. He dropped out of business school to

start Comet Systems, where he proudly makes the world's best cursor-customizing software.

Sara Smith spent four of the most grueling hours of her life sweating in a Mickey Mouse costume, complete with a fifteen-pound papier mâché headpiece, at a business expo in southern Rhode Island. At that point she decided to leave the state, and has since worked in a box office, narrated *Peter and the Wolf* (in Portuguese) in a small Brazilian community theater, done data entry, and discussed the finer points of costuming for drag shows with Kevin Kline. She works for a small but extremely classy publishing firm in Palo Alto, California.

Michelle Sullivan began her professional life on Florida's sunny Gulf Coast, where she spent summers selling snow-skiing apparel and mountain-climbing equipment. She has since puréed hamburgers in the kitchen of a nursing home, traveled through New England, Canada, and Australia as a travel writer, and provided intricate background noise as a theatrical sound technician. She currently writes and edits for an online career exploration service based in Boston.

If this book hits its mark and you follow its advice, we'd love to hear about it. Our e-mail address is nicejob@email.com. Please write us with your own wacky job experiences and any suggestions you have for jobs that belong in our next edition.

Jamie Rosen
New York, 1998

1 Call of the Wild

Pet Groomer

Beekeeper

Holistic Veterinarian

Fish Processor and Deckhand

Aquaculturist

Pet Groomer

Job description: Basic grooming includes bathing the animal (usually twice), and performing a massage and lump check for unusual growths, a nail trim, and an ear cleaning. Dematting (thinning out dense clumps of fur) and clipping are also common services. Show dog groomers do the artful canine topiary that has made poodles notorious.

Compensation: Usually a 30 percent to 60 percent commission. Groomings cost about $20 to $50, depending on the provider, the animal, and the sophistication of the grooming. Show dog groomers make a bit more than domestic pet groomers do.

Prerequisites: No special schooling is required. Grooming schools do exist; it's just that they're relatively small and have the unfortunate habit of going out of business. If you're thinking of opening your own pet grooming establishment, it makes sense to have some business training.

Qualities employer is seeking: A love of animals and lots of patience are the most vital credentials. Aspiring pet groomers often apprentice themselves to established ones and volunteer their time until they've gained the necessary skills to go out on their own. And, of course, allergies are a significant, even prohibitive, handicap.

Perks: Free samples of flea shampoo, pet toys, and the like. If you're on the show circuit, there's the extra glamour that comes with competition and exposure to some of the best groomers in the nation. Pet owners who care enough (and have enough money) to bring in Pooch or Kitty for a grooming are generally a big-hearted and laid-back bunch. The biggest perk, notes groomer Steven Longo, is "a clean animal and a happy owner."

"You can do ten, fifteen beagles a day," says groomer Steven Longo, regarding the capabilities of an efficient groomer.

Risks/drawbacks: Cats are, in fact, more dangerous than dogs, because their teeth are smaller and sharper and they have claws (and, boy, can they be temperamental). In fact, while one person can usually handle the most unruly dogs, it often takes two to handle a recalcitrant cat. In terms of disease, no groomer has ever died of heartworm (it's not transmittable to humans), but tapeworm and ringworm are both transmittable through the skin. Groomers generally don't wear gloves, because they need to feel the animal to check for lumps, so the risk of disease is ever-present. In the northeast, deer ticks carry Lyme disease, a potentially life-threatening illness. Due to the stressful nature of the job, there's a high rate of burnout. Most groomers only stay in the field for five or ten years before moving on, often to kennel work.

Overview

The pet industry is a growing one. Supply stores, retail pet shops, dog obedience schools, and kennels are all on the upswing, and pet grooming is riding the wave. Perhaps it's the recent media attention on the positive effects of pets on human health. Studies have shown that pets are good for you. In fact, some life insurance companies now adjust their premiums depending on whether you have a pet.

Pet groomers, however, hold that a good grooming shouldn't be a luxury; it's a necessity, just like it is for people. "There's nothing sadder than seeing a dog in really awful shape," says Longo. "The owner feels terrible, the dog feels terrible." While some owners bring in their pet religiously, once a month, others only arrive on special occasions—a birthday or a visit to the vet.

The overwhelming majority of pet groomers are women. "It's like hairdressing," admits Longo, who weathers the same jibes that men with a human clientele do. Reasons for this remain as mysterious as reasons for the dearth of male hairdressers. Longo points out that, while a man's brute strength would seem to be an advantage in wrestling a St. Bernard into a tub, it seems that most animals respond better to a woman's gentle touch. (Your clients won't care if you're a man or a woman, or even if you screw up and cut too much off the top, when you're a cosmetologist for the dead; for more, see "Funeral Home Cosmetologist," p. 124.)

Practical Information

Look for job openings in the help wanted ads, or just stop by a local groomer or kennel and inquire. The National Dog Groomer's Association has a job helpline. You can also try contacting the National Kennel Operator's Organization.

For those who want formal training, there are pet grooming schools scattered throughout the country. For example, the Arizona Pet Grooming School, in Fredonia, Arizona, encourages you to "change your career while on vacation!" (Several national parks are in the vicinity.) The standard two-month course includes a full overview on washing, trimming, decorating, and teeth and nail cleaning; according to promotional literature from the company, students are given use of "their own 'hands on' pet to groom in a relaxed modern atmosphere." For more information visit their Web site, www.xpressweb.com/dog-grooming-school, or call 520-643-7377.

There is a virtual cottage industry of pet grooming books. Would-be groomers can check out *Guide to Home Pet Grooming* (Barrons Educational Series) for a general primer on the subject. For those who are interested in starting their own grooming company, pick up *From Problems to Profits: The Madson Management System for Pet Grooming Businesses*. The author, Madeline Bright Ogle, of Santa Clara, California, has for twenty-five years owned one of the world's largest pet salons in the world.

Beekeeper

Job description: Though the word conjures images of graying hobbyists or obsessive entomologists, beekeepers are actually an extremely vital part of agriculture—and not just for the honey. The main service that most professional beekeepers provide is pollination. Orchards and other farms require the help of a few hives of bees to get their yield up each year. A beekeeper's job is to develop and look after the hives, cart hives to and from different farms, and harvest the honey that is the byproduct of pollination. Some beekeepers are also moving into apitherapy, which puts bee venom to use in the treatment of arthritis and multiple sclerosis.

Compensation: While there are large bee farms, most beekeepers would actually call themselves hobbyists or small farmers at best. Many of the hobbyists strive to break even (beekeeping equipment, such as new hives or extracting drums for honey production, can get expensive), and the small farmers just aim to support themselves and their families while still doing what they love. Few people get rich keeping bees.

Prerequisites: A beekeeper must desire independence and solitude, must truly love bees and beekeeping (believe it or not, it can be rough work), and of course, must not mind getting stung. "Bees can sense anger," says one beekeeper. "You have to have a mellow soul."

Qualities employer is seeking: Most beekeepers are self-employed. However, they must be independent, driven, business-minded, and totally dedicated to their craft (especially since the rewards are rarely financial). A strong connection to bees, bordering on instinct, is also essential.

Perks: People become beekeepers almost entirely because they love and are fascinated by bees. So, for most beekeepers, the biggest perk is simply being able to do what they love. Other perks include freedom, self-employment, and honey.

Risks/drawbacks: Getting stung. This can, in fact, be life-threatening. A particularly angry or "Africanized" ("killer") hive can swarm around a person, stinging enough times to actually be fatal, even if that person is not allergic. This is, however, extremely rare. Most beekeepers are stung as many as a dozen times a day, with no lasting adverse affects. Beekeeping can also be backbreaking labor (hives full of honey are quite heavy—especially when you're lifting them in something akin to a spacesuit), sometimes with little financial reward.

"The stings never seemed to bother me," says Emery Hall, a beekeeper in Maine. "I've been stung up to twenty times a day. It's no problem."

Overview

Beekeeping may be the oldest form of agriculture, and looking back to the days before refined sugar, one can guess why. Honey is, literally, like nectar, and to a sugar-deprived population, every taste of honey must have been the Mesolithic equivalent of a bowl of Froot Loops—certainly worth battling swarms of angry, stinging bees to reach. (If you feel ready to take on more than a swarm of fuzzy little fliers, consider a career as a mercenary, p. 26.)

Though most of us have grown numb to the now-tame sweetness of honey, beekeeping is still extremely important, and the taste of honey still intrigues refined palates. Connoisseurs of honey can tell the original flower that fed the honey and its quality, as well as the quality of the hive itself; younger hives produce lower-quality honey than do older, more established hives. The boutique honey business is bustling, though still waiting for micobrewery levels of success. Most American beekeepers produce honey for small brands; big-name honey tends to be imported today.

Even more important than honey production is the pollination that bees provide to farmers' crops. Remember the birds and the bees? In their search for nectar, bees pick up the pollen of one flower and drop it off at the next, helping to fertilize the second blossom. Emery Hall tells of a blueberry farmer who didn't use the services of his hives. When a new owner came in and hired Hall's bees, the harvest rose from five or six tons of berries to twenty-two tons. According to one article, one-third of all food consumed requires bees for pollination.

Credit: AP/Arizona Daily Star

"You never get used to being stung," says one beekeeper.

Bees tend to take the winter off, so a beekeeper's busiest season is the summer, when fifteen-hour workdays are not uncommon. The beekeeper checks on the bees regularly (which often means traveling between several different farms) looking for signs of damage (North American beehives have been hit badly in recent years by parasites) or filled honeycomb frames to cart off and turn into honey. The beekeeper also transports the hives from farm to farm and back home for the winter.

Beekeepers love the mystery and the efficiency of bees. Bees have very developed social structures, can communicate complex directions with a dance, and are almost totally devoted to their work and hive. Perhaps it is that last point that appeals to a certain strain of Yankee who takes immense joy out of working with these cranky creatures.

Practical Information

Anyone with a hive is a beekeeper, but to turn it into a business, you'll need at least 100 hives, and probably close to 1,000. Since each hive has 30,000 or more bees during the summer, you can see that you'd have some work on your hands. You need all of the bees, though; to make one pound of honey, 550 bees need to visit more than 2.5 million flowers. Each healthy hive makes between 50 and 400 pounds of honey a season, and hives are rented to orchards and farms for $30 to $40 each.

Most people new to beekeeping start as hobbyists, which is easy enough to do. Farm supply stores often carry beekeeping supplies, and many communities have beekeeping associations; contact your state or local agricultural office. Of course, you could just find some bees; an unwritten rule in beekeeping is that whoever finds a swarm, keeps it—just be sure you have a hive ready.

On the Internet, you can find information at weber.u.washington.edu/~jlks/bee.html. A good recent article, called "The Hum of Bees," appeared in the September 1998 issue of *Harper's Magazine*.

Holistic Veterinarian

Job description: Use holistic methods—chiropractic, acupuncture, and homeopathy—to treat pets and other animals.

Compensation: All-holistic clinics are still rare. Most practitioners have "mixed practices," supplementing traditional veterinary medicine with holistic services for patients that request them. Sessions of animal chiropractic run from $30 to $100 depending on the location and the size of the animal. An initial exam for animal acupuncture costs $40 to $75, and a standard treatment on a large animal generally runs about $200. Homeopathy costs around $115 per session. By contrast, a twenty-minute session with a conventional vet costs around $60 to $70.

Prerequisites: In general, one must be a licensed veterinarian to practice holistic medicine on animals. In addition, training in various techniques is required. For example, the American Veterinary Chiropractic Association in Illinois requires a $2,500, 150-hour course for certification in animal chiropractic. Also, the candidate must pass a written and practical exam administered by the association with a grade of at least 80 percent. Finally, the aspiring animal chiropractor must submit three case studies to a board for review prior to certification. The International Veterinary Acupuncture

Society has similar certification requirements for budding acupuncturists.

Qualities employer is seeking: Besides a commitment to the health of animals, most holistic vets share a pioneering spirit and an open mind, only natural for the first generation of a field practicing hotly debated techniques.

Perks: Holistic vets are largely able to set their own schedules. Vets who use acupuncture and chiropractic can also create a bustling practice with racing animals, who need treatment to stay in top form. Jan Golash, of the Crossroads Equestrian Center clinic reminds skeptics, "These animals are athletes, and like any other amateur or professional athletes, they become stiff or suffer muscle strain."

Risks/drawbacks: Holistic veterinary medicine isn't sanctioned everywhere; animal chiropractic is still not legal in about half of the states in the U.S. The "practice act" of a state usually means that it is only legal for a licensed veterinarian to treat animals. However, this is changing state by state, as professions like animal chiropractor take hold.

Overview

With Americans increasingly exploring alternatives to traditional health care, it is perhaps inevitable that they would take their pets along for the ride. As pioneering holistic vet Dr. Allen Schoen reports, "Many of my clients are on natural health programs. Then they'd go to a veterinarian who was feeding their animals drugs and they began to think, 'Why not explore alternative medicine for my dog or cat or bird or ferret?' " Holistic medicine encompasses a wide variety of nontraditional medical techniques, all sharing an avoidance of drugs and surgical procedures.

"I thought it was a little unrealistic for a human to manipulate bones in an animal as large as an elephant," says animal trainer Dave Blasko. But I guess I was wrong."

The three major areas of holistic veterinary medicine—chiropractic, acupuncture, and homeopathy—use treatments similar to their human analogues. In chiropractic, animals are adjusted in about thirty minutes; acupuncture substitutes needles and Fido's central nervous system for calipers and braces; and homeopathy involves injecting a variety of distilled toxins (e.g., arsenic, poison ivy, rattlesnake venom) in minute doses to stimulate the body's natural defenses. In practice, these techniques range from placing small needles in the temples, neck, and shoulders of an English setter to cure a brain abscess to simply feeding a cow gallons and gallons of cheap beer to cure a displaced stomach. Carvel Tiekert, a member of the American Holistic Veterinary Medical Association,

takes a more teleological view of the situation, defining holistic medicine as "anything that works." Follow-ups vary according to the nature of the problem. In minor cases, vets simply advise the owners to keep an eye out for signs of recurrence or administer herbal or vitamin supplements.

Proficiency in holistic techniques gives veterinarians a chance to diversify and increase their traditional practice. Advocates of holistic animal medicine also see the field as a way to legitimize holistic medicine for humans. Unlike humans undergoing New Age techniques, animals have no idea what they're getting into, and there is accordingly no "placebo effect." And holistic vets seem to be winning over some human converts. Dr. Schoen reports: "Clients come here and see how well holistic medicine works on the animals and then they say, 'What about me?' "

Animal practice also helps innovate and advance tried and true methods of holistic medicine, most notably acupuncture. In an odd collision between science fiction and centuries-old Asian mysticism, the use of lasers instead of needles is becoming increasingly prevalent in animal acupuncture. The portable laser units create the same physical sensation as the needles and are easier to use, as animals instinctively dislike being poked with needles. At least, this is the explanation tendered by manufacturers of expensive laser acupuncture equipment.

Practical Information

The alternative vet medicine field is small but growing. In 1997, there were 230 certified animal chiropractors in the country. And only 350 of the 60,000 licensed vets in the United States are trained in acupuncture techniques. But the growth has been astonishing. Though the field barely existed fifteen years ago, today there are around 700 members in the ranks of the American Holistic Veterinary Medical Association. As holistic medicine becomes the treatment of choice for growing numbers of Americans, you can bet they'll be dragging even more of their feline, canine, and other friends along.

Unless you're already a licensed veterinarian, you'll need a couple years of vet school before you can start getting paid to put needles in dogs. For additional information, try www.altvetmed.com, a clearinghouse for information related to holistic animal medicine. The American Veterinary Chiropractic Association is headquartered at 623 Main St., Hillsdale, IL 61257, and the International Veterinary Acupuncture Society can be reached at P.O. Box 2074, Nederland, CO 80466.

Interview with Bashkim Dibra, dog trainer to the stars

On getting started in the field: "After being trained in Europe, I started pursuing an academic career here in the United States. You had these lab exercises, to study what is conditioned response behavior, what's operative conditioning—the Skinner principle, rats, do this, do that, open them up to see how they think. But I felt like that's great, now we know, but it doesn't mean anything. So I went to the West Coast and started doing movie work. A lot of celebrities were impressed and would say, 'Can you train my dog that way?' And I would, and soon everybody started using me and I became the dog trainer to the stars, dog trainer to the rich and famous."

Credit: Bashkim Dibra

Bash Dibra, dog trainer to the stars, poses with some of his honor students. (If you prefer working with more docile animals, consider taxidermist, p.121.)

On working with Henry Kissinger: "Kissinger had this Lab, Amelia. He got this little puppy and he loved her so much that he forgot that love is not enough. The dog was jumping, pulling. And the *Post* was doing a lot of stories about him, saying 'Look at Dr. Kissinger, he's a world diplomat and he can't even control his own dog.'"

And some other celebrities: "I worked with Mariah Carey; when she was with Tommy, they had Doberman pinschers. I trained Andy Warhol's dachshund. Woody Allen and Mia Farrow had a bichon frise that I worked with. Carly Simon was great because when she won a Grammy Award for her music, I had her dogs staying with me. We were watching TV together, and she was singing and the dogs started to jump and howl."

When he first became interested in animals: "When I was about one, my family tried to escape a communist country, Albania, which was horrible. But we got caught and were put in this camp in Yugoslavia, where we were until I was about nine. To make sure you didn't escape, they had attack dogs patrolling the camp. But something magical, something spiritual clicked in me, and instead of seeing these as killer dogs, I just saw them as furry lovely creatures. So I put my hand out and touched them and they would lick me. And before you knew it, I knew I had to be working with animals. That became my passion."

The most satisfying parts of the job: "It's great when you take what you know into the real world of helping people with their pet training. A simple example: When I say to people, 'You're giving mixed messages.' And they say, 'What do you mean?' I say, 'You told the dog you didn't want it on the furniture and now you telling them, 'Oh c'mon, Shnupsy, come to me, let me hug you.'"

Bash's advice for would-be pet trainers: "If you're looking to go into this field just to make money, forget it. You really have to love working with animals and you can make a nice living in it but you have to be committed and stick to it. Then down the road you can get lucky and things click for you."

Mr. Dibra is the author of *Dog Training by Bash*, now in its eighth printing, and *Teach Your Dog to Behave*.

Fish Processor and Deckhand

Job description: Fish processors work in salmon processing factories and canneries in Alaska, some land-based, some floating, some on board full "fish-processing catcher" factory ships. Deckhands work on the decks of catchers, hauling nets and doing other manual labor.

Compensation: Workers in commercial salmon fishing typically are paid with a percentage of the catch which can be a blessing or a curse, depending on an outing's success. Fish processors earn about $3,500 to $4,500 per month in the high season, $2,500 to $3,500 during slower periods. Deckhands earn about double that. Both work typically six to eight months per year, which means that a "greenhorn" (processor with no experience) can earn about $30,000 in a year.

Prerequisites: Other than possession of no major disability, very little is required of a fish processor. Deckhands have to have worked a couple of contracts (usually two to four months each) as a processor.

Qualities employer is seeking: All the companies want is that you know exactly what you're getting into (see "Risks/drawbacks"). It's a tough job. Companies don't want someone who thinks he's going to Alaska for the scenery and fresh sea air.

Perks: The bulk of commercial salmon fishing is in Alaska, in some of the most beautiful scenery in the country (when you're not in the belly of a ship). The work is short-term, allowing people to construct workyears around their lifestyles. You come away having done some of the hardest work of your life, which some say builds character. Plus, the money is good.

Risks/drawbacks: Injury and death is possible. "You've never heard a man shout louder than when he falls overboard off an Alaskan fishing boat," said Matt Riordan, a skipper. Falling overboard means certain death unless you are rescued immediately. Factory ships are infamous for their many dangers, everything from processors injuring themselves in machinery to deckhands being tossed overboard. Conditions have improved a lot in recent years, though. Crews are larger now and deckhands wear survival suits. A cottage industry of attorneys—a processing factory of a different sort—has sprouted in Seattle (where most of the companies are also based) to represent former workers with injury suits; their work has helped to keep otherwise exploitative companies in check. Another drawback is the exceptionally grueling work required on the job.

"People have to come in and realize that they're there to work," says Marcio Ferreira, a former processor, deckhand, and ship captain. "It's not a vacation. It can be like slavery."

Overview

Commercial salmon fishing is one of the few industries where someone with virtually no work experience and education is guaranteed a job with pay starting at $30,000 and salaries growing very quickly from there. Marcio Ferreira, a former processor, deckhand and ship captain was a salmon fishing captain within four years of entering the industry and earned as much as $150,000 for four months of work. Let's be frank: The money draws people to Alaskan salmon fishing. It's hard, unpleasant, difficult work. No one does it because they like it; they do it for the money. People might come away having said they're glad for the experience, glad for the skills they learned if they move into higher positions on a ship's crew, but they don't like it when they're there.

The work conditions are harsh. Processors work sixteen hours a day. Deckhands on fish processing catchers work twelve-hour shifts, followed by twelve hours off, while deckhands on smaller catchers are on duty twenty-four hours, catching a couple hours' sleep when they can. As you can imagine, some people can't handle it. The problem is, they're stuck in Alaska, or even on board a ship. And if you stop working, the companies start charging you for room and board and make you pay for your own airfare back. Once you're there, you have to work.

The chance for huge earnings, plus the borderline illegality of the work conditions, means that commercial salmon fishing draws large numbers of immigrants and other foreign workers. Sixty to eighty percent of the workers in Alaska salmon fishing are Hispanic. Despite the harshness of the job, nearly 30 to 40 percent of the workers today are female, which only adds to the frontier-like party atmosphere. The town of Dutch Harbor, where most of the canneries are based, has a resident population of about 1,000, which swells to 50,000 during peak season. The most popular bar there, the Elbow Room, was once named by *Playboy* as the wildest bar in the United States. Chances for romance abound; Ferreira reports that women tend to have more of an eye for the deckhands than for the fish processors.

Practical Information

Without other maritime experience, newcomers enter commercial salmon fishing as fish processors in canneries on land. With a couple of contracts under your belt, you can move up to processor on a factory ship and perhaps up to deckhand from there. Getting a job as a fish processor is easy. The demand for workers is high. The only

real prerequisite that fishing companies have is that you know what you're getting into: They can't afford a slacker.

Many of the people who work in commercial salmon fishing are not interested in moving up the corporate ladder; they're happy to work half the year in a cannery and watch their wages rise with their experience. Therefore, if you're ambitious, smart, hardworking, and willing, you can quickly rise up to ship officer or even into management.

A number of agencies help place interested fish processors and deckhands; most are based in Seattle. One Web-based service with lots of job listings is Maritime Jobs (www.maritimemployment.com).

Aquaculturist

Job description: Raise fish by the thousands, from babies to plate-sized adults, within the confines of an industrial park.

Compensation: The pay varies between $6.50 an hour for an entry-level technician and upwards of $100,000 a year for a manager at an established fish farm. A "culturist" who handles fish can start out making between $20,000 and $30,000, but getting into the $50,000 to $60,000 range requires a specialty, such as feeding, breeding, or waste analysis.

Prerequisites: None, for the technicians who keep night watch while the experienced aquaculturists sleep. For advanced positions, a master's degree in biology or engineering may be necessary. Fish farming combines elements of environmental engineering, biohistory, and animal husbandry. Aquaculturists must be able to analyze and monitor tank conditions in order to keep the fish growing just so. A manager must know how to control variables from feed to water to air to the ammonia that the fish excrete.

Qualities employer is seeking: Important qualities include an analytical temperament, an entrepreneurial spirit, and a "blue thumb"—a light touch with the little critters.

Perks: The excitement of using agricultural and biological training to create market solutions for a hungry world. No, there's no free fish.

Risks/drawbacks: These jobs provide little tenure and few benefits. Culturists need to locate in rural areas where the water is cleanest, keep farmer's hours, and probe fish during their most intimate biological moments (see "Fishy Sex", p.15, to learn where baby fish come from). Having fish die without knowing why and burglary are also problems. A Malaysian fish farm had its stock of siakap wiped out by bandits—who were caught the next day at a fish market.

Overview

Despite what the Marvelettes tell you, there aren't too many fish in the sea: The global appetite for seafood is roughly twice what the wild supplies. To meet this shortfall, Jim Carlberg, founder of Kent Seafarms, and many others have turned to "recirculating" fish farms made up of massive tank systems housed in industrial parks. In the United States, fish farms produce between 800 and 900 million pounds of fish every year, roughly half of which is channel catfish grown in the Mississippi Delta area and sold to chain restaurants like Long John Silver's. These farms and other aquacultural endeavors contributed roughly a quarter of the world's edible fish in 1995.

Broadly speaking, one can enter three kinds of aquaculture. In pond culture, fish spawn after two hot summers. In flow-through systems, dominant among rainbow trout breeders in Idaho, water runs down a hill, into a tank system, and out into a creek. In recirculation, which takes place entirely indoors, aquaculturists direct the life process from fingerling to plate size, staggering development to allow for year-round harvests. Some fish farming is big business; companies like ConAgra support large salmon fisheries in Alaska and Maine or anywhere else deep, cold water can be found. Mississippi's Delta Pride and South Carolina's Southland Fisheries farm catfish for institutional buyers; aquaculturists for these companies pull in crawfish and oysters to the tune of forty to sixty million pounds a year. These farms are big operations subject to intense price competition, and their crops are somewhat unpredictable.

Credit: Josh Goldman/Aquafuture

Josh Goldman nets a profit as a fish farmer.

Hence, the industry engages in an endless quest for new technologies that will reduce their guesswork.

"Economics—greed and everything else—drives aquaculture, not saving the oceans and feeding the starving masses," says Jim Carlberg, founder of the pioneering Kent Seafarms, located 100 miles outside of San Diego.

The pressure of breeding can be as intense as that faced by any farmer. "People have to be aware of the tenuous nature of inventory," says Carlberg, a former marine biologist with the Scripps Oceanographic Institute. "If a feed truck runs over a power line at night, everyone dies." Employees can be fired for muffing processes that maximize survival rates. An advanced operation involves pathology, cannibalism studies, and a sense of breeding—none of which shuts down at 5 P.M. Indeed, even the smallest operation requires twenty-four-hour attention. If Jerry Redden, an aquaculturist for Aquamar Industries in Pocomoke, Maryland, doesn't get his 4:45 A.M. wake-up call from the technician who tends the tilapia in his tanks, he drives up the road to the farm himself.

To what end? Aquaculturists talk of a future in which the water they use will be treated and used to irrigate agriculture land for vegetable crops, producing more food while using fewer natural resources. For his part, Josh Goldman of Turners Falls, Massachusetts, is out to breed the perfect flounder, with a predictability and docility to match that of cattle. Roadblocks on the way include limited supplies of fish meal (anchovies, menhaden, and other little guys), impatient investors, and the relative paucity of decent, clean aquifers. Still, growing fish is a growth industry. "As the technology improves you'll need less labor per pound of fish," says Redden. "This isn't corrupted yet," says Greg Gutchigian, who has carved himself a niche writing aquaculture mortality insurance. "These people have always loved growing fish." Goldman says many of his employees like to hang out in the outdoors during their downtime—and go fishing.

Practical Information

Redden, according to a fan, "wants to be the Frank Perdue of tilapia." But this kind of ambition means a major investment. A beginning aquaculturist can buy a small tank system for around $3,000, but Goldman says it would cost at least $500,000 to start an operation that can match his series of tanks, the largest of which hold 150,000 gallons of water. Pond farmers tend to spend between $8,000 and $10,000 per acre to outfit a farm to pump out hybrid striped bass—and farms need to cover at least five to seven acres to make any economic sense. Impatient investors tend to favor sexy livestock like lobster or abalone

Fishy Sex

You'll never hear somebody belly up to the bar and boast that he "screws like a fish." Bass and tilapia practice a sex that would confound even the most hell-bent independent counsel. To produce hybrid striped bass, growers first let their fish reach sexual maturity, then scoop up a female and three or four males (to control for infertility) and inject each with a hormone. It's a race against time: The female will spawn in ten to twelve hours by secreting eggs. Once she spawns, she is removed from the water and a grower has between half an hour and an hour to strip the eggs out of her body before she dies from exposure to oxygen. To get the male fish to discharge, one must hold it: "There is an art and a science to doing that," says one extension agent. Because the males have been preinjected, the grower can zap them with anesthetic ("so they're not flippin' and floppin'"). He then points the squirt toward the eggs, and the miracle of life begins. Some bass outstud others: "If their testes really make a lot of volume, you can squirt sperm three to five feet."

The tilapia breeding process is courtlier, but no less tidy. Jerry Redden, of Aquamar Industries, strives to "create a little environment that they like." Atmosphere is important in rousing the male to do his reproductive duty. Once a month, the female lays eggs, picks them up, and broods them in her mouth. "The male will make a nest, the female will say 'Hey, good-lookin,' and drop eggs in front of him." Redden and his team, for control, pick up the female fish and shake the eggs out of her mouth, into the male's bachelor pad, where he can fertilize them. This procedure is still experimental, but Aquamar already sells between 20,000 and 40,000 pounds of mature tilapia each month. And Redden's approach may be safer for everyone involved than what goes on in the wild: "A natural spawning forty-pound female will swim up to the top, and you'll have, like, ten males waiting underneath. Most will be eaten by something bigger."

over economically manageable species, but state governments and university extension agents will provide help to burgeoning aquaculture outfits.

Training is available at Woods Hole Oceanographic Institute in Massachusetts, University of Washington, Auburn University, and Texas A&M, and in twenty-nine coastal states through the U.S. Agriculture Department's Sea Grant program. Virtually every fish has its own trade association. And you can subscribe to *Aquaculture* magazine, *Aquaculture News*, or more scholarly journals. The government also sponsors a Web site (ag.ansc.purdue.edu/aquanic), and the National Aquaculture Association in South Carolina can help hook you up with career lines that will keep you from sinking.

2 Risky Business

Wildland Firefighter

Rodeo Clown

Hollywood Stuntperson

Mercenary

Bounty Hunter

Human Guinea Pig

Wildland Firefighter (Smokejumper)

Job description: Every year, thousands of wildfires burn in forests across the country, and thousands of wildland firefighters spring into action to keep them under control. There are several different types of wildland firefighter, most defined by the method of transportation to a fire. Smokejumpers, the most well-known of wildland firefighters, fly to a fire, sometimes several hours into the backcountry, then parachute from as high as 3,000 feet. Once there, the firefighters contain and douse the fires, using far fewer resources than their urban counterparts. During the fire season, wildland firefighters are on call twenty-four hours and can spend as long as twenty-one days straight fighting a fire, sometimes getting only twenty-four hours of rest before heading out for another twenty-one days.

Compensation: Most wildland firefighters are employed by the federal government through the Park Service, the Forest Service, or the Bureau of Land Management (some states have their own crews as well), and so are paid on the government pay scale, typically GS-4 or GS-5. This translates to between $10 and $19 per hour. Firefighters earn time-and-a-half for overtime and time-and-a-quarter for "hazard pay," which means that while fighting a fire, firefighters are often earning almost twice their base pay. The vast majority of firefighters work seasonally, taking other jobs or unemployment during the winter. All this equals about $20,000 for most and up to about $50,000 or $60,000 for a foreman or base manager. (For another job where a few months of hard work can support you all year—unusually high compensation that reflects a similarly high risk of being killed or maimed—consider being a deckhand in Alaska. See p. 10.)

Prerequisites: All that's needed to start is good physical condition and a high school degree. To be a smokejumper, one has to have worked for about four or five years on the ground, at least some of those with a "hotshot" crew (the elite land-based wildland firefighters who are flown around the country to help district crews). Once selected, smokejumper applicants must also pass a training program called "rookie school." Previous parachute experience does not matter.

Qualities employer is seeking: Physical fitness, self-reliance, the ability to make good decisions under a lot of stress. For smokejumpers: proven firefighting ability and excellent references.

Perks: The work is exciting, outdoors, and can save lives and property. You work closely with high-caliber people and forge enduring relationships. Firefighters tend to be smart, competent, and trustworthy. "You see some of the most beautiful parts of the country," says

Bill Cramer, a smokejumper in Alaska. Most of the work is seasonal, which allows a lot of freedom for those who want to pursue other seasonal work or nothing at all. And of course, there's the adrenaline rush of courting a gruesome and painful death.

Risks/drawbacks: Gruesome and painful death. Fortunately, injuries are much more common. Almost every smokejumper will injure himself jumping at some point, and injuries are par for the course in firefighting of any kind. Deaths are quite rare, despite a few well-publicized disasters, such as when fourteen firefighters died in Colorado fighting fires on Storm King Mountain the summer of 1994. According to Cramer, the Alaska Smokejumpers haven't had a fatality since 1966, and there have only been nineteen total smokejumper deaths in fifty-five years.

"You work with people you trust with your life," says Wayne Williams, a smokejumper in Montana, "and you work with people you like to work with. Everything else is secondary. There aren't a lot of jobs left with those qualities."

Overview

There are several types of wildland firefighting crews. The most basic are engine crews, usually based in a district or state, who actually drive an off-road version of a fire truck to the fires. Hotshot crews, the more elite land-based firefighters, are a national resource flown around the country to aid the district engine crews. Helitack crews and smokejumpers are used for fires that engine crews can't reach. Firefighters on helitack crews rappel from helicopters hovering over a fire, and smokejumpers parachute from planes anywhere from 1,500 to 3,000 feet above a fire. Though smokejumpers get the most public attention, firefighters are quick to point out that the main difference between crews is just a matter of transportation. They all fight wildland fires the same way—with a "line," an eighteen-inch-to ten-foot-wide clearing of all "fuel" (what firefighters call anything that burns) on the edge of the fire, to stop the fire's blaze. Sometimes water or another repellent is used, brought in by engine, helicopter, or plane.

Though women are still rare among wildland firefighters, and especially among smokejumpers, this is not because of any overt sexism. "It used to be a male-dominated agency, but not so much anymore," says Syndy Heidt, a female wildland firefighter. "Women are accepted as equal." Because the physical requirements are the same for men and women, and because every firefighter must depend on every other, there is

Credit: Wayne Williams

Out of the flying plane and into the fire. Smokejumpers parachute into the woods to fight forest fires.

little room for discrimination. The 1998 season was the first since 1990 that the Alaska Smokejumpers haven't had an active female smokejumper, according to Cramer.

There are approximately 400 smokejumpers in the United States, 15 of whom are women. Smokejumpers make on average ten fire jumps per season from the ten jump bases in the United States, in California, Oregon, Washington, Montana, Idaho, New Mexico, and Alaska.

Practical Information

If you want to be a wildland firefighter, get in shape and call a state agency or local branch of the Park Service, Forest Service, or BLM. Many firefighters start out working summers on district crews as teenagers and graduate to longer positions as they age. To become a smokejumper, you have to put in the years with engine and hotshot crews and be aggressive. Most rookie smokejumpers are still in their early twenties after four or five seasons as firefighters, and it's competitive. About one in twenty applicants is accepted to rookie school, and 20 to 60 percent of those go on to fail the four-week training. For those who make it, "they look back on it as the best job they ever had," says Cramer. Most smokejumpers last about eight seasons, though some have worked as many as thirty.

So the most important things you can do are getting physically prepared and finding out what's in store. (Wayne Williams, a smokejumper in Montana, notes that a common reason for rookie failure is simply lack of preparation.) Contact a local agency or the National Smokejumpers Association (406-549-9938; e-mail: smokejumpers@smokejumpers.com; www.smokejumpers.com). You can also contact the Aerial Fire Depot in Missoula, Montana (406-329-4900). There are a number of books on wildland firefighting; one recommended primer is *Fire Line: Summer Battles of the West* by Michael Thoele (Fulcrum Publishing, 1995).

Rodeo Clown (Barrel Man)

Job description: Sit in a barrel, tell jokes to the audience to fill dead time between rodeo acts, and taunt angry bulls after they have bucked their riders.

Compensation: Since rodeo clown work is generally conducted on a freelance basis, the salary varies from performer to performer. Depending on booking schedule and travel costs (which the clown frequently shoulders), a rodeo clown can make between $40,000 and $90,000 a year.

Prerequisites: Most rodeo clowns and barrel men were rodeo performers at one time. If you survive your years as a rodeo performer and wish to remain associated with the scene, this job can be a form of semiretirement.

Qualities employer is seeking: Athleticism, fearlessness, and a sense of physical humor. You also need to know how to apply your own makeup.

Perks: See the country, enjoy a life in showbiz, and work with animals, albeit large, angry ones.

Risks/drawbacks: Lots of driving from venue to venue, badly broken bones, and a strong possibility of getting gored by a rampaging bull.

Overview

Roughly three types of rodeo performers fall under the umbrella term *rodeo clown*, though they blur around the edges. The first type is perhaps the most recognizable, the clown. In addition to running around the ring distracting a bull from a fallen rider, the clown is responsible for entertaining the crowd between stunts and does this by donning a standard clown uniform while making jokes and performing tumbling routines. This is the least risky part of the job, yet it requires comic timing and charisma, which do not typically come into play when working with the animals. The second type of rodeo clown is known as a barrel man because he sits inside a barrel and pops up to taunt the bull. The barrel is a protective barrier between you and the bull, but it is still a risky place to be. The third type is the bullfighter, who must draw the bull after it has tossed the rider, allowing the rider to get to safety—this involves more bull-handling than either a clown or a barrel man must do.

A rodeo clown's job is to protect the cowboy from being hurt by distracting the bull. This is a dangerous job, since the bull is usually enraged and bucking wildly within the confines of the rodeo ring. The bullfighter is particularly at risk, since he enters the arena without any equipment and is expected to work in close contact with the bull. The barrel man is also at risk. Bulls have been known to ram their horns into barrels and gore their cargo. In rodeo lingo, an eliminator is a bull that can hurt a rider

(or a clown) very badly; eliminators should be avoided at all costs.

Kirk Guy, a rodeo clown from Pontiac, Michigan, has been hit by bulls no less than seventy-five times. One time, according to Guy, "I stepped to turn a bull back and lost my footing. He knocked me out for fourteen hours. He hit me so hard I hit the dirt and dislocated my shoulder." Despite this setback, Guy, like many rodeo clowns, loves his job. "If I want to quit, I want to quit on my own. I don't want to quit because a bull forced me into it." Among the many injuries sustained by Guy are broken ribs, a gored shoulder, and damage to his teeth. "My teeth aren't mine," he says. "I have false teeth."

Among the expenses a rodeo clown or barrel man must anticipate is the cost of a good barrel. Frank McIlvain, a rodeo clown who also teaches young people how to perform in rodeos, says that his barrel cost $1,000. The reinforced aluminum barrel protects the forty-year rodeo veteran from charging bulls, but outside of his fortified safe haven, McIlvain is constantly at risk. "One time, this bull actually took me out of the arena on his horns," he recalls. "When I woke up in the hospital, I was face down on a bed and they were sewing my head back together." Another time, McIlvain was charged by a bull and ran into a steel pipe. The impact popped his right eye

Credit: Alan Nelson

Bozo never had to worry about getting gored by a three-ton raging bull.

out of the socket. Luckily, his eye was saved.

As difficult as bullfighting may sound, the hardest part of being a rodeo clown, according to Allen Nelson, a sixteen-year rodeo veteran, is the comedy. "The comedy is more challenging [than the bullfighting] because people know what's funny. The comedy aspect of what you do is what's going to carry you through the rodeo." Being funny also helps you to land better gigs: "As a funny man you have more potential to make money," says Nelson. "It's very competitive out there." Nelson performs in as many as 100 rodeos a year.

"I can't believe they pay me, because I love to do this so much," says Martin Kiff, barrel man for the last four years (bull rider for nine years before that).

Practical Information

One way to get started in the exciting world of rodeo clowning is to call the Rodeo Clowns and Bullfighters Association (800-687-4122), a national organization dedicated to promoting professionalism within the field and publicizing rodeo as a legitimate sport and pastime.

You can also find out more at the Web page rodeo.miningco.com/msub_assn.htm or by reading *Fearless Funnymen: The History of the Rodeo Clown.*

Hollywood Stuntperson

Job description: Perform actions that are dangerous (or appear dangerous) for movies.

Compensation: Stuntpeople are actors and members of SAG (Screen Actors Guild). The minimum day rate for SAG actors is currently $559. Adjustments to this rate, which vary from a few hundred to a few thousand dollars, are based on the difficulty of the stunt and the budget of the film. Adjustments are paid per take of the stunt. The number of days you work a year is obviously a relevant factor. An extremely successful stuntperson can take in nearly $200,000 a year. On the other end, some stuntpeople rely on secondary sources of income to get by.

Prerequisites: You have to drive well to do car stunts. You need to be a pilot to fly a plane. Riding well helps with horse stunts. General coordination or experience with gymnastics, tumbling, diving, and martial arts help to round out a potential stuntperson. Since you have to market yourself to get work, charisma and affability are also necessary.

Qualities employer is seeking: Half the jobs require the stuntperson to double for another actor. Employment decisions are often made based on how closely the stuntperson resembles the actor with the speaking role. Similarity of height and frame are primary, since these are hard to fudge. Any extra similarities are a bonus. Between a group of individuals who all look the part, employers will typically hire the person with the most experience in the type of stunts that need to be performed. Nepotism is also a big factor in this field.

Perks: The challenge—many stunt folks think of their occupation as a professional sport. Taking that bullet just right is a matter of personal pride. Adrenaline rushes can be fun—even the most jaded stuntpeople get a thrill jumping ninety feet into a raging inferno. "I enjoy doing something different everyday," says stuntwoman Nancy Thurston. The glamour of the set and potential travel opportunities are added value for some stuntpeople.

Risks/drawbacks: "We always get bruises. We all have bad knees or hips or necks. After a few years we all walk funny. Everybody walks funny. A lot of the times before they say 'action' you know you're going to get nailed," says stuntwoman Ellie Alexander. When you jump out of a vehicle moving twenty-five miles per hour and land on asphalt, something is going to sting. The most perilous of stunts remains the high, high fall. Stuntpeople get killed and paralyzed doing high falls on a yearly basis. The next highest danger is from burns. Says the petite Ms. Thurston, "I've seen friends of mine get burned very badly when the explosion is bigger than it is supposed to be." Broken noses are not uncommon, even when the fight scene has been well choreographed. This is a risk-intensive profession. "You could get hurt, get killed, get paralyzed. Just because you do something a lot doesn't mean it isn't dangerous," says Thurston.

"I never get recurring roles," says Ellie Alexander, commenting on the fact that the characters she plays die violent deaths on screen.

Overview

Once upon a time, "a stuntperson was a guy from Texas who rode a horse well and had a lot of balls," says stuntman Dave Thompson. Women's stunts were done by little guys from Texas wearing wigs. Getting a job was as simple as saying, "Sure, standing on the outside of a plane 5,000 feet in the air, with no parachute, sounds like a good idea."

While throwing yourself headfirst into a concrete wall still requires a good Texan, the industry has changed. Women do their own stunts; minorities do their own stunts; and the stunt coordinator and the stunt actor's job is to minimize the risk in each stunt. This attitude has led to specialization and professionalism. Tumblers and gymnasts are highly sought after. Some stuntpeople do nothing but car chases. Others specialize in high falls or stage fighting. It remains true that the more rounded you are, the more work potential you carry. But being rounded no longer represents a willingness to do

anything, but actual expertise in a variety of stunt possibilities.

Ever since the *Star Wars* trilogy proved that poorly written, poorly acted action films can bring in bushels from the box office, Hollywood has been producing more films packed with stunts. Getting work remains extremely competitive. Just getting into SAG can be tough. "It took me a year and a half to get into the union. I've seen people that took seven years to get in," says Thurston.

The special-effects industry poses a threat to stuntpeople. While blue screening and optical effects have been around for some time, new technology makes it economically and aesthetically viable to use your leading man in death-defying feats. Stuntpeople will undoubtedly be needed in the future, but the amount of work may diminish, leaving only the most genuinely dangerous stunts for the pros.

Practical Information

Schools for becoming a stuntperson have fallen by the wayside. Stuntpeople learn techniques by befriending more experienced stuntpeople and doing "workouts" together. Some stunts are harder to learn than others—not everyone has an eighty-foot ladder in his backyard. Trampoline classes at gymnastics schools are useful. Extreme sports (e.g., kick boxing, rock climbing, scuba diving) offer the novice possibilities for learning needed skills. Live shows at amusement parks, fairs, and circuses are a good way to get started, as these venues typically are more willing to train people without experience.

To get work, you'll need a resume and a head shot. List whatever you can do on the resume (e.g., surfing, in-line skating, skiing). Most of the work is shot or cast in Los Angeles and Florida. Read the trade papers to find out which films are using stuntpeople. Head to a municipal film permit office and get a shoot sheet to find out where films are being shot when. Go to the shoot and introduce yourself to the stunt coordinator. These are the guys (and gals) who will hire you. Give them your head shot. A short videotape showing what you do well is another useful tool to drop off.

Most stuntpeople use a message service that can provide them with information on upcoming jobs and send out copies of their head shot. Teddy O'Toole's (323-462-2301), Bill's (323-469-9980), and Joni's Stuntpeople (818-980-2123) are three of the most popular in L.A. Each runs $50 a month.

There are five different stuntpeople's associations in L.A., three for men and two for women. Eligibility requires sponsorship by a member and a few years' experience in film stunt work. If you can join one now, you probably don't need to be reading this. Aside from bearing an excellent resemblance to Tom Cruise or being a world-class gymnast, the best guarantee of work is good word of mouth. Consider cultivating contacts, the most important aspect of your profession—in the end, this is what will get you work.

Mercenary

Job description: Mercenaries are soldiers for hire, working for private companies that provide military and security services to governments or corporations.

Compensation: Bert Sachse, who works for Executive Outcomes, one of the leading providers of mercenaries, puts it bluntly: "Executive Outcomes is a business, and we're in it, of course, for the money." The soldier of fortune's pursuits are ultimately lucrative ones. Infantry soldiers with only rudimentary training make around $2,000 per month (they are paid on a retainer basis), and pilots and specialists make between $5,000 and $7,000 per month. A retired marine officer doing mercenary duty for Vinnell in Saudi Arabia was able to save several hundred thousand dollars in only five years.

Prerequisites: Would-be kings are unlikely to place manpower, expensive equipment, and the fate of their fledgling regimes under your control if all you've got is a junior marksman badge from your summer camp. Particularly given the new professionalism of today's mercenary companies, formal military or police training is essential, and the more specialized and elite it is, the fatter the paycheck a soldier of fortune can command.

Qualities employer is seeking: A good mercenary should be brave, adventure-seeking, independent, and travel-loving. The ability to follow orders and keep cool under fire is essential. Oh, and you have to be willing to kill people for money. (Prefer to kill people domestically? See "Executioner," p. 103.)

Perks: Travel and adventure come with the territory. In addition, most mercenary outfits these days offer generous insurance benefits. And if you keep your scruples in check and play your cards right, it's not hard to imagine what sort of perks—mining interests, perhaps, or even your own little puppet regime—might fall into your lap. The opportunity to get in on the ground floor of a burgeoning field is always appealing, and the mercenary business is booming. A recent Defense Intelligence Agency symposium cited a "consensus among government officials and the companies that this sort of activity is going to greatly increase during the next few years." And if you want work that'll help you feel good about yourself, it's worth noting that in some cases, mercenaries have the high moral ground. They perform unsavory but ultimately productive tasks without compunction, while recognized powers stonewall progress and wring their hands. One Executive Outcomes official commented, regarding the company's Angola operation, that "we also have principles. We agreed to help the military regime because they promised to move towards elections. Without Executive Outcomes, there would be no democracy here."

Risks/drawbacks: When you're killing for a living, there's a very real chance that you'll end up dead. Although mercenaries tend to be better trained and equipped than their adversaries, casualties are a way of life. Executive Outcomes lost twenty soldiers during their 1993 operations in Angola. Imprisonment is also a real, if unlikely, possibility. International law still tends to turn a blind eye to mercenaries—only twelve nations signed the UN's 1989 Convention on Mercenaries, condemning mercenary activity, and the policies of individual nations are rarely more strict. The attitudes of most First World governments range from condemnation or ignorance of these firms' existence to tacit approval (and funding) of some of their operations. And though freelance military activity is illegal in most countries, action is rarely taken to curtail it. The U.K., for example, hasn't convicted a mercenary in over a century.

Overview

Since Washington and his whiskey-drinking, squirrel-eating band of minute men sent George III's Hessian mercenaries packing some 200 years ago, the soldier for hire has fallen into disrepute. For the last two centuries, national armies, relying on conscription and the backing of strong federal governments, have increasingly been the rule. In the past fifty years, however, as empires and armies have begun to downsize, the nature of warfare has changed yet again. As European powers evacuated their African and Middle Eastern colonies and territories, volatile power vacuums were created. Mercenaries have stepped in to fill those vacuums, particularly in areas, most famously Angola, Sierra Leone, and Saudi Arabia, where vast fortunes in mineral resources are at stake.

An anonymous Vinnell employee: "We are not mercenaries, because we are not pulling the triggers. We train people to pull the triggers. Maybe that makes us executive mercenaries."

These first new mercenaries were opportunistic, independent freeloaders, often remnants of the evacuating colonial armies. Blackguards to some, macho heroes to others, they roamed postcolonial Africa propping up and tearing down regime after principality after fiefdom. Perhaps the most famous of these is Colonel Robert Denard, a former French officer, who spent much of the last thirty years providing freelance military support in a number of notorious struggles in the former Belgian Congo and the Comoro Islands. But Denard and his ilk are a dying breed, as even the mercenary trade falls prey to the conglomeration inherent to global capitalism.

Today's mercenaries put forward a vastly different face than their rape-and-pillage forebears, and one entirely in step

with 1990s corporate professionalism. Leading outfits—among them Britain's "military consultancy," Sandline International, South Africa's Executive Outcomes, and the U.S.'s Military Professional Resources, Inc. (MPRI), and Vinnell—flaunt sleek corporate headquarters in Alexandria, Virginia; Pretoria, South Africa; and London, U.K. They hand out glossy brochures outlining their services and have strict codes of conduct bordering on the politically correct. Most outfits vow to abide by the Geneva Convention, though, by their own admission, it is nearly impossible to hold them accountable in the event of an infraction. Executive Outcomes's Eeben Barlow asserts, "We're not going to get involved in countries where atrocities and genocide are being committed.... We won't get involved in religious wars or conflicts where we don't understand the particular politics."

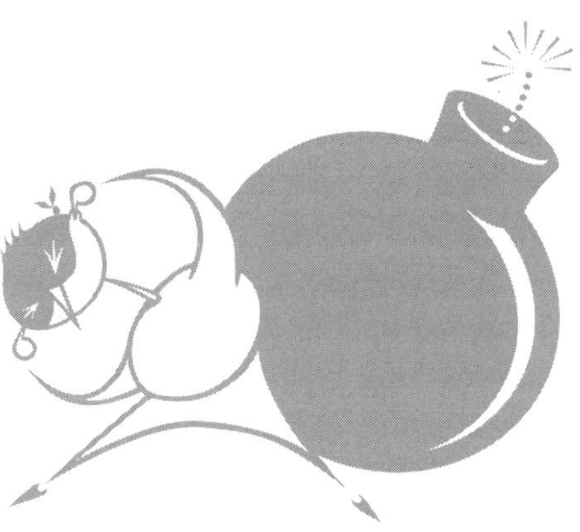

Actual battles are few and far between. Mercenaries are hired now by upstart governments largely to train their own indigenous soldiers, to protect leaders, and to safeguard valuable mining and other commercial concerns. In a business where public relations is becoming increasingly important, many mercenary execs go so far as to claim that their men also work on civic projects, including building irrigation systems and digging wells. But fat paychecks, the constant threat of armed combat, and a basic lack of humanitarian motivation make it clear that today's merc business still ain't the Peace Corps.

Practical Information

Mercenary companies don't hire applicants lacking military experience, so the best place to start is with a tour of duty with your own nation's armed forces. If you're unable to make the cut there, the French Foreign Legion has a century-old reputation for turning even the most downtrodden outcast into a francophonic killing machine. The only catch is that you have to sign up in person in one of their French recruiting offices. A personal favorite of ours is Fort De Nogent, (near Paris), 94120 Fontenay-Sous-Bois (011-33-1-48-77-49-68).

Bounty Hunter (Bail Enforcement Agent)

Job description: Hunt people down, kidnap them, and haul them back to face trial.

Compensation: The salary range at one company is $18,000 to $48,000, with full benefits. However, most bail enforcement agents work freelance, not on salary. The industry standard is 10 percent of the bond at stake. A good hunter can make $50,000 a year.

Prerequisites: In some states, there are no restrictions whatsoever. Other states require some training, a license, a clean criminal history, insurance, etc.

Qualities employer is seeking: The ability to think independently, work in an unstructured environment, and kidnap armed and dangerous felons.

Perks: Be a legal vigilante with a business card like Drew Hinkle's, which says: "Senior Special Agent, Fugitive Retrieval Unit, K-9 Team." Many bounty hunters are former law enforcement officers who left jobs in the government sector because they couldn't stand red tape and politics getting in the way of their efforts to bring criminals to justice. As a bounty hunter—a law enforcement entrepreneur, if you will—you're liberated from many of the civil rights "nuisance issues" facing cops. As Hinkle says, there's "no micromanagement" in this corner of the private sector.

Risks/drawbacks: Getting into brawls with —or possibly killed by—armed fugitives; also, tedious stakeouts.

Overview

Many alleged criminals, arrested but not yet tried in court, are released from prison on bail—that is, in exchange for a large sum of money, until their trial arrives. Since the accused parties may not have the money up front, a cottage industry of bail bondsmen has sprung up to loan alleged criminals bail money for a fee. Every so often, however, the criminals skip town, leaving the bail bond company responsible for the money. It is the job of a bail enforcement agent (also called a *fugitive recovery agent*) to retrieve these bail jumpers.

The job boils down to outfoxing the fugitive, using the bounty hunter's bag of tricks. Successful bounty hunters are adept at making up stories while speaking with relatives, neighbors, and the fugitives themselves. Many people think that bail enforcement is an exclusively shoot-'em-up profession, but there is an important element of strategy and cunning needed to convince people close to the fugitive to relinquish information about the fugitive's whereabouts. Most often, bounty hunters pretend to be deliverymen, long-lost friends, or new acquaintances when speaking with a fugitive's intimates.

Bounty hunters need to be competent with firearms and in hand-to-hand combat, since fugitives—many of whom were arrested for violent crimes in the first place—are understandably eager to avoid being hauled back to jail by anyone, much less some busybody private citizen. Bail enforcement agents, who often hunt in teams, use state-of-the-art weapons, bulletproof vests, and cutting-edge communications equipment. When apprehending a fugitive, they sometimes resemble SWAT teams, right down to their imitation black-and-white police uniforms.

"No body, no booty," according to Bob Burton, the patriarch of the bounty hunter community.

The Supreme Court decided back in 1873 (*Taylor v. Taintor*) that this occupation is 100 percent grade-A legal. A person who jumps bail forfeits his or her civil liberties and can be kidnapped and brought back to jail with virtually no restrictions. The bail bondsman has authority to retrieve the fugitive and may transfer this authority to a third party, who then has a license to make a so-called "private arrest."

Sometimes, a bounty hunter will throw a fugitive into the trunk of a car and drive back to the place where the fugitive is wanted. Not surprisingly, there have been cases in which overzealous bounty hunters have gone a little too far. One bounty hunter nabbed a bewildered woman off the street in New York and whisked her off to a jail in Alabama before discovering that she was in fact an innocent woman walking down the street, not a fugitive. Lawsuits in such cases have yielded substantial damages.

Practical Information

It's blissfully easy to break into this line of work. Compared to the substantial training and time involved in becoming a police officer, you can be out on the street nabbing criminals in no time as a bail enforcement agent. Bob Burton, the nation's leading bounty hunter and a one-man lobbyist for the industry, trains hundreds of men and women every year at the National Institute of Bail Enforcement in Tucson, Arizona, and in seminars he conducts all over the country. (*Police Magazine* has refered to this seminar series as 'the Harvard of Bounty Hunters.') For $360, you get a three-day course in the basics and registration in the National Association of Bail Enforcement (520-290-8051; www.bountyhunter.net/home.htm; weapons training not included).

Be forewarned, however, that there is more to bounty hunting than just traveling around the country kidnapping folks. This is a business, after all, and according to Burton's promotional materials, you will need to learn a host of surprisingly white-collar skills, including "advertising, management of resources, subcontracting

arrests, local and federal laws, and contracts." Between learning how to collar a man and how to quickly reload your semiautomatic rifle, the seminar can feel like law school. Students memorize all sorts of arcane rules: where it's a felony to carry more than 2 percent pepper gas; where it is legal to have handcuffs in your possession "without good reason"; and what to do if, when handcuffing a prisoner, the prisoner asks for his or her "medicine," or a small child enters the room as you are about to take away the only guardian at the scene. "What do you do with the child?" asks Burton. "These problems are addressed at the Institute. The complexities of this unique form of contractual arrest must be confronted and addressed daily."

Trackdown is a bimonthly publication of the National Institute of Bail Enforcement for the agents it certifies (annual subscription fee is $25). It is free to certified agents for one year from the date of certification. They run articles on all facets of this business, from the dramatic ("How Secure Is Your Prisoner?") to the more mundane, such as insurance and legal matters. Other publications to check out are *Bail Enforcer: The Advanced Bounty Hunter* ($21) and *Bounty Hunter* ($15), both by Bob Burton, who served as technical advisor to Robert DeNiro for the movie *Midnight Run*. The books are available from the NIBE. The foreword for *Bounty Hunter* is written by Ralph "Papa" Thorson, who was the inspiration for the movie *The Hunter* starring Steve McQueen.

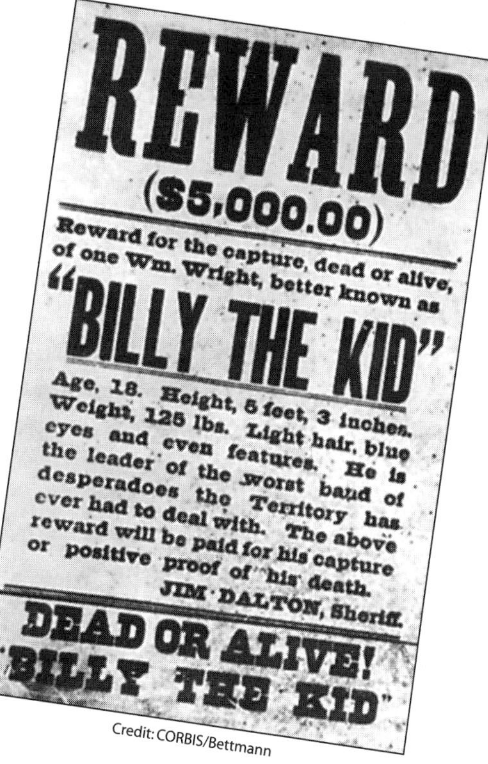

Credit: CORBIS/Bettmann

Bounty hunters must be able to think independently, work in an unstructured environment, and kidnap armed and dangerous felons.

Human Guinea Pig

Job description: Receive cash stipends for participating in clinical drug trials and other scientific experiments involving human test subjects.

Compensation: According to DataEdge, a medical research firm in Fort Washington, Pennsylvania, stipends for in-patient clinical trials run about $200 a night, $600 to $1,000 for a weekend. Stipends vary considerably from trial to trial, depending on factors such as the amount of blood taken, inconvenience, and time commitment.

Prerequisites: Some studies require having a specific medical condition. Allergic to bee stings? Got genital herpes? Addicted to heroin? You could be in luck.

Qualities employer is seeking: A human guinea pig must be fearless in the face of blood, needles, tubes, spinal taps, rectal probes, device implants, cerebrospinal injections (involving extra long needles to cross the "blood-brain barrier"), and other invasive procedures. Eleonora Florance, a nurse in Annandale, Virginia, was paid $450 testing a drug for seasonal mood disorder during which she had to give a blood sample every half hour and spend the night with a heat-sensitive probe up her rectum. "Doing these studies is not for the squeamish or weak," according to John Sanchez, a veteran guinea pig.

Perks: Being on the front lines of scientific or medical breakthroughs. Also, free food, shelter, and videos during hospital stays.

Risks/drawbacks: If you're lucky, you'll be in a placebo group and get paid to take sugar pills for a few weeks. If you're not so lucky, you may end up helping scientists discover new and unpleasant side effects—from none to death, and everything in between—for the drugs they're testing. Mike Yeager, of Cleveland Heights, Ohio, has seen it all in more than seventy-five trials and medical tests. One drug introduced him to premenstrual syndrome, making him bloated and cranky. In another, an impotence study, he got shot at the base of his penis with a substance that produced an erection. When the doctor gave him another shot to counteract the first, the doctor said, "OK, if it comes back up again, you need to get to the emergency room because it's not going to go down." His penis reerected later that day, sending him to the ER. It did not return to normal for six hours.

Overview

Volunteer testing on humans has come a long way since Walter Read, an army bacteriologist, pioneered the practice around the turn of the century by paying people to participate in yellow fever experiments. He offered subjects $100 in gold, plus another $100 to be paid to their estates in the event that the test treatment proved lethal.

The infamous Tuskegee study, where government researchers withheld treatment for syphilis to African American men in Alabama without their consent, highlighted the need for the guidelines that now govern all human testing in the United States. Such guidelines were adopted in the 1960s, after "flipper kids"—children born with deformed arms and legs—resulted from an improperly tested drug called thalidomide. The guidelines mandated that patients be warned of potential risks on a consent form and that an independent panel approve experiments before they are conducted. Nowadays, there are typically 400 different doctors, and multiple institutions, involved in reviewing studies before their methodology (or "protocol") can be approved by the FDA.

Most studies soliciting healthy volunteers are so-called "Phase One" studies: testing on humans for the first time, after the drugs have been proven safe after extensive testing on animals. Phase One is intended to discover whether there's some "unpredictable response to the human body," according to Mark Hovde, vice president of Data Edge.

Practical Information

It is difficult to earn a living as a human guinea pig. Besides the pain, inconvenience, and hazards, being enrolled in multiple trials can be problematic, as researchers—who invest considerable time and money in each patient—do not want their subjects contaminated from other experiments. "This is not something you can make a living at, to be honest," said Christopher Hendy, president of Novum, a pharmaceutical company that conducts paid tests. "Most people come in to supplement their income." In fact, most studies take place at research institutions and rely on student volunteers.

A more realistic approach is to view this as a part-time job opportunity and stay abreast of opportunities in your area, especially condition-specific studies for which you may be qualified. If you find yourself with strep throat or another ailment, call local research institutions, teaching hospitals, and drug companies to check to see if you qualify

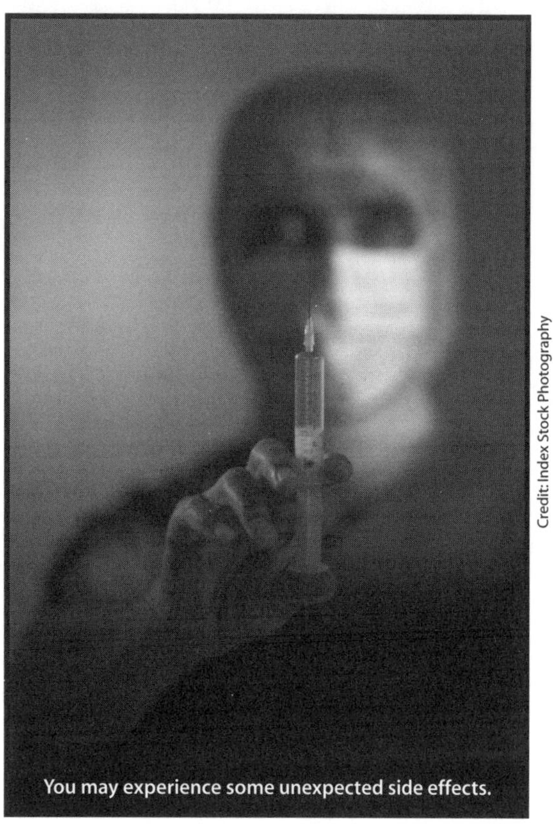

You may experience some unexpected side effects.

Credit: Index Stock Photography

for any ongoing studies; you might get treated and paid for it at the same time. The Camino Medical Group, in Sunnyvale, California, for example, paid people with the flu $100 for an overnight observation.

"I wouldn't do it," said Mark Hovde, vice president of DataEdge. "I've been around this industry and I just don't like the idea of getting poked and probed." Describing an experiment where researchers paid subjects $800 to fly to a clinic on Long Island where the researchers dripped a test substance into the subject's cerebrospinal fluid for five hours and then waited twenty-four hours to discover any unforeseen side effects, he balked. "Who would want to do that? I wouldn't. I would rather be home helping my kids with their homework."

Studies are often advertised in the classified sections of local papers and on bulletin boards at local colleges. Some are fun and noninvasive, such as a metabolism study at MIT. Subjects were paid for their involvement and given all their meals for free in exchange for having their weight monitored periodically. Some research institutions will let you sign up for upcoming studies and call you when something arises.

This is not for the faint of heart. There is often a correlation between pay and bloodlettings. Take, for example, a study of omeprazole, a drug that inhibits the secretion of stomach acid. For $510, patients spent three twelve-hour days at the facility and gave a total of fifty-three blood samples. The disclosure form listed possible side effects, including constipation, vomiting, diarrhea, bloody urine, painful urination, and "unusual bleeding and bruising." Although he was turned down for the omeprazole study (because he took daily vitamins), one man was prepared to go through with it because he needed the money. "I wasn't really looking forward to it," he said. "But I just bought a bass guitar, and I'm behind on my credit card bills."

In addition to unpleasant procedures, there are also serious risks, including death, as in the case of Hoi Yan (Nicole Wan), a nineteen-year-old University of Rochester freshman who died as a result of an air pollution and smoking study. The research involved harvesting lung cells during a procedure called a *bronchoscopy*. "In this procedure,"

Selling Your Body

Can I sell one of my kidneys? The answer is yes, and no. You cannot simply walk down to your local hospital and cash in a kidney. Although you do have an extra one, and the end result may be to extend the life of someone with kidney dysfunction, this practice is illegal in the United States, Canada, Mexico, and all of Europe. Reportedly, India has tolerated paid renal donation in the past but is cracking down on the practice. According to Jeff Punch, a surgeon at the University of Michigan, "Although paid donation may occur in parts of the world, the lack of accountability of the unscrupulous individuals that engage in this practice means that it is unsafe to donate a kidney through such an organizer."

Instead, sell body parts that regenerate, such as hair, plasma, and sperm. The Community Bio Resources, Inc., in Cedar Rapids, Iowa, for example, pays $25 the first time you donate plasma and $20 for each additional donation. The procedure takes about an hour: they draw blood, separate out the liquid, and give you back your red blood cells. They also give you a free sub sandwich.

Sperm banks pay you to masturbate into a vial. What could be easier? With some experience as an amateur, you turn pro in no time, making $50 a pop, but you must generally commit to making one or two trips a week for a year. They insist that you "abstain" for two to five days prior to each "collection."

Wig and hair-extension manufacturers buy human hair, but rarely in small quantities. Most buy it in bulk (by the ton, in fact) from India, China, and Indonesia. If you have really long "virgin" hair (never colored or processed), you can sell it in the States, but don't plan to get rich harvesting your hair: a fourteen-inch head of hair only weighs about four ounces, and at $6 an ounce, that's only $24.

Eggs don't regenerate, but if you're a healthy young woman, you've got more than enough. You can make $2,000 to $3,000 by joining a six-month egg donation program.

Scientists will pay top dollar for you to sleep with a heat-sensitive probe in your rectum, take dozens of blood samples, and undergo new, experimental treatments. Not for the squeamish, there are more than 8,000 clinical trials a year seeking human guinea pigs.

according to an account in *Guinea Pig Zero*, a zine devoted to human guinea pigs, "a bronchoscope measuring 7mm x 40cm is inserted down the subject's windpipe, and the anesthetic lidocaine is sprayed down the throat to control gagging....The NY State Department of Health found that Dr. Mark Frampton...had given Wan four times the maximum dose of lidocaine, had failed to state clear maximum dosages in the study's protocol, had violated the stated guidelines, and had failed to properly monitor the young woman's condition after the procedure."

Before participating in any study, read all the protocols carefully and do not enter into any study where you are not comfortable with the credentials of the researchers. For more, check out the zine *Guinea Pig Zero: A Journal for Human Pharmaceutical Research Subjects*, edited by Bob Helms, at www.geocities.com/Hot Springs/Villa/2529. You can write to *Guinea Pig Zero* at P.O. Box 42531, Philadelphia, PA 19101 ($10 for a four-issue subscription). Additional companies can be contacted at the following addresses: Novum (412-363-3300), PPD Pharmaco (512-447-2663), or Phoenix International Life Sciences (513-541-2800). A useful Web site is www.medville.com/cta.html.

WARTS -ACNE

TESTING NEW THERAPIES FOR ACNE IN WOMEN/ WARTS IN MEN & WOMEN AT NYU. STIPEND

ADDICTED TO COCAINE?

Want to stop using? Receive up to $330 for your time. If you are an otherwise healthy male or female 21-50 you may be eligible for free & confidential treatment in a research study at the Medication Development Research Unit at the NYVA Medical Ctr. Treatment incl a physical exam, lab evaluations & counseling. Info call

3 Up on High

Forest Fire Lookout

Blimp Pilot

Helicopter Traffic Reporter

Bush Pilot

Flight Attendant

Airshow Pilot

Forest Fire Lookout

Job description: Fire lookouts work in tall towers, usually sitting atop mountains in forested areas. They scan all they can see for signs of fire, estimate the location of fires, and report the location to the proper authorities. There are a number of volunteer lookout organizations in areas that no longer have the funds to support a paid staff.

Compensation: For the most part, fire lookouts are paid around $9 to $10 an hour, but earn time-and-a-half for overtime (which is common in fire season). Indeed, lookouts can work up to twenty-one days straight before getting a day off, if they're badly needed. In recent years, agencies like the U.S. Forest Service and the U.S. Park Service have begun taking bids for lookout work; candidates submit their price for a season's worth of work, and the agency chooses the best price.

Prerequisites: A high school education and proven responsibility are the only requirements. Skills such as map reading are highly valued.

Qualities employer is seeking: Good eyesight, attentiveness, and trustworthiness are important qualities. The ability to hold one's cool in the middle of a huge lightning storm, perched on a glass-insulated stool to avoid electrocution, with lightning exploding directly overhead, sometimes several times a second, sometimes so close that you go blind for thirty seconds at a time, also helps.

Perks: Solitude, peace, quiet (unless there's a storm). The time to pursue other projects (see "Erotic Screenwriter," p. 93). The satisfaction of helping to stop a fire that could have endangered lives. (If spotting the fires isn't enough, and you want to get down there and put it out, check out "Wildland Firefighter," p. 17.)

Risks/drawbacks: Extreme boredom. Getting struck by lightning. Downsizing (as technology improves, lookouts are being phased out in some places).

"You have to be into nature," says former lookout Don Scronek.

Overview

Such places (where the Scripture is observed) however wretched they may be, will be loved as though they were famous memorial parks and monuments, to which countless pilgrims and sages will come (to Desolation Peak!) to offer homages and speeches and dedications. And over them the angels of the unborn and the angels of the dead will hover like a cloud.

—Jack Kerouac, in his journal, on his last night as a fire lookout on Desolation Peak, Washington.

Lookout towers have always provoked strong emotions and artistic outpourings. What draws almost every lookout to the job is either nature or

solitude. Those who enjoy working as lookouts and do it year after year are rewarded by amazing views from their mountaintop perches, and they treasure the peace of their nearly monastic lives. A few famous artists (Jack Kerouac, Edward Abbey)—and many unknown ones—have retreated to lookout towers to devote themselves to their work, be it writing *Dharma Bums* or painting a landscape watercolor.

However, there are quite a few career fire lookouts, and they're quite good at it. "A good lookout," says former lookout Dan Scronek, "can look at smoke and tell location, size, intensity, type of fuel, give access routes, and suggestions for retardant." Lookouts are trained in map reading and the use of a specialized tool called a *fire finder*, which, well, helps find fires. After reporting a fire, a lookout is often asked to communicate changes and suggestions on firefighting method. During quiet periods, fire lookouts make weather reports, do maintenance work, act as communication relays, and scan, always scan.

Fire lookouts take a lot of pride in their work, and not just from the service they provide. There's a history to fire lookouts and organizations to preserve the towers and the institution. The towers themselves become homes, sometimes an only home. Lookouts have been known to take their whole families along for the season ("That gets a little weird," says Scronek). Some areas that can't afford to pay full-time lookouts have a network of devoted volunteers that keep the towers manned.

The pastoral solitude is often interrupted. Lightning storms (often the cause of fires) can strike with a vengeance. Standing atop the tallest thing around (a structure made of metal) can pose a problem. During storms, lookouts have to climb on top of a stool with glass insulators at the feet and wait it out. Of course, they do this while witnessing great light shows (that is, unless lightning strikes a part of the tower; then the flash is so strong that the lookout can be temporarily blinded).

Practical Information

Fire lookouts are hired by the forest or park that the particular tower is in. Therefore, interested applicants should contact the supervisors of the forests or parks directly. A directory of office numbers is available from the U.S. Forest Service, the U.S. Park Service, the Bureau of Land Management, and state forest offices. Most of these agencies have offices in major cities.

A good place to start learning more about fire lookouts is at the Web page of the Forest Fire Lookout Association (www.paulbunyan.net/users/quam/ffla.htm).

Blimp Pilot

Job description: Float around from sporting event to sporting event in the gondola of a helium-filled airship.

Compensation: Pilots are paid $25,000 to $60,000 per year, depending on experience and seniority. In addition, they receive a per diem stipend to cover hotel and living expenses while on the road (which is always, for some companies).

Prerequisites: A Federal Aviation Administration lighter-than-air pilot certification for airships is required of all blimp pilots.

Qualities employer is seeking: Being an experienced general aviation pilot alone won't land you one of these select flying jobs. More important is the ability to be a militantly cheerful company spokesperson, answering the same questions over and over from guest passengers, typically bigwig corporate clients. "Pilot qualifications all come second," said an official of Airship Management, a large blimp operator. "What we're hiring, primarily, is a public relations representative. It's really a PR job when it comes down to it."

Perks: Bird's-eye views of sold-out sporting events: the Indy 500, the Super Bowl, the World Series, etc.

Risks/drawbacks: Since the *Hindenburg*, which crashed and burned in 1937, there has been a transition from highly flammable hydrogen to inert helium inside the dirigibles. As a result, blimp travel has become the single safest form of traveling, with zero fatalities in civilian blimp travel since the *Hindenburg*. The primary drawback is a rigorous travel schedule.

"I'm a very lucky person. I have an office with a view that changes all the time," said John Crayton, one of the pilots on the *Goodyear Eagle*.

Overview

"We fly low and slow," said Dominique Maniere, member of the Fuji blimp team. Flying at altitudes of 1,000 to 2,000 feet, and moving only a little faster than a bicycle, you get a better view and more interaction with people below (who often look up and wave) than you can get from an airplane. At one point, when the Fuji blimp was flying over the Midwest, a school bus stopped and everybody got out and lay on the ground spelling the word *HELLO*.

Top cruising speed for a blimp is about thirty-five miles per hour, which can make for long, slow legs between destinations. (If you're craving a flight job with a little more zing, read about airshow pilots on p. 52.) The pilots have it good, however, compared to the support crew, who travel in a caravan of buses, vans, and trucks, slowly chasing

the blimp from the ground and anchoring it at night. (Perhaps as a deterrent to anyone contemplating stealing a blimp and taking it for a joyride, Goodyear mentions repeatedly in its marketing materials that its blimps are "never, ever left alone.")

The Goodyear blimps, perhaps the most famous in the field, have an entourage of seventeen crew members (riggers, engine mechanics, ground handlers, and electronic technicians), five pilots, and a public relations manager. Goodyear maintains three blimps: one that covers the West Coast, one that covers the East Coast, and one that anchors in Akron, Ohio, at Goodyear's headquarters. Other companies that use the floating billboards include Budweiser, MetLife, Tommy Hilfiger, Fuji, Blockbuster, Izod, Blue Cross-Blue Shield, and Pizza Hut.

The sausage-shaped vessels are not used strictly for advertising. They are used to entertain celebrity and VIP guests (corporate clients, winners of charity events, etc.) for their parent companies. They are also occasionally used for aerial photography and scientific studies, such as observing whale behavior.

Despite their relatively benign reputation today, blimps have gotten into trouble in the past. There is the mysterious case of the "ghost blimp": Two pilots of a Navy L-8 airship disappeared while on a routine antisubmarine mission (blimps were used extensively for this purpose in World War II). Their ship was spotted nestled against a cliff near San Francisco, but when rescuers approached, it suddenly dislodged and drifted inland, making a perfect landing at an intersection in Daly City. The blimp was found empty, and the pilots were never seen again.

Approximately fifty years later, in 1993, a Pizza Hut blimp with an experimental new design petered out rather spectacularly over New York City. The airship, known as *Bigfoot*, was on its maiden voyage when it suddenly lost control and heaved down in an emergency landing onto a roof on West fifty third Street. On the roof of Midwest

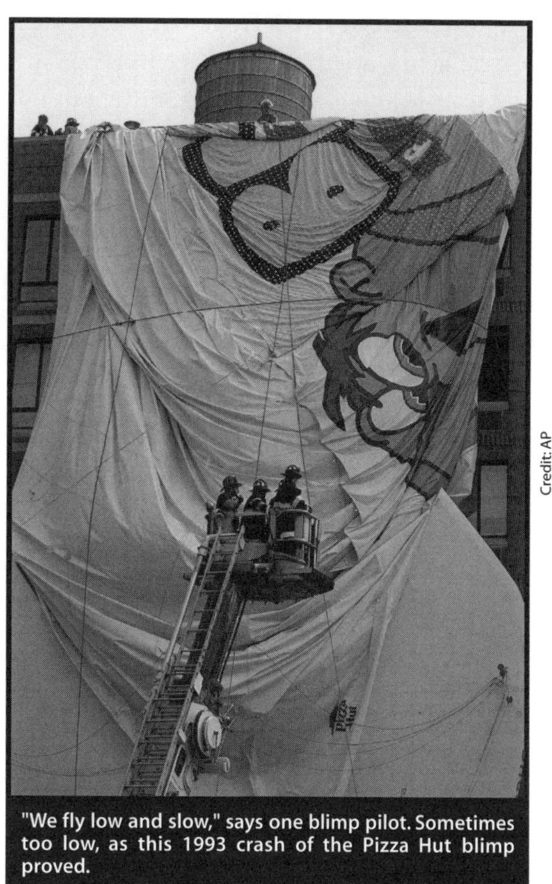

Credit: AP

"We fly low and slow," says one blimp pilot. Sometimes too low, as this 1993 crash of the Pizza Hut blimp proved.

Court Apartments on West Fifty-Third Street, two women and three men were sunbathing. According to the account the next day in the *New York Times*, "They looked up, astonished, as the airship came toward them, skimming the rooftops. Three ran into a stairwell, but two men stayed to watch, fascinated, as it landed beside them, hissing in its death throes." The two pilots escaped from the wheezing wreck, and watched, disoriented and slightly injured, as their airship expired into a flaccid tarp, drooping over the sides of the ten-story apartment building.

Practical Information

There is no fixed career path to becoming an airship pilot. There are only about fifteen airships in the world, and becoming a pilot can be a competitive and time-consuming pursuit. Some pilots spend years working on the crew before they are handed the controls. One of the challenges is that there are no blimp-flying classes per se. Blimp pilots get their training after joining a crew. At Goodyear, for example, current pilots are trained as instructors, and the next generation of pilots is taught on the job, by these senior crew members. One pilot said that his company prefers candidates who have worked as fixed-wing flight instructors, as they are both experienced aviators and comfortable interacting with people while flying.

Getting a job on the crew is easier and does not always require specialized skills, except in the case of mechanics and technicians, who are required to be FAA-certified in their fields. There are many semiskilled support jobs, from driving the trucks that follow the blimp to monitoring the anchored blimp at night to managing the public relations logistics surrounding the blimp's outings.

If you opt to pursue blimp work, be prepared to travel—a lot. Unlike airplane pilots, who tend to have certain routes and a home base, blimp pilots are always on the move. "You have to actually love to travel, not just like it. You have to be ready to do it permanently," according to a pilot for Airship Management Services, which operates a number of blimps for corporate clients. Unlike the Goodyear airships, most blimps are in a fleet of one and are perpetually peripatetic, canvassing the entire nation on a never-ending tour of sporting events. The crew of the Fuji blimp, for example, lives on the road all year. While this job can be a dream—seeing the country in style with all your expenses paid by your employer—it is incompatible with a normal family life. John McHugh, chief pilot of the Fuji blimp, does not have a wife or children. "I'm married to the blimp," he says, with no trace of regret.

For more information, contact these or other blimp operators: American Blimp Company (410-544-6507), Goodyear Blimp Operations (330-796-2121), or Airship Management Services (203-625-0071).

Helicopter Traffic Reporter

Job description: Fly above a major metropolitan area; report on automobile traffic patterns.

Compensation: The salary range for these jobs can vary widely, depending on the size of the city and a traffic reporter's popularity on a station. A well-known reporter, who also flies the aircraft, can make up to $300,000 a year.

Prerequisites: A heartland voice that bespeaks knowledge of cars and roads is necessary; for pilot-reporters, the ability to fly and talk at the same time.

Qualities employer is seeking: Traffic reporters almost never read from any sort of script. You need to be able to speak fluidly and extemporaneously—and sometimes jawbone with a slow-witted disc jockey, who may be scavenging for material.

Perks: Begin each morning by getting into a million-dollar chopper with a name like Zambo, Astar, or Bell 206 Jet Ranger, starting the propeller, and lifting into the skies; getting to say "rubbernecking" and "jack-knifed tractor-trailer" a lot; learning to master that secret language known only to a city's commuters, such as "Sumner's halfway back to the airport roadway."

Risks/drawbacks: "There was the time a goose smashed through the windshield and landed right in the middle of the aircraft," says Neal Busch, a traffic reporter in New York. "Naturally, we had to do an emergency landing."

"If you can do traffic, you can do anything in radio—this is the beast," says Jeff McKay, a New York traffic reporter and columnist.

Overview

Being an airborne traffic reporter is tough work. It frequently requires getting up as early as 4 A.M., peering out the side of the aircraft's window and looking straight down for several hours on end, and cramming as much information as possible into short broadcasts without seeming rushed. Reporters who fly their own helicopters, need to be able to do all this while still maintaining control of the aircraft. Yet, the job is uniquely satisfying—you can do it unshaven, in shorts and a T-shirt; for aviation enthusiasts who dislike the long distances required of commercial pilots, it's practically a dream job. The business, additionally, does not have much turnover. "Traffic is a very stable thing," says Jeff McKay, who works for 1010 WINS in New York and writes a traffic column, "McKay's Way," for the *New York Post*. "You rarely get fired unless you're the ultimate screw-up."

Traffic reports, communicated by UHF radio, can last as long as forty-five seconds and occur as frequently as every ten minutes. Few reporters are able to summarize all of a city's traffic news in one spot, so the job requires a calculated cycling—over a series of traffic broadcasts—through a city's most crucial roads, tunnels, and bridges. "We have to guard against forgetting anyone," says Neal Busch, who has been a traffic pilot-reporter for thirty-one years, with over 18,000 hours of flying time, and currently works with WCBS Chopper 88 in New York. "We have to keep in mind that when we're doing a traffic report that people all over the tristate area are listening. You've got Connecticut, New York and Long Island, and New Jersey—it's a really broad geographic area."

Most modern helicopters are capable of speeds of up to 150 mph and can cover a city's layout at a fast enough rate to keep up with changing traffic patterns. A helicopter is considered one of the more challenging aircrafts to maneuver; it requires solid coordination. Al Verley, a pilot-reporter in Colorado, keeps his right hand on the control joystick while using his left to not only keep the helicopter balanced—flicking knobs and switches and handling a smaller control stick—but also to jot traffic notes on a pad strapped to his leg. "I'm lucky," says Verley. "I'm left-handed."

An affable personality is a necessity for this job. Many morning and afternoon disc jockeys, particularly on FM stations, where there's lots of time to schmooze, engage the traffic reporter in witty repartee—brief chat about local restaurants, movies, or anything else local or contemporary. When invited, the traffic reporter is obliged to join the banter. "I love that part of the job," says Robert "Whit" Baldwin, a pilot-reporter in Richmond, Virginia. "I've got a gift for gab that my mother gave me."

Traffic reporters may also get called away to cover citywide celebrations: the Macy's Thanksgiving Day parade, hooplas for the Rangers and Yankees, and the Gulf Storm parade were all covered by helicopter traffic reporters in New York. (Get an aerial view of sporting events and parades, without the hassle of having to monitor traffic, as a blimp pilot. See p. 40.) Breaking stories may also demand immediate coverage. When Flight 800 went down in East Moriches, Long Island, the airborne traffic reporters swarmed the scene first. "At that moment, you stop being a traffic reporter and start being a news reporter," said Jeff McKay. "You've got to wear a number of different hats."

Practical Information

There are two ways to get into this business: through aviation or broadcasting. If you want to be a pilot-reporter, you will naturally have to choose the former route. A sizable number of traffic reporters begin first as escorts for non-pilot broadcasters and eventually end up on the air. Getting a commercial pilot rotorcraft license (which is the bare minimum for traffic reporters) requires

Interview with Chuck Street, aka "Commander Chuck," Los Angeles traffic reporter

Job description: Report traffic from high above the streets of Los Angeles for KISS FM.

How he got the job: "At the time, Rick Dees was just starting to get a following here in Los Angeles, and I'd always had a goal of being a pilot-reporter. I ended up flying alongside Rick Dees's nineteenth floor radio studio window on Sunset Boulevard with a topless girl one morning, and he went crazy. I ended up having dinner with him that night, told him my ideas about having their own traffic reporter—at the time, they were taking taped feeds from the highway patrol that usually didn't get on the air for about twenty minutes, so they weren't very fresh. This was about a year before the 1984 Los Angeles Olympic Games, and they were talking about gridlock traffic, and I said, 'Look, you need to have your own guy in a helicopter,' and I had bought a helicopter with my two best friends about a year before that. I wasn't really making it, flew a lot of photo missions for the *New York Times*. And they gave me a shot—they said, 'We'll try you for ninety days,' and now it's been almost fifteen years. It really worked."

significant time and financial commitments. Once you've factored in instructor fees, aircraft rental costs, and fuel (most helicopters burn through over twenty gallons of jet fuel per hour), the cost of learning how to fly can hover in the $225-per-hour range; a complete course costs around $25,000.

Many seasoned pilot-reporters create their own companies and offer scenic trips, corporate travel, real estate development scouting, and in some areas, vineyard and orchard frost patrol. Television and movie flying gigs for filming aerial shots are particularly lucrative. ("Whit" Baldwin provided helicopter work, most recently, for *Deep Impact*, *Enemy of the State*, and Ken Burns's *Thomas Jefferson* series.) These additional sources of income help defray the costs of owning and operating a helicopter. Chuck Street, of KISS FM in Los Angeles, gets money from carrying another traffic reporter (who broadcasts from the backseat) and from a sponsorship with Mountain Dew—the soda company covers one-third of the helicopter's costs, and in exchange, has emblazoned the aircraft with its colors and logo.

Those who are interested in taking the broadcasting route should consider an internship at a local radio station (one that generates its own traffic reports rather than relying on existing feeds) or enrolling in broadcasting and radio classes. Completing a few courses may make one a stronger job applicant,

although entry-level radio jobs—which may offer some on-air time—are not unheard of, particularly on the late-night shifts. One of the country's most popular news radio stations, 1010 WINS in New York, frequently has part-time positions for off-peak traffic reporters, when helicopters aren't used, according to WINS traffic reporter Jeff McKay. (The pay for this particular position is around $21 an hour.) Finally, certain jobs in the traffic-broadcasting field can improve one's knowledge of a city while offering a toehold on a prominent station. Tom Kaminski, who now works as a helicopter traffic reporter for WCBS in New York, got his start doing ground research stints in a beat-up jalopy—driving around the city, monitoring jams, and communicating the traffic patterns he observed with a two-way radio back to the station.

Bush Pilot

Job description: Fly airplanes from the farthest outposts of civilization into the backcountry. Bush pilots must perform a number of tasks in the line of duty. Depending on the trip, depending on the client, depending on the weather, a bush pilot may play such roles as travel consultant, babysitter, and skilled aviator. Of course, in performing every one of these tasks, the successful bush pilot must exude the rugged confidence that clients expect from those who spend their lives navigating uncharted travel routes and landing on dirt (or water) runways.

Compensation: Bush pilots are often independent contractors whose incomes fluctuate greatly depending on the number of regular clients they have. A pilot with a fleet of four planes can gross upwards of $200,000 per year, before deducting the considerable sums for maintenance and gasoline costs associated with air travel.

Prerequisites: In addition to steel nerves, a bush pilot also needs to possess an official FAA-approved license, mechanical expertise, and the ability to pander to clients.

Qualities employer is seeking: Self-employment demands confidence in oneself and a clear vision for the future of the business.

Perks: You fly, drive, hunt, and fish in some of the most splendid terrain on the continent, whether in California, Washington, or Alaska. Your clientele—often composed of the beautiful people who can afford you—shower you with the respect that your job deserves. Perhaps most important, you are your own boss, with a daily schedule organized according to your altimeter-equipped wristwatch.

Risks/drawbacks: Injury, death, and financial ruin. The happy depictions of bush piloting seen on *Northern Exposure* are pure fabrication. Bush piloting is an extremely dangerous profession. In some parts of the world, bush pilot crash rates are as high as 100 percent (i.e., every pilot will crash once); of these crashes 20 percent are fatal. Unsophisticated flying equipment, poorly maintained runways, oxygen-depleted mountain air, and Arctic temperatures below minus 100 degrees can mean death for the bush pilot. In addition, most pilots bear the burden of financing their own operations, either through personal savings or bank loans. Needless to say, few flying companies stay solvent in the competitive world of bush piloting.

Overview

The allure of bush piloting is as strong as it is haunting. These pilots make a job of exploring our last frontiers. Where there is no other access to the wilderness, there are bush pilots, and where there is no other access to the wilderness, it is beautiful. The job is a labor of love for those with stable piloting businesses, a number of planes, a regular client-base, and enough savings to ride out the slow patches in the off-season. Yet, even for these operators, a few inches of landing space, a few feet of altitude, a few extra particulates of oxygen, and a few degrees of temperature can bring a beautiful day to a deadly close. This is not a job for the faint of heart, nor is it a job for the indecisive. Flyers must be daring and quick, and they must be lucky. (For another dangerous wilderness job, see "Wildland Firefighter," p. 17.)

"The other night I was camping on a new lake, scouting territory for a cabin, when a Kodiak decided that he'd cut a hole in my tent," said one bush pilot. "It can be difficult on your nerves."

In places like Alaska, where almost everybody knows how to fly, entering the bush pilot business is difficult, if not impossible. In less traditional markets (i.e., those outside the Caribbean and Alaska) finding a niche may be easier—finding clients may be slightly more difficult. However, shuttling clients to exotic fishing locales is not the only reason to fly a bush plane. Flying doctors, aid, and food to needy recipients in developing countries can be an equally rewarding—if less lucrative—alternative. In many African countries, pilots provide such vital functions as mail delivery, food transport, and medicinal aid to

communities inaccessible by car. Frequently organized by agencies rather than by independents, these international flying engagements can provide an easier starting point for bush pilots because they do not require large upfront outlays of capital. Additionally, Africa supports a large tourist population that draws the bush pilots who work for safari groups.

Although flying jobs have been opening up to a more diverse range of entrants in the past few years, the bush piloting profession continues to be dominated by men. Many of these men have attained flying experience through training in the armed forces (both in the United States and abroad). Others have learned their trade from a family member; the famous bush pilot Paul Klaus operates a flying business that was founded by his father. But tradition need not deter other applicants. The world of piloting is a meritocracy of the highest order. "If you can't hack it, you'll know," is a mantra among professional pilots. Indeed, clients and others respond more to an impressive flying record, intelligence, and mythical tales of pilot savvy than they do to a pilot's pedigree.

Practical Information

Unless you already have an FAA license, the first step on the way to your career as a bush pilot is flight school. Flight school traditionally begins with an FAA medical exam (cost $60). Those who pass the physical exam must then pass a written exam. Materials for the exam typically run about $180, and the test itself costs an additional $50. The most significant cost for an aspiring pilot comes from plane rental fees. Most schools suggest fifty hours of flying time (twenty-five dual and twenty-five solo hours) before matriculation. Airplane rental costs for this period average about $2,500. Thirty hours of instruction account for another $750. The final exam, another FAA test, is $175. All told, flight school costs about $4,000. In choosing a flight school, look for one that offers ground school instruction for free. This will help cut down on costs.

Prospective bush pilots should know that one of the benefits of flight school is learning to fly in the types of planes used in the bush. These planes—two- to four-seat Cessnas, Piper Cubs, etc.—are easier to maneuver and considerably less expensive than jet planes. Although high-altitude flying, water landings, and grass field landings require additional training, at least the planes will always be the same as those you use in flight school.

Finding a flight school in a convenient location should not be difficult. There are hundreds of schools throughout the United States. One easy way to begin your search is to browse a phone directory for local flight schools. Even if nothing is listed, local airports (particularly those that do not handle much commercial traffic) will have information on flight schools in the area. Searching for flight schools on the Web can also be fruitful.

Flight Attendant

Job description: Assuring the safety of passengers, serving meals, tending to boozy businessmen, embodying the corporate personality of the airline.

Compensation: Beginning attendants earn $10 to $20 per flight hour, depending on the carrier, with guaranteed payment for a minimum number of hours each month (sixty-five to eighty). With annual raises, attendants who stick it out for the long haul earn as much as $40 per flight hour (in some cases, more for international routes). Many airlines also offer "incentive pay" for working on holidays, night flights, and understaffed flights, putting in overtime hours, or taking positions involving on-the-ground organizational duties.

Prerequisites: Gone are the days when (U.S.) airlines could discriminate on the basis of gender, age, marital status, and weight. Today's prerequisites relate to the applicant's ability to do the job and keep passengers safe. Each airline sets its own standards, but all require applicants to be at least eighteen years old and have a high school diploma or GED. Some airlines impose height requirements, or look at an applicant's "reach height," to ensure that he or she can reach all of the on-plane emergency equipment. Airlines that use weight requirements have, in recent years, adopted the rule that a flight attendant's "weight must be proportional to his or her height," thereby veiling their tendency to discriminate against overweight candidates.

Qualities employer is seeking: Airlines receive approximately twenty applications for every open position, so they can afford to be picky. Applicants with foreign language skills are currently in high demand, but past favorites, including applicants with nursing experience or psychology degrees, still do well. A flexible schedule is a must. Attendants rarely learn of their schedules more than a month in advance. It's also good to be in shape; meal service on a 727, with 100 to 200 trips up and down the aisle in an hour and a half, can be quite a workout.

Perks: The biggest perk is the (almost) free flights—contrary to popular belief, attendants are assessed a service charge for their personal trips, but compared to what outsiders pay, the prices are a steal. Then, of course, there's seeing the world, visiting friends in faraway places, and on some routes, access to the best shopping on Earth.

Risks/drawbacks: Attendants find it hard to maintain normal family lives, and even pets may feel neglected when left alone fifteen nights a month. On the job, one overly flirtatious or demanding passenger can make a flight into a nightmare, and the increasing incidence of "air rage" among passengers is causing airlines to implement creative new disciplinary tactics to ensure the safety of flight attendants and other passengers.

(British Airways passengers who earn two soccer-style warning cards on any one flight are banned from the airline.) According to the Air Transport Association, passenger violence, which is often fueled by alcohol, resulted in three times as many complaints by flight attendants and airlines in 1997 as in 1994. In one particularly notorious case, a passenger exposed himself to a flight attendant and then urinated all over her and the airplane galley.

"People just love to drink on airplanes. They feel adventurous," says flight attendant Terry Mason, summing up a timeless truth of her profession in Studs Terkel's 1972 oral history *Working.*

Overview

Working as a flight attendant is more than a job; it's a lifestyle. Attendants have fought long and hard to reduce the airlines' influence on their lives, overturning rigid weight requirements, rules against marrying and having children, and discrimination on the basis of age and gender, but there's no way to change the one basic demand of the work: frequent overnight travel. Attendants spend two to four days a week away from their families, in the company of their co-workers. In exchange for the stresses placed on their families, attendants gain exceptional friendships. Gail Sullivan, a thirty-year veteran with American Airlines, says, "I love the group of people I work with. We spend two to three days together each week, so the friendships are unusual for a working group."

Training for new flight attendants lasts from two to seven weeks, depending on the type and size of the airline, and focuses mainly on emergency skills. All flight attendants are certified to use the emergency equipment found on an airliner and have basic EMT training that qualifies them to stabilize and monitor an injured person's medical condition until medical personnel arrive. Applicants aren't considered employees of an airline until they finish training, so keep in mind that you may be disqualified during the training process. (If you find yourself in a position to choose between airlines, compare the training packages offered; some airlines pay trainees, while others charge newcomers for the instruction.)

The daily ups and downs of the job depend largely on the passengers. "The worst part of the job is dealing with passengers who are used to being in charge all of the time and getting whatever they want," says Sullivan. Every veteran knows what it's like to find someone locked in the bathroom, to help an overweight passenger down the aisle, or to care for someone who's had one (or several) too many. Then, there are the truly unusual passengers who populate attendants' most vivid memories.

On one Caribbean-bound flight in 1997, two American Airlines flight attendants got a shock when they tried to help a portly passenger to the lavatory. The woman claimed that she couldn't walk, so as one attendant supported her weight, lifting her into the aisle, another attempted to help move the woman's legs. Before the trio could take a step, the second attendant started in horror as she felt the passenger's leg come free from her body. The woman had failed to explain that she was unable to walk because her legs were in fact crudely fashioned prosthetics that did little to support her weight (to find out about the art and science of building prosthetics, see "Prosthetist" on p. 107).

Extra tips: Seasoned attendants advise newcomers to volunteer to work the coach section of the airplane. You might think that the first class has caché, business class leads to connections, and coach has nothing but squealing babies. However, it turns out that coach passengers tend to be grateful for any extra attention. The most popular flights among flight attendants are the long hops that provide lots of hours, well-appointed layovers, and lots of days off. By flying a cross-Atlantic route, for example, attendants can top their guaranteed monthly hours and get into lucrative overtime, while working fewer days than their domestic counterparts.

Practical Information

Job postings are easy to find. The employment section of your Sunday newspaper should carry announcements for open house interviews being held in your area. The Flight Attendant Corporation of America posts a biweekly list of airlines that are hiring on its Web site (www.flightattendantcorp.com); you can contact the group by mail at P.O. Box 260803, Littleton, Colorado 80163.

All of the major airlines have Web pages that list their openings and their hiring requirements. It makes sense to pursue work with an airline that has a flight hub in your area. These areas of high traffic must be well staffed.

Don't be discouraged if you can't find current job postings for a specific airline you want to work for. All of the airlines accept resumes by mail. If you meet the company's minimum requirements, you will be contacted for an interview once a job becomes available.

Airshow Pilot

Job description: Fly death-defying spins, rolls, and dives; bring smiles and gasps to children of all ages.

Compensation: Top performers take in $6,000 in a weekend and average twenty to twenty-five weekends over the annual seasons, from late spring to early November. A small number of airshow participants, ten or so per year, derive their income from corporate sponsorships. These pilots receive full-time payments and expenses in exchange for flying a plane bearing ample corporate identification. During the off-season, pilots work on planning the next year, and many teach aerobatics courses. Few have nonaviation jobs.

Prerequisites: An airshow pilot must have a pilot's license, access to a very strong little plane (a quality aerobatics plane can withstand up to seven times the stress that an airliner can), and a desire to please the crowd. Shocking as it sounds, there is no special licensing required to perform aerobatics (or to teach it). Good pilots should also be conscientious and meticulous; it takes more than a devil-may-care spirit to perform maneuvers correctly and live to tell about it.

Qualities employer is seeking: Aerobatics pilots come in all shapes and sizes, according to Guenther Eichhorn, a research professor at the Harvard/Smithsonian Observatory in Cambridge, Massachusetts, who participates in aerobatics competitions as a hobby: "There are no special traits. All kinds of different people do it. You don't need to be a daredevil." Yet, the more dangerous brand of flying practiced in airshows draws a more adventurous element, and audacious flyers are rewarded with renown in some circles. (For less dazzling aerial pursuits, read about being a blimp pilot, p. 40.)

Perks: According to Michael Goulian, the 1995 U.S. National Champion in competitive aerobatics and a major player on the airshow circuit, the best part is "the excitement the kids get out of it." He also mentions flying in an airplane that's the airborne "equivalent of a Formula One race car."

Risks/drawbacks: The airshow business loses two to three people a year. "Most of the accidents are caused by the pilots themselves," says Goulian. "If you're not completely concentrated, disciplined, and conscientious," it's not hard to lose control. Air sickness is a more common worry for beginners.

Overview

Competitive aerobatics, as practiced in International Aerobatic Club contests all over the United States, is a highly technical and extremely controlled adventure hobby, but the men and women who make their living on the airshow circuit don't play the game that way. "Airshow performers are pilots, entertainers, wanderers, minstrels, business people, and dedicated professionals all rolled into

one," says Patty Wagstaff, perhaps the best-known aerobatics performer in the country and a three-time U.S. National Aerobatic Champion. As a crowd-pleasing subset of the aerobatics community, airshow pilots push themselves to the top of their field by creating ever-more-daring maneuvers that allow them to sweep in over the crowd and make the onlookers squirm. "Airshow flying is strictly for the enjoyment of the audience," explains Michael Goulian, and this means flying fast and low. (The FAA restricts aerobatics to altitudes above 1,500 feet, but offers airshows a special dispensation, so pilots can fly both lower and in more congested areas than would normally be allowed.)

The complex maneuvers performed by airshow headliners are similar to those practiced in the most-advanced, or "unlimited," classification of aerobatics competition, though not all performers get their start in competition. Beyond the basic rolls and spins taught in most introductory aerobatics courses, pilots practice for years to master Immelmans, Cuban Eights, Lomcevaks, torque rolls, and the inverted ribbon cut. The goal is to achieve grace and safety at a low enough altitude to give the crowd a good view. Other pilots specialize in show openers or comedy and novelty flying, the less-exact flying styles that fill out a show's program.

"You don't really have to work for a living," says Michael Goulian, summing up the perks of the airshow flying business.

During the season, an airshow pilot's week falls into a familiar routine, despite the unfamiliar locales in which the routine plays out. Monday through Wednesday are for recouping and traveling. Thursday is for the media; pilots visit hospitals to see children who won't be able to see the weekend's shows, answer questions on the tarmac from journalists, and treat the most intrepid reporters to a bird's-eye view of airshow practice. Friday may be a press show or a real performance, depending on whether Sunday has been reserved for rain delays or another scheduled run. Saturday, though, is the big day on any airshow schedule. On performance day, pilots gather at the airport

High and dry: Airshow pilots rarely indulge in three martini lunches.

around 8 A.M. for a briefing, to be told the order in which they'll fly and any other necessary details. Meanwhile, their crews ready the airplanes for a practice run. (All told, there are about 100 people involved in staging an average airshow.) Each pilot has up to twenty minutes of flight time in the show, so performance days involve a lot more waiting than working.

Practical Information

Many airshow pilots grow up in flying families. Patty Wagstaff was born to an air force family, and Michael Goulian's family runs a flying school. However, it is possible to learn aerobatics on the weekends, and if you're daring enough, ascend to the ranks of airshow professionals.

Of course, flying comes before aerobatics. If you do not yet have your pilot's license, consult the Yellow Pages or the Internet or call your local airport to find instructors in your area. You'll use the same resources to locate aerobatics instructors.(Try to find someone who has a flight instructor's license; they're not required, so there are plenty of instructors without one.) After ten to twelve hours of aerobatic training, most pilots are competent to fly aerobatics solo, according to aerobatics hobbyist George Norris. Once you feel confident to embark on competition, contact the International Aerobatic Club (acro.harvard.edu/IAC/iac_homepg.html) to find out about contests near you.

Though not all airshow pilots come from the competitive aerobatics circuit, Michael Goulian recommends starting out in competition before breaking into the performance business. Because competition is based on the execution of standard maneuvers within limited airspace, it's a perfect training ground for pilots who want to get comfortable with the basics before learning to perform controlled careening in a crowded area. "Once you work up through the basic levels to unlimited, you're better than 90 percent of the airshow pilots going," Goulian encourages.

One major player on every pilot's team is the plane in which he or she performs. Eichhorn estimates the cost of an aerobatics aircraft at $18,000 for a simple single-seat plane to $150,000 for the latest high-performance craft on the market. Everyone in the business agrees, however, that purchasing a plane isn't necessary until you're ready to make a time investment that matches your monetary stake in the sport. It's not unusual for competitive pilots to use rental planes until they reach the higher levels of competition.

4 Voyeurs and Poseurs

Mystery Shopper
Pilgrim
Mall Santa
Cartoon Character Impersonator
Drag Queen
Private Investigator
Paparazzo
Audience Member
Celebrity Autobiography Collaborator

Mystery Shopper

Job description: Pose as a shopper in a store, a guest at a hotel, or a diner at a restaurant and thoroughly scrutinize products and services.

Compensation: A mystery shopper may get between $10 and $25 for a thirty-minute report on a retail store; mystery diners may get less in formal payment ($5 or $10) but have the cost of their meals reimbursed.

Prerequisites: None.

Qualities employer is seeking: Basic evaluation and writing abilities are important, and a certain finickiness may be helpful, although relentless criticism rather than observant and objective documentation is unwelcome.

Perks: The small rush incurred by concealing one's identity. Some mystery shoppers are also given certified checks of as much as $100 to give out if they have a particularly good encounter with an employee. (For more information on the excitement of surprising people by giving them money, see "Publishers Clearing House Prize Patrol Member," p. 254.)

Risks/drawbacks: The embarrassment and buzz kill when your undercover status is blown. At a Circuit City in Alabama, one employee notes that he's actually established an easy rapport with one of the frequent "mystery" shoppers: "It gets to where you don't worry about it, and you say, 'How're you doing, buddy?' "

Overview

Retail stores and restaurants have, in the last decade, begun seeking feedback more scientific than comment cards, customer complaints, and letters to management from angered patrons. "Because competition has gotten so fierce," says Bruce Van Kleeck, vice president of the National Retail Federation, "retailers need some way to evaluate themselves. A disinterested third party is the best way to get a fair assessment." Are the medium-sized dresses scattered about? Is the cheese too syrupy? Are the employees pushing super-sized shakes too aggressively? These are some of the questions that mystery shoppers are paid to answer. "We try to evaluate the total shopping experience from the eye of the target consumer," says Lea Kubas, president of Kubas Consultants, a Canadian mystery shopping service.

Mystery shopping organizations give assignments to their shoppers outlining the details of the visit and any pertinent issues that the retailer or restaurant is focusing on. Recent instructions for scrutinizing the Sonic chain of fast-food restaurants, as described by W. F. Orillo & Associates, a California mystery shopping organization that specializes in restaurants, read as follows: "Please order ONLY the items we have asked you to order. For this round of audits, you need to order: 1. A SONIC #1 or SONIC #2 Burger; 2. A Dr. Pepper; 3. After giving the speaker attendant the opportunity to suggest a side order, you must order a side order of Fries, Tator Tots, or Onion

Rings. Also, give the speaker the opportunity to suggest a LARGE Dr. Pepper." If the assignment is accepted, the mystery shopper usually is asked to conduct the visit within the week and fax in the evaluation less than twenty-four hours after the visit.

In some cases, mystery shoppers may be asked to pose as a certain kind of visitor or bargain hunter. "I went in there, to the Gap," says Harold Blumeno, sixty-eight, a mystery shopper in Michigan who does approximately 600 restaurant and retail visits per year, "and I was supposed to ask them about a camp outfit for my grandson, who was supposedly going off to camp. So I was to ask what did they have in khaki slacks, or shorts, that kind of stuff."

Some mystery shopping gigs may involve more than just cruising aisles or gorging on daily specials. Many mystery shopping organizations have begun branching out to offer analyses of accommodations, meaning citizens are paid to take working vacations at local motels. It's not as easy as it sounds. "These people have stopwatches on their wristwatches to time service," says Carl Braunlich, an assistant professor in Purdue University's Department of Restaurant, Hotel, Institutional, and Tourism Management. "They may eat four or five meals a day and order room service at all hours of the night. Some go so far as to make small pencil marks somewhere on their sheets to find out if the maid actually changes them.... They are so busy recording and monitoring, there's not much time to enjoy themselves. Believe it or not, some mystery guests become so familiar, they have to wear elaborate disguises and use phony names."

"He ever so carefully hid a piece of roast beef in between my slices of bologna," says Jim Jolly, a mystery shopper in New Jersey, reflecting on a less than satisfactory experience with the butcher at a national supermarket.

Mystery shopping organizations hold their workers to high standards and frequently weed out freeloaders who might gobble the complimentary meals but offer shallow evaluations; thus, many mystery shoppers adopt particular techniques to comprehensively record their experiences and impressions. "I'm always afraid I'm not going to get enough information," says Candace Radar, a mystery shopper in Virginia. She and her husband, Tim, have begun relying on a small concealed tape recorder to bolster their reports: When no employees are looking, Tim whispers a "play-by-play" of the meal and Candace later transcribes and faxes the report. Another mystery shopper, Noah Goldstein, twenty-eight, who's done a slew of California Pizza Kitchen evaluations in San Diego, recalls trying to surreptitiously detail his visits:

"You have to be covert about it. I generally posed as a student, so I'd just be taking notes—but in my notebook I'd be writing, like, soup arrived at 7:15, drinks arrived at 7:18. Sometimes I would write on my leg. And since you always have to check if the bathroom's clean, I'd go in the bathroom and write everything in there."

Practical Information

Finding work as a mystery shopper is becoming increasingly easier. The number of mystery shopping companies nationwide has doubled to 500 over the past five years. While a few large chains employ their own shoppers directly, the majority rely on third-party mystery shopping companies to handle the work for them. The best tactic is to blanket as many national organizations as possible. In general, these national organizations have clients spread out around the country. Don't limit yourself only to those mystery shopping companies that might be based in your area.

A number of helpful newsletters (many operated by successful mystery shoppers themselves) contain updates about companies seeking workers in specific areas. The *Mystery Shoppers Network* newsletter is published quarterly and includes general advice about finding work, as well as company listings and specific contact information. To order, send $29.95 to The Mystery Shoppers Network, 33228 West 12 Mile Rd., Suite 331, Farmington Hills, MI 48334 (800-579-4847).

Feedback Plus (972-616-8989) is one of the country's oldest and largest mystery shopping organizations, with over 72,000 contractors working for it.

Pilgrim

Job description: Present a historically accurate and engaging portrayal of one of the early English settlers in colonial New England.

Compensation: Some colonial-era living history museums pay interpreters, as the Pilgrims are officially called, as little as minimum wage, but the industry leaders, such as the interpretation department at Plimoth Plantation in Plymouth, Massachusetts, bump up the range to between $7 and $11 an hour. The hardest part of the Pilgrim compensation package is that the work is seasonal. The real Pilgrims might have toughed out the winters, but their modern-day counterparts don't even get the chance to try. When the New England interpretive centers close for the winter, usually in early November, the Pilgrims find themselves out of work until late March or early April. (If you're willing to relive the American Revolution again and again, you can find a longer work season at Colonial Williamsburg, Virginia.)

Prerequisites: An avid interest in history and education and some experience interacting with the public. Contrary to what you might think, most people break into interpretation work as apprentices, without any field-specific training. Some interpreters come from acting, some from history, and others from trades like carpentry that could pique one's interest in the crafts of the Pilgrim era.

Qualities employer is seeking: Ability to draw even "Old Surly, by the door" (as one militantly engaging Pilgrim calls aloof museum-goers), into the early 1600s. You have to love this enough to study hard and to put everything you have into making sure you're giving a performance that will captivate everyone in the audience, from the four-year-old who's more interested in a lollipop than obsolete methods of smithing

Credit: Michael Hall/Plimoth Plantation

A Godly pilgrimme from Plimoth in the New Worlde contemplating Sin, Salvation, the Harvest, and also where he left the keys to his Volvo.

horseshoes to the businessman who got dragged to the museum by his niece.

Perks: Interpreters emphatically agree that interacting with the public and seeing people learn is the best part of the job. Steven Angel, who plays William Palmer, Jr., the son of the town blacksmith, at Plimoth Plantation, says that his best on-the-job memory is of overhearing a young boy explaining to his father how the roofs on the plantation were built, based on a description Angel had just given the boy moments before. Training in the lost arts of colonial life may be a motivating factor for some Pilgrims, while others see learning carpentry, sailing, gardening, or smithing as an unexpected benefit.

Risks/drawbacks: Making ends meet during the off-season, in order to continue performing during the summers, is a challenge for most latter-day Pilgrims. And the off-season work options for a professional Pilgrim aren't extensive. It's been a long time since a competent blacksmith could rest assured he'd find work in any town. Even the most useful colonial skills may be considered esoteric in today's job market.

Overview

Falling somewhere between acting, lecturing, and split personality disorder, the job of interpreter requires extensive study of the history, religion, dialects, customs, and skills of daily life attributed to the English colonists. In addition to participating in preseason training provided by a museum, interpreters devote considerable personal time to perfecting their understanding of the world inhabited by the historical figures they represent. They may read books about these colonial characters, and when possible, books that these historical figures themselves were known to have read. Interpreters also learn the skills, such as carpentry, gardening, and farming that colonists used to survive. A Pilgrim's knowledge of Pilgrim life must be deep and detailed if he or she is to sustain improvisations for up to four hours at a stretch, talking with tourists and acting out life in the colonies.

Michael Hall, who now spends his days evoking the spirit of Miles Standish, first visited Plimoth Plantation when he was ten years old. According to family legend, he left declaring, "I want to be a Pilgrim when I grow up."

Because of the elevated station given to the Pilgrims in American elementary school history classes, interpreters sometimes face a challenge in overcoming the positive and negative misconceptions people bring into a museum. Plimoth Plantation employee Michael Hall finds it difficult sometimes to convince visitors that Miles Standish, the fictional pilgrim he portrays, didn't necessarily experience the tale of lost love told in Henry

Wadsworth Longfellow's poem "The Courtship of Miles Standish," and many visitors come with ready notions about how the Pilgrims and the Native Americans got along. "I'm always looking to turn people," says Hall.

Interpreters form tight-knit working communities, due to the many cooperative activities that go into keeping a living history site up and running. People often socialize together outside the museum and feel a familial bond within their historical setting. "There's a great community here. You get this team feeling. You party and socialize together," says Angel.

Practical Information

To learn more about first-person interpretation, find a copy of one of Jay Anderson's books, including *Time Machines: The World of Living History*, *Living History Sourcebook*, and *A Living History Reader: Museums*. All come recommended by Plimoth Plantation's Angel. Only the third is currently in print, but it's possible to find all three in libraries or through online book sources.

The Association for Living History, Farm, and Agricultural Museums (ALHFAM) is the field's best-known professional organization. The association's Web site (www.alhfam.org) includes membership information, a glossary of interpretation-related terminology (for example, *ghost interpretation*: When a first-person character travels into the present and may acknowledge the present), a bibliography of books on living history, and job listings for interpretation positions across the country. *Bulletin,* the ALHFAM newsletter, is free with membership. The New England and Southeast regional representatives for ALHFAM are, respectively, Tom Kelleher of Old Sturbridge Village in Sturbridge, Massachusetts (508-347-3362, x 279; www.osv.org) and John Caramia of Colonial Williamsburg (804-220-7493). Though their own living history affiliations date to eras later than the Pilgrim period, they should be able to direct you to opportunities in Pilgrim portrayal in their regions.

For the full-time, firsthand Pilgrim interpretation experience, go straight to the source, Plimoth Plantation (508-746-1622), and ask to speak to someone in the interpretation department. All of the interpreters are eager to talk about their work and encouraging of people's interest. Seasonal layoffs lead to a steady rate of turnover at the plantation, so each season brings new faces to replace the Pilgrims who found that the bills of the present outlast the past. After years of accepting interns on an irregular basis, the museum has organized an internship program, which provides another excellent introductory opportunity for aspiring pilgrims who still need to learn. Interns participate in preseason behind-the-scenes preparation, the interpreter training course, and genuine Pilgrim portrayals.

Mall Santa

Job description: Sit in the mall, wear a red suit, and listen to children's requests for Christmas. Get your picture taken. Laugh merrily from time to time. Be prepared for everything from leaky diapers to women with Santa fetishes.

Compensation: Pay is generally by the hour, starts around minimum wage, and can go up to $10 an hour. For the big-time Santas who work the advertising and commercial circuit, personal appearances can bring in upwards of $7,000.

Prerequisites: No special schooling, although the studios that provide seasonal photography (that means Easter, too) usually run training sessions for novice Santas. These workshops teach recruits everything from how to put on makeup to politically correct conversational techniques. First lesson: Don't ask about the child's "parents," since many today are lacking one or both. More advanced lessons include perfecting the belly laugh and learning how to deal with beard pullers.

Qualities employer is seeking: It's a man's world when it comes to the Santa gig, although the market for Mrs. Clauses and elves is growing. In addition, it usually helps to have a natural beard and a stomach large enough to shake "like a bowl full of jelly" when laughing. Not surprisingly, mall Santas tend to be overweight retired men, although unemployed people of all shapes and sizes flock to the profession as well. (If the Santa suit fits, wear it; if not, prospective Santas too slim and fit for Santadom might want to investigate opportunities as a cartoon character impersonator; see p. 65.)

Perks: Santas bring joy to children around the world, and without a strict workout regimen: the fatter the better. Perks for dead ringers include good tables at restaurants and free airline upgrades—everyone wants to be nice to Santa.

Risks/drawbacks: Brady White, a Santa so successful that he's known as the "Santa to the Stars," laments the attention he garners off duty. "I was in a bar having a martini and a woman came up to me, shook her head, and said, 'Santa shouldn't be drinking.' " Solemn occasions like funerals and wakes can be awkward if people titter, "Look! It's Santa Claus!" as he tries to pay his respects to the dead. Beside the emotional strain, the job can also be physically taxing: The suit is hot; the artificial beard (for Santas without the real thing) is scratchy; and kids can get heavy (hence the growing market for helper elves, who are often recruited to do Santa's heavy lifting).

Overview

For readers unfamiliar with two mainstays of American culture—Christmas and malls—starting in late November or early December, malls across America display Santa Claus look-alikes. Children can have their pictures taken with

Santa to the Stars

He's been profiled in the *New York Times* and *Cosmo*. Liz Taylor sat on his lap and told him that he was the best she'd ever seen. He drives a red Mercedes, doesn't have to diet, gets free airline upgrades, and makes upwards of $60 a minute. In other words, he's the sort of guy you'd love to hate.

Except that he's Santa Claus.

Brady White, the Santa to the Stars, started out as an unemployed actor with a Yuletide Santa gig at a mall. All it took was winning a contest sponsored by a local paper to find the best Santa Claus in L.A. Agents came crawling out of the woodwork, and so did the jobs. Twenty years later, White works for Cartier, Nieman-Marcus, Saks Fifth Avenue, and Lord and Taylor. He flies to Honolulu, Tokyo, and the Swiss Alps for photo shoots. His beard is insured "to six figures" by Lloyds of London (see "Ice Cream Flavor Developer," p. 218, for someone else with an insured body part).

But it isn't all fun and games—being Santa can be hard work. There's the simple physical strain of having a stream of tots, not always pint-sized, perch on your knees for hours at a time. The suit is hot, and parents can be awful.

White recounts the time a little girl's mother forced her to approach him, despite the girl's visible terror at the prospect." She was shaking like a leaf," he recalls. The mother kept pressuring her to "sit on Santa's lap, sit on Santa's lap," until a small puddle appeared around the little girl's feet. White, ever the professional, assured the little girl that "the reindeers do that all the time" and smoothly went on to ask her what she wanted for Christmas. "I tried not to make it a traumatic experience."

Tinkling tots aside, big-time Santahood has other challenges. As far as professional community goes, forget it: "Small-time Santas get resentful," says White. And he can't ever really retire. The older and fatter he gets, the more work he has. Last in the list of occupational hazards, White can't go anywhere without being recognized and treated like he's, well, Santa Claus. This is fine when it gets you a first-class seat on an airline, but imagine getting a death-stare every time you walk into a bar, order a martini, and light a cigarette. It's like you just ran over the Easter bunny.

"Santa" and tell him what they want for Christmas. Adults sometimes join in the fun, too. Depending on the establishment, the setup can go from simple to baroque. (See David Sedaris's essay "SantaLand Diaries" for a harrowing account of the Macy's holiday colossus.)

The job isn't all fun and games, especially in this age of dysfunctional families and sexual-harassment lawsuits. Santas have to be careful not to ask invasive questions about parents or home life, and heaven forbid they accidentally touch a young bottom as they're picking

up their pint-sized suppliants. The photography studios that hire and train Santas usually include the new etiquette as part of the crash course to Santahood, but you can never be too careful.

He's kind, generous, and great with kids. No wonder some women think he's the ideal man. "You'd be surprised how many women have fantasies of Santa," says White. During a mall engagement, a woman in a fur coat asked to have her picture taken on his lap. When she sat down, her coat revealed only a skimpy bra and panties. He stood up immediately: "I felt it was the wrong situation."

Practical Information

The Santa gig is a seasonal one unless you're the best in the business. For the lucky few, the work never stops: Commercials and print ads can be shot anytime. Open casting calls for Santas can bring in literally hundreds of portly and bearded aspirants, but it's up to the whim of the casting agents who gets picked. Sometimes they look for a "halo Santa" (balding à la Friar Tuck, with a fringe of hair at the sides), and sometimes they look for a Santa with a full head of hair. Sometimes Santas are short, sometimes tall; sometimes black, more often white. It's more a business of looks than of talent, so most Santas stick to holiday-time mall appearances. They're in it because they have some free time, they need to make some money, and most of all, they love kids.

Most malls start advertising in the classifieds and in the mall around September or October. You can also try approaching the photography studio that the mall uses. Dedicated Santas start growing their beards in June. Engagements are usually about six weeks, part-time (four- to five-hour shifts). And during your Santa stint, there's no smoking or drinking on the job.

Cartoon Character Impersonator

Job description: Dress up as and pretend to be a cartoon character. Adults occasionally request these services for charity functions, but the bulk of the work is at children's birthday parties. Many character impersonators refer to themselves as "children's entertainers."

Compensation: Independent contractors for established companies make $25 to $50 per party (about ninety minutes) plus tips. If you work for yourself, you can charge $165 or more per party. The bulk of the work is on weekends. Income for contractors can range from $50 to $250 in a weekend. Working independently, an impersonator can make triple that range. One impersonator claimed she made $1,000 in a single weekend. Another interviewee gave up the profession because he wasn't able to turn more than $250 a week.

Prerequisites: An interest in performance, a love for kids, enough dexterity to make balloon animals even when you can't see out of the eyeholes on your poorly fitted Barney headgear, and your hands are covered in fur.

Qualities employer is seeking: Charisma and perkiness, the ability to maintain the rapt attention of thirty children for ninety minutes, a clean-cut appearance, some resemblance (either by nature or through costuming) to the cartoon character you are impersonating, and the ability to make great balloon animals.

Perks: "Kids are amazing. They're like sponges. They just want you and want your attention. It's really fulfilling when you have thirty kids who want to hug you and kiss you. Eighty-ninety percent of the time it's really fun," says Shanine Chandler, who, at six-foot-one, most commonly impersonates Barbie and the Pink Power Ranger. Some entertainers get a kick out of putting on big funny costumes.

Risks/drawbacks: Having thirty kids kicking you and screaming, "You're not Barney," as you baste in sweat inside a fur costume, where the temperature can rise above 100 degrees on a summer afternoon, is one possible inconvenience. You can also get sued for copyright infringement. While all of your clients will want well-known characters from recent films or television shows, you may not advertise the specific names of characters that are copyrighted. Your costume must have some distinct differences from the character you are representing. While Disney has never been known to go undercover to catch every entertainer with a Pocahontas outfit, some companies are sticklers, and the law is on their side.

The Spanish Barney and the Drunk Barney

Cartoon character impersonator Stephen Raymonds, discussing his first day at work: "You have to park a block and a half away, so the kids don't see you changing into your costume. I get out of the car and a bunch of Hasidic elementary school kids began to push me around 'cause I'm dressed as a purple dinosaur. I arrive at the party, and it's for two-year-olds. In my distraction, I left the tape player in the car. I start singing the Barney song, and the kids start screaming. So I say, 'Barney needs to go look for Baby Bop,' and head back to the car, running down the street full speed in a dinosaur costume, [with] people honking at me and trying to run me over. The kids never got over that initial scare. All the balloons that I had were melted 'cause it was ninety-seven degrees. Then I get a page from the office and they tell me there's a party all the way on the other side of the city, and the other Barney didn't show up because he was drinking all day. So I drive down there in my costume, and I look across the street, and the other Barney is there. I call the office and they say, 'Steve, he's drunk, you have to go and fire him,' so I go in to the party, and I say, 'Hey, it's me, I'm the real Barney.' It turns out that none of the kids speak English. Luckily, I speak some Spanish so I become Spanish Barney and got rid of the other guy. He was a good [balloon] animal maker, but he was drunk as a skunk."

Overview

The business of cartoon character impersonation took off in the early eighties. The abundance of work reflects the willingness of baby boomers to spend outrageous amounts on their kids, as well as Hollywood's successful takeover of children's entertainment. In the seventies, a grab bag and a cake made for a decent party. A magician or a piñata was a special event. Today, a kids' party is a drag without a live character from the latest animated film in your living room.

The pantheon of characters grows yearly. At press time, favorites include Barney, Barbie, Power Rangers, Cinderella, Snow White, Pocahontas, Batman, Winnie the Pooh, Buzz Lightyear, Big Bird, Lamb Chop, Bart Simpson, Casper, John Smith, the Lion King, Captain Hook, Mulan, and Jasmine. Whatever characters Disney puts out tend to make it into suburban backyards within two or three months.

Many cartoon character impersonators are out-of-work performers: Your weekends are shot, but you can attend auditions all week. Chandler reports that some cartoon character impersonators double as adult entertainers: "You know, Tommy the Tank by day, and Ted the construction worker strip-o-gram by night."

Practical Information

To do independent contracting, look through your phone book for companies that offer the service. The company will probably give you a training session that doubles as an audition. At the session you will be taught how to perform some magic tricks and otherwise keep kids entertained for ninety minutes.

"Some kids will fall for the old hot dog balloon, but jaded ones will insist on giraffes, swans, lions, and so on."

Since most companies will keep 60 to 70 percent of what the parents pay, you'll make a lot more doing it on your own, but you'll have to shoulder the investment risk and marketing costs. "People just don't realize how easy it is," says Chandler. Costumes run from $50 to $300, depending on how complicated they are. Disney sells costumes of their characters, but many costume shops can create something more durable for less.

On the job, you're basically a glorified babysitter. Some ways of keeping the kids happy are singing, storytelling, face painting, teaching martial arts, parachute games, piñatas, magic tricks, cutting the cake, and of course, making balloon animals.

Jobs are acquired through word of mouth and referral. Advertise in local parenting magazines and the phone book. Leave flyers at party supply stores. Try to get a gig at a school event, from which classrooms of kids can go home and beg their parents for you to come to their birthday parties.

(If your calling is to don a big furry costume and romp around, you should also consider becoming a sports mascot. See p. 196.)

Drag Queen

Job description: Dress in women's clothing and entertain an audience. Performances generally include some combination of musical numbers (either sung or lip-synced), celebrity impressions, and stand-up comedy.

Compensation: Drag queens are paid either by the song or by the show. Some leave with nothing more than the joy of having entertained, while a successful performer can bring in up to $100 to $200 a night, including tips. In general, though, only a handful of drag queens actually make a living in drag. Like everyone else in show biz, they temp, take other acting jobs, or wait tables while waiting for that big break.

Prerequisites: A few sparkly gowns, a wig, some makeup, and a lot of gumption. Being gay—or at least being in tune with gay culture—is also helpful, since most audience members at drag shows are gay men.

Qualities employer is seeking: Looks are unimportant—the success of departed 300-pound drag legend Divine is proof of that—but the look is essential. Whether she's going for sexy and glamorous, coy and girlish, or just plain trashy, a drag queen often spends years perfecting her persona. Other key attributes: vocal and dancing ability and a razor-sharp wit.

Perks: Artistic freedom and being able to offer your commentary on the world—and look absolutely fabulous doing it. Plus, as New York drag performer/Queen-of-All-Media Hedda Lettuce reveals, "You get away with murder. Any man who says he's straight and you find him attractive—you can have sex with him."

Risks/drawbacks: To avoid any unsightly bulges, a drag queen must tuck, also known as "hiding your candy." First, the testicles are pushed back into the inguinal canal (it happens naturally to males when they're immersed in cold water). Then, to remove the evidence, the penis is tucked under the legs and held back between the buttocks with—ouch—duct tape.

Overview

The term *drag* is nothing new. It was common usage in the 1800s to refer to the swish or "drag" of a woman's dress along the ground. The concept of men dressing in drag has been around even longer, from the flowing robes of the Greeks to the Shakespearean tradition of male actors playing female roles, all the way to Harvard University's 150-year-old bastion of undergraduate cross-dressing, the Hasty Pudding Theatricals. Drag crosses cultural boundaries as well, with traditions among Native American shamans, African tribesmen, and the Noh and Kabuki actors of Japan. Indeed, it seems that as long as there have been ladies' dresses, there have been men willing to wear them.

Interview with "Charlene Unger," aka transgender performance artist Peter Mohawk

Job description: "Well, I work at a Brazilian restaurant called Rhumba here in Chicago, where I'm the entertainer—the entertainment. My job is to sing songs, woo the public, make them laugh, make them cry, make them enjoy themselves, make them feel special, and also to delight them, mesmerize them, and fascinate them."

Her military background: "I've been singing and performing since I was a little girl. From the USO back in WWII—I was the Shirley Temple of the Big One, you know—to being in Bob [Hope]'s and Dean [Martin]'s shows, I was always singing, always entertaining, always bringing a special joy to people. I'm always giving. I guess I've given so much that's all I know how to do!"

What she meant to do: "I've had many jobs. I worked at the Russell-Stover Candy Company. I stuffed chocolate-covered cherries for quite some time. But after I was married and my daughter was born, I thought that that's what I'd be doing: I'd be a mom and a housewife, and I'd live the life of the average American gal. But history wouldn't let that happen."

Why she loves her work: "I can see the delight in people's eyes and hear their shouts of pure joy when the number is going well, and when it's over, I know that I've been able to move someone."

The worst thing that can happen on the job: "When people stand up out of their chairs, and they just turn around and walk out."

The best thing that can happen on the job: "A marriage proposal!"

Her last big break: "A few years back I was invited to audition to be part of the chorus for Cyndi (Lauper) when she sang 'Girls Just Wanna Have Fun' on Oprah, while Ms. Winfrey interviewed Patrick Swayze, Wesley Snipes, and John Leguizamo about their movie *To Wong Foo, Thanks for Everything, Julie Newmar*. And Cyndi and I bonded, and she picked me to stand front and center right behind her for the whole song!"

Her dream: "Well, my big dream is to have my own talk show, called Charlene's Garden Party. I fancy it a sort of combination of the old *Dinah Shore Show* and the *Carol Burnett Show*. That's my dream."

Advice for aspiring transgender performance artists? "You have to find that kernel of truth inside you, no matter how you're dressed or what sort of character they ask you to be or what costume you wear. There's that kernel of truth, and that's what you're giving to the audience—because in the end, you're telling your own story."

"You're born naked and everything you put on after that is drag," says drag superstar RuPaul.

Only recently, though, has drag found its way into the mainstream, thanks to movies like *Tootsie*, *The Adventures of Priscilla, Queen of the Desert*, and *To Wong Foo, Thanks for Everything, Julie Newmar.* With the success of those movies, drag has come into its own as a form of entertainment; no longer merely the realm of cross-dressers, drag today is an art form that is caught up in camp, self-conscious excess, and the over-the-top subversion of societal norms. And while it may not fly in Peoria, some form of drag culture can be found in any metropolitan area.

Drag is about individuality; there's no typical drag queen profile. Other than that, like any actor, drag queens are drawn to the spotlight and driven to perform. Some are classically trained singers and dancers; some have no training beyond the complete works of Patti LaBelle. Most are gay men. Some are transsexual (which means that they believe they're actually of the opposite sex, and perhaps have taken steps toward having a sex change), and this has raised a controversial point: How can it be drag if you're not really a man? Which, in turn, raises another question—exactly what is a man? And that's what makes drag fascinating: It blurs gender lines and makes an audience question traditional ideas of sex. Of course it's also, as Divine once commented, "just a way to give people a good laugh."

One issue that drag performers must face is career longevity—or lack thereof. "Drag queens are not like fine wine; we don't get better with age," confesses Hedda Lettuce. In a job where glamour is essential and thirty-five is over the hill, aging drag queens have two options: cake on the makeup ever more thickly, or as geriatric go-go dancer Charlene Unger encourages, "Keep on reinventing yourself. Always, always, always."

Practical Information

It's easy to be a drag queen. Just tape up your genitals, throw on a dress, some makeup, and pumps, and strut out into the night. But to be a successful, working drag queen is a different story. In this highly competitive field without a union and without regulations, it's every girl for herself. To get started, think about karaoke—obviously it doesn't pay, but many a drag queen has worked out a number with informal sessions at the microphone on Karaoke Night. From there, aspiring queens can move on to local pageants, parades, nightclubs, and maybe even the queen of them all—New York City's annual Wigstock Festival in September.

The e-zine *Drag Hag*, at www.fortunecity.com/westwood/vivienne/5, has helpful hints, book recommendations, and pop culture commentary about and of interest to aspiring drag queens. Two other Web sites of interest are www.rupaul.net and www.hedda.com, homes to Supermodel of the World

RuPaul and up-and-comer Hedda Lettuce, respectively. Required reading includes *Hiding My Candy: The Autobiography of the Grand Empress of Savannah* by The Lady Chablis (of *Midnight in the Garden of Good and Evil* fame), RuPaul's *Lettin' It All Hang Out*, and finally *Miss Vera's Finishing School for Boys Who Want to Be Girls*, about a real Manhattan drag academy, by Veronica Vera.

Private Investigator

Job description: Engage in all kinds of investigative activities: high-level surveillance work, missing person searches, extramarital affair documentation, personal injury investigations, etc.

Compensation: Most P.I.s make between $60 and $100 a hour; top-level investigators, who work for large corporations or wealthy public figures, can make as much as $2,000 a day.

Prerequisites: Requirements for a state license vary: Some states require that the aspiring investigator be only of a certain age (generally eighteen or twenty-one), while others require that an individual has either logged several years in public law enforcement or has worked an equivalent period of time for a licensed private investigator. The states may also require applicants to attend a certified training seminar and take a written test.

Qualities employer is seeking: A good intuitive sense for theft and fraud; conversational tact in order to extract precious information from skittish interviewees; for some surveillance cases, the ability to disguise oneself as a convincing bush for hours on end.

Perks: The satisfaction of bringing a complex and unwieldy case to a close. There is also, as private investigator-

turned-writer Edward Pankau states, an exciting unpredictability inherent in the job: "The next person in the door may be a dreamer looking for a lost love, a business owner who's been swindled, or a little old lady who thinks the Martians are stealing her brain waves."

Risks/drawbacks: Investigators can be attacked or shot, particularly those involved in prickly domestic disputes.

Overview

A P.I. may spend one day searching for a runaway child or cruising an office for evidence of employee theft and the next hunting down a celebrity stalker or peering through a telephoto lens to document evidence of industrial toxic waste. Some P.I.s work within large, specialized agencies that focus on one particular niche—be it video surveillance or domestic disputes; others may choose to live more as independent pavement prowlers, conducting all of their investigations by themselves and rarely, if ever, contracting out their sleuthing skills to other investigators.

There is also a distinct group of private investigators who make their living as so-called information brokers: "These guys go around buying databases, microfiche, public record data, anything they can find," says Robert Venezia, a former New York police officer who now works as a P.I. in California. "They make a lot of contacts throughout the country and the world, and when you need a specific piece of information, you call them up."

"In this business, the commodity you're selling is yourself," says private investigator Anthony Dellaventura, the real-life inspiration behind the CBS television series *Dellaventura*. "If I'm some 300-pound fat guy, or I'm wearing a $99 Alexander's suit, what kind of message does that send out? I have to be able to discuss a case in a lawyer's office and also work on the street. Not a lot of guys can do both of those."

Those P.I.s who choose to meddle in personal relationship cases may find themselves immersed in heated and potentially threatening situations. "A lot of investigators consider matrimonial work the most dangerous kind there is," says Bruce Haskett, a California P.I., "since you're dealing with people who are in some kind of dispute, and emotions run high—people, men and women, can do some very strange things under pressure."

Investigators who take on these relationship cases must also be sensitive to the possibility that the information they unearth can ignite fits of jealous rage. Misinformation can be catastrophic. In New Orleans, in April 1998,

after a private investigator working for a worried husband revealed that he'd seen the man's wife in a "romantic hug" with a co-worker (the hug was neither photographed nor videotaped) the husband shot his wife's co-worker. The sheriff's deputy later revealed that the husband had made promises to the P.I. of a full-scale paid investigation if the investigator turned up any inklings of an affair.

Some of the biggest clients for private investigators are insurance companies, which frequently hire investigators to scope out the legitimacy of certain compensation claims. Tony Passanisi, a private investigator in San Francisco, recalls doing surveillance on a man who allegedly had injured himself at work and was unable to move without the use of a walker; Passanisi trailed the man and found him loading hefty packages into his van. "He looked like death warmed over," says Passanisi, "until he needed to lift a few hundred pounds."

Another lucrative—although, by some standards, rather dry—area of P.I. work is employment background checks. (The U.S. Chamber of Commerce says employee theft costs U.S. businesses between $20 to $40 billion annually—more than $400 per year for every working citizen in the U.S.) "Almost all companies put more research and effort into checking out their next copier machine than a human being who is going to have a major impact on the company, good or bad," says Thom Wagner, a Milwaukee-based investigator who makes a living primarily through conducting background checks—each of which can cost up to $300.

Practical Information

State regulations regarding private investigators vary from just an age requirement and license fee to actual law enforcement training. Some states require a written examination, which may focus heavily on legal questions, since private investigators must frequently understand what kind of evidence collection work (recording conversations, videotape surveillance, etc.) is legal and admissible in local courts. For information on individual state requirements, Paladin Press offers a handbook, *Obtaining Your Private Investigator's License*,

Credit: AP

"There's just one more thing I don't understand."

for $10. Write to Paladin Press, Inc., P.O. Box 1307, Boulder, CO 80306, or call 303-443-7250.

Another good resource, also from Paladin Press, is Edmund Pankau's poorly titled book, *How to Make $100,000 a Year as a Private Investigator.* The book includes an overview of the various public information databases available to private investigators, recommends some important legal reference books to build an investigative library, and has a useful appendix of sample P.I. billing forms and contracts. One of the best online resources is P.I. Mall (www.pimall.com), which has links to both individual P.I. company pages and state-level investigation organizations. The site also offers newsgroups and an unusually well-populated P.I. chat room.

Finally, those who are interested in becoming private investigators might explore apprenticing with licensed and experienced local investigators. Also, certain security jobs, although slightly less glamorous, may provide useful training. Thom Wagner, now a private investigator in Wisconsin who focuses on corporate theft, says he culled his investigative techniques while working as an undercover detective at a racetrack in New Jersey. "The main things we worked on were narcotics, both human and equine," says Wagner. "Part of my job was to buy drugs for the state police on the tracks. That taught me a lot. For starters, I learned that I had to have a set of names to use, otherwise I'd say my name was Tim, and two minutes later, I'd tell them my name was Dave. It takes a little bit of acting."

Paparazzo

Job description: Photograph celebrities and sell the pictures to magazines and tabloids.

Compensation: Pictures of celebrities sell for as little as $35 (to fan magazines) and up to $1,000 to $1,500 for cover shots for *People.* Freelance photographers generally retain rights to their works and can earn ongoing royalties if a picture runs in multiple publications. The photographer who captured Elle McPherson right after she gave birth reportedly grossed more than $50,000 in international syndication royalties. Rare exclusives can be lucrative; the first pictures of Diana and Dodi reportedly sold for a million dollars. A hard-working paparazzo on the celebrity circuit can expect to clear (after expenses) about $4,000 a month.

Prerequisites: A camera with a flash.

Qualities employer is seeking: Pertinacity to brazenly stalk celebrities who would, if given the chance, have their bodyguards beat the crap out of you. Ability to take focused pictures, in all lighting conditions, of sometimes uncooperative, occasionally belligerent, moving subjects.

Perks: Set your own hours. Suing for pain and suffering damages after getting assaulted (see "Risks/drawbacks").

Risks/drawbacks: Getting assaulted. Ron Galella, who has been shooting celebrities since the 1960s, has been roughed up by Secret Servicemen, bodyguards, and occasionally celebrities themselves. In 1973, Marlon Brando sucker-punched him and knocked out five of his teeth. R. J. Capak, a New York paparazzo, claims he was mauled outside a New York club by Q-Tip, a rapper, and Leonardo Di-Caprio's handlers. They knocked into him, smashed his video equipment, and took his camera. "So I go up to the window [of DiCaprio's Range Rover] and I'm like, 'Hey, Leo, you know, this is like really uncool, man. You guys assaulted me and stole my video camera.' And he looks at me and he shrugs and is laughing and everything. And then another guy got out of the back of the truck and spit on me. I couldn't believe it. I was like, 'Hey, buddy. That's the best you can do, spit on me?' So I was pleading with Leo to get the video camera back. He laughed and just drove away."

Overview

Thomas Hinton lived next door to O. J. Simpson in Brentwood and had the presence of mind to go around back and snap O.J. being placed into handcuffs. By the time O. J. was led out in front of his house, where the rest of the photographers were waiting, the police had removed the handcuffs. Hinton, an opportunistic photography student at the time, got the only shots of O. J. in handcuffs. He sold the pictures to the *National Enquirer* for $15,000.

An insider joke:

Q: What's the difference between paparazzi and Sammy the Bull?

A: Sammy the Bull stops shooting when you're dead.

The difference between a good paparazzo and a great one is a combination of photographic talent, a businessperson's sense of what will sell, and a knack for being in the right place at the right time. Like seasoned fishermen who know where the fish are, successful paparazzi develop a sixth sense for knowing which bars, clubs, and restaurants are likely to disgorge hot stars on a given night. The effects of luck and serendipity are further reduced over time as veteran paparazzi, barnacles on the celebrity circuit, accumulate archives of pictures that may become valuable someday. "These people around me might have missed a shot, or might not even want it," said Capak. "Tomorrow, that person might be locked up for murder. And all of a sudden that picture has become very valuable. Things happen. Princess Di. Nobody expected her to die."

In the United States (primarily in New York and Los Angeles), a core of about 200 men and women make a living slogging it out behind a never-ending ropeline at openings, promotional events, and premieres. While there is competition between the professionals on the circuit, there is also camaraderie. "Everybody talks. We're all friends," said Capak. "Until it's time to take the photo. And after that we're friends again."

Given the premium for exclusives, outfoxing the competition is a constant challenge. Capak recounts with pride his exclusive shots of David Beckham, an English soccer player who flew to New York to meet his girlfriend, Victoria Adams (Posh Spice), after his team lost in the 1998 World Cup. "When he came into the country after he lost the soccer game for England, I'm the one that nailed him at the airport. Everybody was at the wrong door and when he came through customs. Yup, I nailed him big time."

In Europe, particularly England, where tabloids maintain an insatiable appetite for voyeuristic, privacy-violating photographs, paparazzi have grown increasingly aggressive. In an unusual reversal, American paparazzi tend to be more civilized and restrained than their European counterparts. Congress is now considering antipaparazzi bills, sponsored by lawmakers from California, which would make it a crime to threaten someone's safety in order to get a photograph or make a recording. Another would make using a zoom lens akin to trespassing.

Practical Information

The barriers to entry in this business are low. All you really need is a camera with a flash (preferably an autofocus camera with automatic aperture and shutter speed selection). Most pros work with

Interview with paparazzo Ron Galella

Ron Galella is the author of *Jacqueline*, a photo-documentary of his favorite subject, Jacqueline Onassis. He followed Jackie everywhere for five years until a court found that he had violated her privacy and levied an injunction, preventing him from taking pictures of Jackie, or her family, for the rest of his life.

His brush with stardom on June 12, 1973: "Marlon Brando was with Dick Cavett. He did the *Dick Cavett Show*. I followed him to Chinatown. That's where it happened. He called me over and he said, 'What else do you want that you don't already have?' I said, 'I'd like a picture without the sunglasses.' It was at night and both of them had sunglasses on. And I looked at Cavett—see, Dick Cavett knew me and I thought that perhaps he would get Brando to do it—but Brando gave me a right to the jaw. That was his answer. He socked me in the jaw and knocked out five teeth. Right-hand shot."

Why Marlon Brando still has Ron Galella's teeth marks scarred on his knuckles: "I wound up in Bellevue [Hospital] trying to patch up the damage. I got ten caps. The funny thing is the next day, Brando was at the Regency and his hand swelled up. His hand was swollen with infection. Dick Cavett took him to the New York Hospital of Special Surgery to fix it up over three days. He has my teeth marks on his knuckles. Permanently. Scarred. It was an ironic twist."

A year's salary: "I got an out-of-court settlement with Brando for $40,000."

an agency, so they can concentrate on taking, rather than selling, the pictures. Agencies usually take care of the selling and billing in exchange for a percentage of sales, although some agencies employ photographers on a salaried basis. To get agency representation, assemble a portfolio of celebrity pictures. It's also helpful to cultivate a specialty, for example, shooting rock stars onstage, that distinguishes you from the field.

In addition to attending promotional events, paparazzi must keep abreast of the volatile celebrity market. Who's dating who, who's hot, who's working on a movie in town. *Celebrity Service* newsletter, which costs $1,500 a year, is an industrial-strength version of *People*: a daily fax-based service that provides exhaustive information about the comings and goings of celebrities. Celebrity Service, Inc., has offices in New York and Los Angeles, as well as sister companies in London, Paris, Rome, and Washington, D.C. (212-757-7979 in New York; 310-652-1700 in L.A.). Short of subscribing to this, local newspaper gossip columns are a good source of information. Also, police departments provide locations of movie shoots.

Audience Member

Job description: Sit in on shows with a live studio audience. Clap on command.

Compensation: Audience members are paid about $5 an hour. Days are usually eight hours long, although you only get paid for the time the show is taping—usually four or five hours, maximum.

Prerequisites: To be in an audience, you must fit into a standard auditorium seat, and when appropriate, make a clapping sound. Other than that, the requirements aren't strict. Since a taping can take anywhere from a few hours to a day, it's good to have a flexible schedule.

Qualities employer is seeking: You should have a sense of humor, or at least be easily amused. Those who survive in this high-turnover business actually enjoy game and talk shows enough to watch them for five hours a day. It's a great asset to be patient. After all, you spend most of your time sitting and waiting.

Perks: There's a chance of running into the nearly rich and once famous. Former "clapper" (as they're known in the industry) Andrew Smith reports having once run into Sherman Helmsley on the set of Wink Martindale's game show *Debt.* "He was showing up for a taping of *Celebrity Debt.* We had pizza together during the lunch break." Smith cites free lunch and T-shirts as two other big pluses, not to mention getting paid to watch live television, something plenty of people do at home (amateurs).

Risks/drawbacks: "Once I saw this guy jump out of his seat and run four rows down. He punched some guy in the face," recalls Smith. It's hard to tell if watching game shows makes you crazy or if only crazy people watch game shows, but there seems to be some correlation.

Overview

Some shows with live studio audiences are very popular; many are not. Unpopular shows, because they can't find enough volunteers to attend tapings, hire professional audience members to fill their seats. While it would be cheaper to just insert a laugh track, shows use clappers in the interest of the performers—they need an audience to react to, even if they know the audience is getting paid to laugh.

All told, the job is a bit of a grind. L.A. studio lots (and this work is found almost exclusively in L.A.) are notoriously poorly run. Clappers can show up in the morning, wait around till the afternoon, and then be told that taping was canceled for the day. They're usually paid for a portion of the wait, but this can translate to $5 to $10 for the morning— less than subsistence-level wages.

Beyond these bleak periods, clappers also have the once-in-a-lifetime opportunity of honing their game-show skills to the point of succeeding as a

contestant. The work is bearable, and even fun, if you alternate clapping engagements with some other form of temporary employment. (Like the idea of winning money? Check out what it takes to be a habitual radio contest winner; see p. 211.)

Smith, on getting fired: "The standards they set make it impossible to be fired. All you have to do is put your fucking hands together." He does, however, admit that the face puncher was fired, or at least ejected from the building.

Some people have even managed to make careers out of professional clapping. The regular clapping community is close-knit and active on the game-show circuit. People have been known to visit as many as five shows on the same lot in a day and then return on weekends for special engagements. A fair number of clappers are out-of-work actors looking for a lucky break. "I don't know what they're thinking," says Smith. "It's not like you're going to find a casting agent just sitting in the audience of the *Keenan Ivory Wayans Show*."

Practical Information

Becoming a clapper involves more than just showing up on the studio lot at 9 A.M. Shows work exclusively through talent agencies, which take around 50 percent of the payment. This means that the studio pays about $10 for every hour you're in, only $5 of which you'll ever see. Agencies advertise in the backs of trade magazines like the *Hollywood Reporter*, as well as on flyers posted around L.A. Watch for want ads looking for "extras," a term sometimes used as a euphemism for clappers.

Celebrity Autobiography Collaborator (Ghostwriter)

Description: Help a celebrity or high-profile public figure write his or her autobiography.

Compensation: What the collaborator receives depends on a number of factors—his or her previous titles, the celebrity's popularity, and the book's sales. It isn't inconceivable that a collaborator could make well into the mid-six figures from a single project.

Prerequisites: There are no formal requirements for this job. Celebrity collaborators are freelance writers, and therefore, will generally get more work as their writing portfolio and list of successful projects grows.

Qualities employer is seeking: An easygoing personality; the ability to construct a compelling and readable narrative; adherence to deadlines.

Perks: Flexible hours and partial fame. In many cases, the collaborator may travel with the celebrity, getting a rare opportunity to hobnob in the celebrity's circle.

Risks/drawbacks: Those who fancy themselves fiction writers may find the work stifling. Many eventually perceive that they are contributing to a commercially successful, but creativity-starved, area of the publishing industry.

Overview

The past few years have seen the rise of the celebrity autobiography in the publishing industry. Many popular comedians, actors, singers, models, and other public figures are choosing to tell their own life stories in book form—and they are profiting handsomely from doing so. Yet, nearly all of these stars have neither the time nor the skills to put pen to paper and compose the books themselves. Without the assistance of professional collaborators, their books might never happen, or might end up poorly crafted.

Collaborators immerse themselves into the celebrity's life and may end up with fruitful experiences from the endeavor. Daniel Paisner is a successful collaborator whose start in the business was with weatherman Willard Scott, ten years ago. "When I did the book with Ed Koch, I got a crash course in NYC politics," said Paisner, who lives in New York. "When I did a book with Maureen Reagan, Ronald Reagan's daughter, I got a crash course in the Reagan family and in California." Paisner's list also includes books with Malcolm Jamal-Warner, Montel Williams, Geraldo Rivera, plus-size model Emme, Governor George Pataki, and actor Anthony Quinn. ("He lived in Italy for twenty or thirty years," says

Paisner of his trip to Europe with Quinn, "and to drive around these backwater towns with 'Señor Quinn' was pretty cool.")

"No one ever grew up dreaming of being a ghostwriter," says William Novak, who has collaborated with Lee Iacocca, Oliver North, Sydney Biddle Barrows, Tip O'Neill, and Magic Johnson on their autobiographies. "I had done a few books of my own—one on Jewish humor and another on marijuana smokers—before I got into this line of work. But the Iacocca book was the first time I had done anything like that. And the book did so well I kept doing it. I suddenly had a career."

A collaborator must be someone who can listen attentively for hours on end, as the project necessitates conducting lengthy interviews, frequently not only with the celebrity but also with the celebrity's friends and family. The work requires the ghostwriter to be a sympathetic ear, continually expressing surprise, amazement, and pleasure at the celebrity's own life. In many cases, the story might be truly compelling, which will make the collaborator's job far more intriguing. At other times, the celebrity may be dull and self-important, rendering the collaborator's job downright painful. Perhaps, however, the worst-case scenario is when the subject just isn't very verbose. Noted ghostwriter William Novak says, "I don't get writer's block because I don't have to come up with the material, but sometimes I get the equivalent. I've worked with one or two people that didn't have a whole lot to say. That's always a problem, and you just try to make due with what you have."

The financial rewards can be considerable. Celebrity autobiographies are considered one of the most bankable literary genres, and thus, publishers are willing to invest large amounts of money in them. The phenomenal success of books by Jerry Seinfeld, Paul Reiser, and Howard Stern, whose *Private Parts* was the fastest-selling book in Simon & Schuster's history, have fueled this trend. Marcia Clark reportedly received a $4.2 million advance for her book, Drew Carey, $3 million, and Whoopi Goldberg, $6 million. Although collaborators frequently get only a fraction of what the

LL Cool J and Karen Hunter, his collaborator on *I Make My Own Rules.*

Credit: Courtesy of Karen Hunter

celebrity receives—both in the advance and in downstream royalties—even a small percentage of these sizable sums is significant.

A celebrity collaborator may take ghostwriting jobs in order to pay the bills and still work on writing projects that bring a greater degree of personal and creative satisfaction. William Novak says that he enjoys "writing long essays for obscure Jewish magazines." Daniel Paisner is equally matter-of-fact. "Ghostwriting is my day job," says Paisner. "It's my waiting tables. Hopefully when one of my own books hits, I can be a bit more selective in what I choose to do."

Practical Information

Becoming a celebrity collaborator is undeniably a challenge. Publishing houses, conservative by nature, are more inclined to link a celebrity with a writer who has a proven track record doing this kind of work. "Particularly in this field, doing one helps you do a second, and doing three helps you do others," says Jim Jerome, a ghostwriter who has done books with Kathie Lee Gifford and Roger Corman, among others. If there is any sort of training ground, it is probably journalism. A newspaper or magazine reporter who has done a series of celebrity profiles may catch the eye of an agent or an editor. *New York Daily News* reporter Karen Hunter expanded a short newspaper profile of LL Cool J into a book-length autobiography collaboration entitled *I Make My Own Rules*. Similarly, David Rensin, a *Playboy* magazine interviewer, has parlayed many of his feature stories into full-length books—he aided Tim Allen in writing *Don't Stand Too Close to a Naked Man* and worked with Garry Shandling on his 1998 book, *Confessions of a Late Night Talk Show Host*.

A piece in *Writer's Digest*, "Four Points in Ghostwriting Contracts," weighs in on some of the following topics: byline credits ("ask to have your name on the cover of the book"), length limit ("establish how long the manuscript will be"), expenses ("make sure that all travel costs related to researching the manuscript will be reimbursed by the publisher"), and payment ("the contract should guarantee to pay the ghostwriter half of the total payment up front and the other half on completion").

Jack Hitt, a magazine editor, wrote an insightful article on celebrity collaboration, "The Writer Is Dead: But His Ghost Is Thriving," for the *New York Times* (March 27, 1997). Hitt, who has himself worked as a ghostwriter, writes that the need for talented collaborators is growing quickly: "On any given week, up to half of any nonfiction bestseller list is written by someone other than the name on the book. Add those authors who feel enough latent uneasiness to bury the writer's name in the acknowledgments and the percentage, according to one agent, reaches as high as eighty."

5 Sex Sells

Stripper

Porn Star

Geisha

Erotic Screenwriter

Dominatrix

Romance Novelist

Stripper

Job description: Dance naked or nearly naked in front of strangers.

Compensation: Strippers make most of their money from tips. Few clubs in the United States offer a wage. In fact, most charge the dancers a stage fee each night. On top of the stage fee, dancers must tip out to the bartenders, the security, and the disc jockey, and pay a portion of their private dance fees to the management. Take-home pay from a shift can vary from $20 to $700. A big night usually results from a single client tipping big ($300 to $500). Typical take-homes vary with the type of establishment. Contrary to expectation, the less you take off, the more you make: bikini dancers can expect $200 to $400; topless dancers can expect $150 to $250; night-shift full nudes average $100 to $200; day-shift full nudes make $50 to $100; peep show girls take in $200 to $300 a shift. Strip-o-grams and bachelor/bachelorette party dancers take in $250 for topless and $300 for full nude (plus tips), half of which goes to the management agency.

Prerequisites: A willingness to take off your clothes and the appropriate clothes to take off. "Most regular lingerie is not meant to be taken off twenty times a night. It's really flimsy. You have to have stuff that's made for what you're doing," says Molly Traffican, a petite blonde who is a strip club and peep show vet of nine years. A g-string runs $15 to $20, and more elaborate costumes run into the hundreds. A complete wardrobe, including shoes, will run $400 to $500. Most dancers purchase handmade items directly from lingerie designers who visit the clubs one or twice a week.

Qualities employer is seeking: "When getting hired by a club, they ask you one question: 'Would you like to start tonight or tomorrow?'" says Traffican. Club managers audition dancers by asking them to take the stage and get naked. If you can do that, they'll give you a shot. The younger and more attractive applicants get the more lucrative night shifts. "It's a self-selecting process. Girls who are fat are embarrassed about their bodies and aren't going to want to take their clothes off. It's girls who have a good image of themselves that are even willing to do it," says Traffican. Very high-end clubs, such as Bare Elegance (on the Sunset Strip in L.A.), may hire only stunning women without tattoos, but these clubs are the exception. Most clubs will only turn away dancers suspected of being prostitutes or junkies. (Suspicion of illegal activity by neighbors or clients can result in police raids and/or the loss of the club's license to operate.)

Perks: You can work as little or as much as you want. Few clubs ask for a schedule more than a day in advance. The industry offers geographic flexibility as well, since strip clubs are scattered all over the United States. In fact, some dancers pay for their vacations by dancing wherever

their travels take them. Says a stripper who goes by the stage name Quail, "I can't think of a more flexible job or a job where you can call your boss an asshole, scream, cry, do drugs in the bathroom, and come back the next day." She adds, "Once you have your costume and your stage act, you can work anywhere—they need girls."

Risks/drawbacks: Dancers receive free drinks from the management, so as with any job that takes place in a bar, the risk of becoming an alcoholic is ever present. Most clubs have excellent security, but there is always a chance of an overzealous client posing a physical threat. You also may run into discrimination outside the club. Says Traffican, "People—especially women—will judge you based on your profession. And men tend to put you in the category of bad girl, not the girl you want to take home to meet Mom. That can make it tough in a relationship."

Overview

You show up, change into your costume, give your CDs to the disc jockey, and do your stage dances in rotation with the other dancers. When you're not on stage, you're talking to customers, trying to get them to pay for a private dance (also called a *table dance* or a *lap dance*). Private dances are where the money is. Most of the guys are only going to pay for one or two dances, so while the atmosphere of the club may appear laid-back, competition can be cutthroat. Dancers are expected to approach and engage the clients. (For naked work of a more interactive nature, see "Porn Star," p. 87.) Says Molly, "Women who aren't pretty brazen don't last very long." Shifts run six to eight hours. When your shift is up, you pay out your tips, and get a security walk-out.

In peep show clubs, customers and dancers are separated by glass. Customers purchase tokens that allow them

The International Sex Worker Foundation for Art, Culture, and Education (ISWFACE)

ISWFACE (pronounced "ice face") is an organization devoted to "trying to get people to accept us as who we are, that we have families, that we have lives, and that jail is not an appropriate place to put us," according to founder Norma Jean Almodovar. Almodovar started ISWFACE to protect the rights of all sex workers, a group including, but not limited to, prostitutes, escorts, porn stars, exotic dancers, and phone sex operators. "Prostitution laws are so vague that they can get you for driving down the street by yourself. Entrapment is legal for prostitution. You can be arrested for intent to commit prostitution. If the individual is carrying condoms, they use that as evidence. These are laws enacted by liberal Democrats to protect us for our own good!" complains Almodovar, who spent three years in prison. ISWFACE publishes a booklet entitled *What Me, Get Arrested for Prostitution? But I'm a Lap Dancer, Stripper, Masseuse, Porn Actress, Porn Actor, Etc.* The booklet explains what the laws are and how they can be used against you. ISWFACE goals are more broadly focused than the political realm. The organization also has a cyberspace museum and a gallery in the works.

to view the dancers. Dancers masturbate in front of the clients, engage with other dancers, and sometimes use toys (dildos, vibrators, etc.).

"I really enjoy the artistic expression. You get to meet a lot of people from all over the world. And they're really happy to see you, which you don't get in other jobs. I've made some really good friends out of customers," says stripper Molly Traffican.

Male strip clubs are few and far between. Some gay clubs operate as strip clubs part time. The bulk of work for men is in strip-o-grams and bachelorette parties. The pay for these jobs is excellent (see above) but the flexibility is lost. You have to be there when the client wants you there.

Dancers work primarily for the money, but some have personal reasons as well. "I was raped when I was nineteen, and I had huge issues with sexuality. And any stripper you talk to will have issues like that. To be naked in front of somebody and to be able to do what you want, and they can't touch you, is really freeing," admits Quail. Quail also says, "There's something about people appreciating just your looks that gives you an adrenaline rush. There's something about the shallowness that's special."

Practical Information

Laws regulating strip clubs vary from community to community. Some have specifications for what can and cannot be worn. Find out before you buy your costume. Numerous laws affect the clients more than the dancers. Most states won't let full nude clubs serve alcohol. Topless bars usually can. In Oregon bars, people can drink beer and watch a full nude at the same time.

The strip club offers a sexually charged environment. Many strip club dancers are bisexual, or become bisexual. Involvement with management or the clients is also not uncommon. Your co-workers, management, and clients will hit on you. If this sounds creepy, this isn't the right job for you.

Seasoned strippers offer some tips to novices. "The way you look, how beautiful you are, has very little to do with how much you make. I've seen very beautiful women make nothing at all, and I've seen girls who don't look like they should be in the industry make bank," says Traffican. Clients can watch the stage show all night without paying a dime. "They pay for attention. They pay for girls to like them. It's this fantasy they're paying for. The successful strippers make their money talking to the clients. These men are lonely," says Quail.

The first few days you work, don't try to make a lot of money, just watch the other girls. This is the only way to learn what behavior sells and what's too nasty. The most common mistake of the

first-time stripper is dancing too quickly. Says Traffican, "Slow it down. There's a lot of power just to being naked on stage. Let your body speak for itself."

Strippers don't get laid off for being too old. They retire. It's rare for a dancer to keep stripping past her mid-thirties. Says Traffican, "Girls know their [own] aging process. And their money goes down. And if you've had kids and you're in your thirties, you're probably ready to retire." Some strippers become waitresses, DJs, or management. Some marry clients. "They're hitting their early thirties and this doctor or lawyer has been coming to see them strip every lunch for five years. I've seen weddings in clubs—bachelor party and ceremony in one," says Traffican.

Porn Star

Job description: Have sex, and act, on film for money.

Compensation: Porn stars are paid by the scene, which can take anywhere from a couple of hours to a couple of days to film. Straight men have the lowest wages, usually between $150 to $500 a scene. Women earn three times this or more, since they're typically the draws in straight porn. Male performers in gay porn probably earn the most, as much as $1,800 to $2,000 a scene, according to former gay porn star Bill Crane. Prices vary depend on the sex act: women earn less for a lesbian scene, more for anal sex, and still more for multiple simultaneous partners, for example. Most porn stars are not members of the Screen Actors Guild, and thus are not subject to film industry payment standards.

Prerequisites: Working genitalia, no diseases, and preferably good looks (though there's always the fetish market) are the important requirements.

Qualities employer is seeking: For women: not much, really, though a slim, athletic body and big breasts help (nothing surgery can't provide). For men (straight and gay): a working penis and the ability to "get wood." It turns out that getting and keeping an erection for several hours on an uncomfortable set, surrounded by a crew of strangers and hot, bright lights, and then ejaculating on

command is difficult. In straight porn, looks are secondary for the male stars. In gay porn, actors usually must be in good shape and attractive.

Perks: Lots of sex. Hordes of lusting fans (except for the straight male stars).

Risks/drawbacks: AIDS and other STDs, of course, are a danger. All performers must take special HIV tests, which test postive within one week of infection, the week before filming a scene and show proof on the set. The industry can be militant about it: Actress Rebecca Lords was reportedly not allowed to film a solo masturbation scene because she didn't have her test results. And recent allegations of porn stars faking their tests have renewed worries. Being a porn star has also taken a toll on the sex lives of some (blurring the distinction between work and leisure); it can wreak havoc on marriages and relationships. Also, it will effectively bar a performer from mainstream acting roles; and the emotional costs it exacts can be high.

Overview

Connoisseurs of adult film often refer to the golden age of the late sixties and seventies, when porn had a brief flash of mainstream success and actors were drawn to porn for the fun and rebelliousness of it; porn star Paul Thomas even performed on Broadway. Since then, video has taken over, and porn has hunkered down and become big business (porn accounts for about a quarter of all video rentals and sales). Films are mass-produced—sometimes two or three at a time, during one day of shooting—and in the age of video, quantity has long since replaced quality.

With the exception of a few mainstays, porn stars today are just passing through. Most of the female (and gay male) stars are actually exotic dancers who realized that a few porn credits could push their dancing earnings to as high as $8,000 a week. "Girls make much more money on the road dancing," says adult film actress Brandy Alexandre. "A great number of actresses today are doing movies just to enhance their marketability as strippers." Most straight men are quickly chewed up and spat out by the harsh treatment of men in the straight porn industry. ("Men are just props," says producer Mickey Blank.) There are only about thirty men in straight porn who work regularly enough to make a career out of it, whose longstanding reputations for being able to get wood protect their jobs from eager newcomers, even as the stars age.

While scripts were important in the golden age, they've been reduced today to vessels for the sex scenes; often the scripts are written on the spot, depending on what props happen to be lying around. A fifteen-minute scene can take several hours to film, because of pauses to switch positions or reinvigorate a softening male star. Performers are often asked to do a couple of scenes in a day. Many stars do genuinely love their work and those who, through luck or skill, become big stars can make a fortune. But for

most, it's tough, demanding work. Few porn stars last more than a couple of years before going back to dancing or disappearing into oblivion. Some move on to directing or producing.

"It has more to do with work than sex, more to do with gender identity than genital excitement," says former porn star Bill Margold.

Being a porn star is a job, and like all jobs, people are often asked to do things they wouldn't otherwise want to do. Almost all women must do lesbian scenes, whether they're attracted to women or not, and some stars of gay porn maintain that they're straight in their private lives. It may be all fun and sex games from the perspective of the viewer, but it isn't always that way for performers. "People don't sit around and say, 'I'm going to dump all my stock in Coca-Cola and buy Xerox today, and then I think I'll make my way over to the porn agency,'" says former star Sharon Mitchell. "Working in porn is typically one of the last stops on the food chain."

Practical Information

Becoming a female or gay male porn star is relatively easy. Exotic dancers have the easiest time, since they're already in the loop, but the major casting agencies also have frequent "talent calls," to

Show me the money shot! Earn your cumuppance as a porn star.

Credit: Newline Cinema

which anyone can go. Becoming a male star in straight porn is extremely difficult: Supply far exceeds demand, and the primary required skill—getting an erection on command and maintaining it for what may seem like an eternity—is rare. There are really only two ways to get a job as a straight male porn star: (1) have a good contact in the industry (the best being a female star who wants to have sex with you—women call most of the shots in the industry), or (2) do some amateur porn to build up a "video resume" of your performance skills (in amateur porn, you provide your own partner and rarely get paid). Almost every actor has to do a screen test before getting a job, which may or may not include having sex, but for men it will usually consist of getting an erection and masturbating to ejaculation in a room full of producers and directors—consider yourself warned.

Almost all of the straight porn industry is located in the San Fernando Valley in Los Angeles. One agency there, World Modeling (818-986-4316) handles almost all of the movie casting, as well as placement in porn magazines. Gay porn is more scattered, with agencies and production companies in most large cities with gay populations. Aspiring performers can also get information from the industry magazines, *Adult Video News* and *Gay Video Guide*. Susan Faludi's seminal article, "The Money Shot," in the *New Yorker* (1995) is required reading. The Adult Movie FAQ at www.rame.net is comprehensive.

Geisha

Job description: Entertain very wealthy, Japanese men.

Compensation: A "geisha party" for five men might cost up to $12,000. A popular *maiko*, an apprentice geisha, makes $2,500 per month in tips alone, though her matron deducts for expenses such as kimono silk dresses, which can cost up to $20,000 each. The privilege of *mizuage*, deflowering a *maiko*, can cost a man hundreds of thousands of dollars. According to Arthur Golden, author of *Memoirs of a Geisha*, most geisha don't get rich in their profession. "Many retire early to marry, or they save," he says. "The main money-earning years are twenty-five to thirty-five, when you have the potential to land a big fish." Many geisha end up earning the bulk of their income from single clients.

Prerequisites: The training for a geisha is long and arduous; with outfitting, a geisha's preparation is thought to cost as much as $750,000. In ancient days (the profession dates back to the 1600s), geisha started training as young as six or seven. Most began training at age twelve and had to quit or become geisha by age seventeen. These days, because of Japan's education requirements, many start later (at fifteen or sixteen) and become geisha at age twenty-one. Learning to become a geisha requires learning ancient, highly cultivated artistic traditions; *geisha* literally

means "art person." Along with singing and dancing, a geisha must play traditional drums and *shamisen*, a three-stringed banjolike instrument. She must also learn to perform the tea ceremony, tell stories, recite poetry, and behave within a certain highly restrictive code of etiquette.

Qualities employer is seeking: Jodi Cobb, a *National Geographic* photographer who has written a book about geisha, says the greatest skill required of geisha is an ability to "pamper the male ego." According to Golden, unusual beauty isn't required. "You don't have to be beautiful, though it certainly helps," he explains. "To be successful at it, you have to excel at one quality: that you're really beautiful, or funny, or entertaining." If you think beauty's your trump card, note that Japanese men are said to have a fondness for attractive necks. Generally, proficiency in the geisha's arts is the main prerequisite; mastery requires discipline and dedication. Geisha must also take a vow of silence; they're held to strict confidence about their clients and their trade, so blabbermouths need not apply. (Another job that shuns blabbermouths, but which doesn't usually involve pampering Japanese men, is cryptographer; see p. 184.)

Perks: The chance to watch hugely powerful businessmen and politicians get drunk and fall prey to your charms; big bucks for relatively simple private performances; the opportunity to wear exquisite, ultra-expensive kimonos.

Risks/drawbacks: The major danger facing geisha today is extinction. In the 1920s, there were approximately 80,000 geisha; today, the number is said to be closer to 8,000. Some geisha develop calluses on the tops of their feet from constant kneeling on rice mats.

Overview

While the world of the geisha is shrouded in mystery, one aspect of the job is clear: A geisha is not a prostitute. Despite Western notions of geisha as exotic, snow-faced hookers who deliver back rubs in hot tubs, geisha sleep with clients at their own discretion (though many choose to do so following a long, involved courtship entailing a substantial exchange of cash). The only exception to the no-cash-for-sex rule is the deflowering ceremony, which takes place before a *maiko*'s transformation to geisha.

"If you're one of those doughy faced, uninteresting girls with bad teeth, maybe you can wrap yourself up in a kimono and sit in a corner so nobody minds having you around, but you're not going to be that successful."

—Arthur Golden, author, *Memoirs of a Geisha*

The centuries-old tradition of the geisha has always been restricted to the upper echelons of Japanese society. The first geisha were male entertainers, but womanly charms combined with the usual song, dance, and storytelling proved a successful combination, and the profession has been all-female since the 1600s, an era when women were perceived as property, and the geisha were perfection personified.

A geisha's job is to make clients happy and drunk and provide social lubricant as they carry on business or political meetings. She helps clients take off their shoes, put on slippers, and get merry. A geisha may play stripping games with a prime minister, but she always maintains control, pulling out hairpins while the man takes off his pants. Her main challenge is upholding the strict regimen required of the job: walking with tiny steps, toes pointed inward, holding the kimono in precisely the right way, satisfying the dictates of the communelike geisha house in which she lives.

Credit: Index Stock Photography

"We can drink in parties, but we can't eat," said one geisha. "And some parties last from four in the afternoon until four in the morning."

As one geisha reported to the *London Times* in 1996: "A good geisha must have stamina. We can drink in parties, but we can't eat and some parties last from four in the afternoon until four in the morning. There are three rules: no smoking, no whiskey pouring, and we must always kneel, sitting back on our feet so they don't show. Anything we hear is a secret. Politicians and the heads of the most powerful companies in the world get drunk and say things but we mustn't tell anyone. Of course, some geisha remember the odd remark and make a lot of money in the stock market."

Practical Information

"In the old days, women didn't have a choice about becoming a geisha. They were down on their luck, or they were sold into it," reports Golden. "Nowadays, it really is a career choice; I don't know whether you'd say prostitution is a career choice."

It's believed that only one non-Japanese woman, Liza Dalby, has ever

become a geisha; her book, *Geisha*, is considered the definitive book in English on the subject. To give a go at the geisha life, your best bet is to head to Osaka, Kyoto, or Tokyo, where certain neighborhoods (such as Miyagawacho, "flower town," in Kyoto) serve as centers for the seductive entertainers. The *Times* of London reported that some geisha have started to use the Internet to publicize their services. In considering turning geisha, keep in mind that economic recession in Japan has put a damper on business in recent years. A safer, cheaper alternative to full-fledged geishahood has cropped up during the same period, though. In March of 1997, the *Los Angeles Times* reported that businesses have sprung up in Kyoto that will help women dress up and look like geisha for $80 to $160. Real geisha see their franchise threatened and have retaliated. Now, a worker must follow the pseudo-geisha around on the street with a sign declaring she's not the real thing.

Erotic Screenwriter

Job description: Write scripts heavy in nudity and sex.

Compensation: Ranges from $4,000 to $12,000 per script. Please don't think you're going to make this for writing hardcore porn films. Not surprisingly, few people, if any, get paid to write screenplays for hardcore (XXX) films; the scenarios are invented by the producers and the dialogue is written on the spot and often improvised by the actors. We're referring here to softcore films, with substantive screenplays.

Prerequisites: All the standard requirements for screenwriting apply—some knowledge of filmmaking, an ear for dialogue, some sense of what might be visually stimulating, and enough imagination to write a tidy three-act plot and subplot. Says writer Jay Sycamore, "A dirty mind isn't what they want. It's more important to be able to justify a sex scene in the plot or to be able to figure out how to make the scene different from the six other [sex] scenes in the film without making it graphic or weird."

Qualities employer is seeking: "People might expect a whole script in two or three weeks. This is a hack writing job. If you can't come up with something they like quickly, they'll get someone else to do it," says Sycamore.

Perks: "Expectations are on the low end sometimes, which means that so long as you work within the genre and write the appropriate number of romantic sequences, you can experiment with style and material," says writer Duncan Tamarind. "There is a bizarre amusement to having your not-so-witty dialogue, awkward scenarios, and semi-explicit material played out on film," said one writer. "I like the fact that I don't have to leave my house much, and that I set my own hours," says Sycamore, "and if you can make a living writing anything at all, I think that's pretty special all by itself."

Risks/drawbacks: Despite the fact that you are simply doing your job, most of the production team (as well as many people you meet) will think of you as a pervert. The rest of the people you meet will insist on telling you their sordid sexual fantasies in the hopes that you will script them. "Some of the less reputable companies may renege on a contract, and entertainment lawyers aren't interested in helping you," warned one writer. Job security is low. "A lot of producers can be pretty whimsical about who they want to write the scripts," says Sycamore. You probably won't win any humanitarian or literary awards for your work.

Overview

Erotica has a long and respectable heritage, from the ancient Greek writings of Sappho to the Latin poetry of Catullus. Erotic writing enjoyed immense popularity in France just before the French Revolution, and had a subterranean cult following in nineteenth-century England. The once-banned works of Anaïs Nin and Henry Miller are now part of the canon of literature taught in higher education. Erotica screenwriters do not take part in this history. (Industry self-esteem is low; all of the writers interviewed requested that their names be modified to protect anonymity.)

"A producer I worked for explained what he wanted like this: The audience member should be able to go to the kitchen, get a beer, drink it, come back, and still understand what is happening," says writer Duncan Tamarind.

"A film with people getting beaten and their heads getting shot off can be high art, but if you've got a bunch of sex scenes in a movie, it's considered smut," says Sycamore. "The culture doesn't respect the field, and that means that the writers don't respect their work." Most scribes of adult material consider it a way of paying the bills until their respectable Hollywood or indie career catches fire. "There's not a lot of incentive to hone dialogue when you know the actors are gonna flub it and that it's gonna be upstaged by a pair of tits," says Tamarind.

Market forces also contribute to the schlockiness of the material. "Even if

you write something good, it'll get ruined. They'll shoot fifteen pages in a day, and the nudity and low pay means the actors aren't exactly the top of their profession either," complains Tamarind. Erotic films primarily go straight to video or to late-night cable stations. Since expected income from these sources is low by Hollywood standards, budgets are tight, and production values (the quality of the sets, wardrobe, music, and cinematography) drop.

Writers have to work within a world of regulations. The number of speaking roles and sets is limited by the tight budgets and shooting schedules. Frontal nudity of men is nonexistent and infrequent on women. "There's kind of a schizophrenic thing going on, 'cause on one hand you're supposed to be turning people on, and on the other the producers are desperately afraid of offending any potential buyer, so you can't even hint at anything kinky. That's why people call 'em tits-and-ass films,' 'cause that's all you end up with. Some places won't even let curse words into the dialogue," says Sycamore. "At production meetings you have to call the sex scenes romantic sequences. There's a lot of self-deception going on about the nature of the material."

Practical Information

Different companies have each carved out their own niches. There is a multitude of genres: erotic thrillers, erotic mysteries, erotic comedies, erotic nostalgic dramas, etc. Some companies target male audiences and some aim for both sexes. Material is strictly divided between heterosexual and homosexual films, except that many heterosexual films will include lesbian scenes. To get a grip on who's making what, go down to the video store and rent twenty or thirty recent direct-to-video releases. The *Hollywood Creative Directory* lists over a hundred direct-to-video companies, and can be extremely useful for tracking down the appropriate person to contact at a company.

Most producers and development people will want to see a "spec" script (a sample script written on your own) before giving you a chance. While some of the works they produce might not be well written, your spec needs to be sufficiently superior to what they are accustomed to if you are to convince them to sign you instead of writers they already know. The easiest way to break in is on a series with recurring themes or characters. The creator of the series will attempt to write more of the episodes than he is able to, or the company will be dissatisfied with some of the episodes, which may result in a willingness to try new writers.

Dominatrix

Job description: To dominate, or train, the mind and body of your submissive, primarily male, clients. Common requests from submissives include teasing, humiliation, servitude, cunnilingus, analingus, breast worship, bondage, nipple torture, forced homosexuality, yellow showers, penile penetration, cock-and-ball bondage and torture, foot worship, spanking, whipping, gags, hoods, diapers, and cross-dressing. Some form of role-playing is usually required, with a master/slave relationship being the most common scenario.

Compensation: Hourly charges range from $40 to $300 an hour. The most common price range is $100 to $150 an hour. The hourly wage is deceptive because many hours are spent on the phone (some dominatrixes—or doms—charge for calls to offset this), preparing for appointments, and waiting for clients who never show. Income ranges vary from $1,000 to $10,000 a month.

Prerequisites: A dominatrix must have a strong will and the ability to understand what people want and give it to them. Many clients (subs) prefer women over forty, but women barely past the age of consent have managed to make a living. Appearance is relatively unimportant. Potential clients may expect an appropriate wardrobe (e.g., lacy items, stretch PVC, flowing dresses, leather) and some semblance of a dungeon (facilities for bondage, torture, cross-dressing, etc.). Dungeons aren't cheap (if you're not careful, you can easily drop $10,000), but initial expenditures can be limited to under $100. Says Mistress Kali Ward, of Buffalo, New York: "I could go into your kitchen and pick up your spatula, [some] rubber bands, clothespins, paper clips, some rope, and some extension cords and do a full-fledged scene. All you need is somebody who knows what to do with it."

Being a woman (by birth or by choice) is pretty much obligatory. The ample number of men willing to offer their services as a dominant for free largely obliterates the need for professional masters. While some professional doms manage to succeed on acting skills alone, head-, gut-, and genital-level interests in S/M are highly advantageous. The most successful doms are lifestyle doms—individuals who live out their day-to-day existence as mistresses with personal submissives. If the job description made you gag (and gagging is not appealing to you), this probably isn't your cup of tea.

Qualities employer is seeking: Trust, respect, sincerity—subs seek out doms with these qualities. A dom must understand the sub's fantasy and deliver it.

Perks: Ever had someone pay you $40 an hour so they can wash your floor, mow your lawn, and clean your toilet? Some doms receive round-trip plane tickets in the mail (which they may refuse or accept) five to six times a month. Set your

Credit: Courtesy of Goddess Glory and Mistress Mona

Do you get enough bonding in your workplace? Consider a career as a dominatrix.

own hours. Never clean your dishes or pay for dinner. Nor is the ego boost of having people beg (and pay) to lick your feet to be discounted. Then there is the pleasure of the scene or session. ("I really enjoy whipping men," said one dom.) But for many doms all these gains are vastly outstripped by the warmth and love they feel in their relationships with their clients.

Risks/drawbacks: As long as no sexual acts take place in exchange for money, nothing illegal has transpired. Definitions of what constitutes a sexual act vary from community to community (and from president to congressperson). The greater potential danger lies in inviting strange men into your house. The best advice is to get to know each client well over the phone before initiating personal contact. Take down his address, phone number, license, credit card, etc. Have a friend call the police if your friend doesn't hear from you by a certain time. Incidences of trouble from submissives are rare, but it's best to be safe.

Overview

The acceptability of S/M has had a huge upswing in the nineties. Popular songs and films on the subject abound. Most major cities have at least one support group that offers lectures, parties, and classes. Fetish gear has become standard clubbing material. Kink is everywhere on the Internet, and S/M ranks as one of

People Empowering People

PEP (People Empowering People) is a nationwide organization that provides counseling, support groups, and information for those involved in the S/M industry. Nancy Eva Miller founded PEP in 1986 and spent the next four years traveling the country to start S/M support groups in Albuquerque, Washington, D.C., Tucson, Phoenix, Dallas, Nashville, and Philadelphia. Says Ms. Miller, "One of my phone counselors met a man over the phone line and married him. I have started about twelve or thirteen (PEP) groups personally. Out of all those groups, there have been thousands of couples that have gotten married and had kids in the last twelve years. I could cry when I think about it. Of course, there were divorces, too." In 1990 Ms. Miller began to work professionally as a dominatrix. Ms. Miller presently employs about thirty dominatrixes around the country who do phone domination and in-person sessions. If you don't know where to look for S/M information, try contacting PEP (to leave a message call 908-284-8028; to reach the office call 505-256-5206; also check PEP out on the Web at www.peplove.com).

the hottest kinks. Traditional bars across the country are replacing Karaoke Night with S/M Night. Recently, the American Psychiatric Association removed sexual sadism and sexual masochism from their official registry of psychiatric illnesses. For an informative and interesting overview of S/M, try *S and M, Studies in Sadomasochism* (edited by Thomas Weinberg and G.W. Levi Kamel). For more titillating material, go to your local adult toy store.

In spite of the spread of S/M, doms complain about the stereotyped viewpoint that their profession is all about sex and violence. Doms and their clients maintain that the essential feature of any scene is psychological. Many subs aren't interested in physical pain, and most clients understand that sexual services will not be provided. "A dominatrix is anything but a hooker. We do not perform sexual acts for money," states Ward.

"Give me three hours, maybe five, with the head of every country across the globe, let me figure out their kink, let me get them that happiness, and you'd get world peace," claims Mistress Kali Ward.

Still, both physical pain and sex are part of the game. "Most doms will tell you no sex. But a lot of us will at least have the guys lick our pussy. If he looks good to us, and we know the guy is not a vice cop, why not?" says Nancy Eva Miller, a lifestyle dom and the founder of PEP (see sidebar). The real distinction between doms and most other sex industry workers may be that doms take pride in their work and believe that they are truly contributing to the psychological well-being of their clients.

Practical Information

The proliferation of information on S/M has provoked a surge of patrons and professional dominatrixes. There's

still plenty of work to go around, but hourly prices are dropping as a result of the competition. Some doms recommend working areas already bubbling with activity (primarily the coasts). Others feel you can make more working areas with less competition. Different fetishes require different time commitments. For some doms, cross-dressers are their bread-and-butter patrons, because they may request services for entire weekends.

Successful dominatrixes recommend receiving training. Says Ward, "This isn't something you pick up by deciding to call yourself mistress. Inevitably the clients will recognize that you're nothing more than an ex-hooker with a whip in her hand." Many doms learn their trade by training as a submissive to a male or female master. Others hook up with an experienced dom and learn from her. Either way, plan to spend at least a couple of months learning tricks of the trade. Taking a class in first aid is also advised.

"There's no reason to reinvent the wheel," says Ward. Novice doms today can benefit from the vast array of support groups. It's also possible to work for an existing dungeon or service as an independent contractor. While management will take 50 percent of your draw, they can also help build your clientele, alleviate uncomfortable situations, and generally show you the ropes.

Romance Novelist

Job description: Plan, research, and write romance novels. Additional activities include answering correspondence and conducting business transactions and dialogue with agents or publishers.

Compensation: Earnings vary widely, depending on publisher, agent, demand, and volume of material. There is no fixed reimbursement for a manuscript, though solicited novel proposals tend to sell for more than unsolicited ones. A single book written for a publisher commanding nationwide distribution earns an average of $7,000 to $8,000.

Prerequisites: "A thick skin and nerves of steel," says Dallas Hamlin, who has written more than forty books for Harlequin. Writers need the skill to compose interesting, appealing, and romantic fiction, as well as the drive to weather scores of rejections. Above all, the aspiring romance writer needs to love and respect the genre, and to want to improve it.

Qualities employer is seeking: Publishers look for unique voices in new writers and new twists on old story lines. Readers seek books "that entertain and provide an escape from real life," says Holly Harte, author of *Texas Silver.*

Perks: The greatest perk is being able to do what you love for a living. Though

the work naturally entails a great deal of concentration and commitment, you can write at home and set your own hours. Receiving fan mail is a "tremendous thrill," according to Harte.

Risks/drawbacks: Drawbacks fall into both financial and creative categories. Pay depends on business, and many romance writers supplement their writing with day jobs—not only to keep themselves fed but also to separate the pleasurable exercise of writing from the mundane tasks of survival. Also, once the book is finished, it's the publisher and not the author who has final say on cover art, cover copy, marketing, and distribution.

Overview

The romance novel is a literary genre whose hallmarks have long been mass-marketed: seemingly identical titles, pseudonymous writers, and a lack of clout in the publishing and literary worlds. Today, romance writers are gaining acceptance in the trade and becoming known individually as they help to expand and improve ever-diversifying genres. Most authors are women, and men usually write under female pen names. Not so long ago, romance meant chivalric and knightly tales, and though modern-day romances deal mainly with love affairs, most authors maintain as essential a great deal of adventure in their books—from the medieval court to space travel to the Civil War.

Romance writing makes up 55 percent of mass-market paperback fiction published in the United States. These books generate $1 billion in annual sales and are read by over forty-five million people in North America alone. Recognized genres place love stories in the present day, medieval times, the Old West, the Civil War, Victorian England, or the antebellum South; on pirate ships, mythical worlds, or other planets; in religious contexts, or African-American or Native American settings and themes; and feature ghosts, angels, vampires, and time travelers. New writers should try to write for series romances, which deal in contemporary or historical settings and are sold as part of a package, often issued monthly. Once a writer has this experience, he or she can move to writing single-title romances, released independently.

Practical Information

Romance writers come from all sorts of backgrounds and maintain a great variety of interests, but most seek through their writing to effect a momentary diversion from mundane concerns. Unfortunately, mundane concerns will plague the aspiring writer; rejections will probably come left and right, and the creative wellspring will sometimes dry up. The first step to breaking in is to choose the genre you love best and write in it; you'll write more easily if you enjoy doing it. Join the Romance Writers of America (281-440-6885) and read *Romantic Times Magazine Online* (www.romantictimes.com), unbeatable sources of information, advice, support,

feedback, and industry contacts. Attend writers' conferences and get critiques as often as possible. Most important, persevere. Selling the first book is the hardest, and many writers wait years before a publisher picks them up.

You get to write some cool stuff, such as this excerpt from *His Royal Pleasure,* by Leanne Banks: "He mastered her mouth and her body until she was weeping with it. He murmured brokenly in French, and her arousal gushed through her like a tidal wave, a solid wall of incredible pleasure that took her past the point of return."

To submit a book or idea to a publisher, you must meet several industry requirements. First, write a query letter: one page explaining who you are, what you've written, and your familiarity with the publisher's books and the romance market in general. With that, send a ten- to twenty-page synopsis of the book, in present tense with no dialogue, revealing all major plot points, characters, relationships, and the end of the story. Become familiar with the publishers, their series, and the things they look for in a story. If you're devoted enough to the genre to write for it, you probably know these things already.

Lists of publishers, publishing contacts, and agents can be found in *Romantic Times Magazine Online*, along with a drove of other resources. Romance Writers of America can be found on the Web (www.rwanational.com). Numerous Web rings are also devoted to romance novels, which can be explored at www.webring.com.

6 Civil Servant

Executioner

Executioner

Job description: Kill human beings on cue.

Compensation: The pay for an executioner varies from state to state and depends on method of killing. Florida pays $150 cash for electrocutions. Nebraska pays $200 to $300. New Jersey reportedly uses three "execution technicians" who receive $500 for administering injections (one has a "dummy" benign dosage, one has a lethal dosage, and one person is kept on hand in case either of the others gets cold feet).

Prerequisites: The classified advertisement for an executioner in the Bradford County Telegraph in Florida called for no prior experience. However, in some states, certain skills are helpful. In Louisiana, state penitentiary warden Frank Blackburn interviewed only certified electricians to operate the state's electric chair. In states where lethal injections are involved, some medical training is a plus (in Texas, with an inmate with a history of drug use, it took forty minutes before they could find a vein that would take the lethal injection). Note that doctors and nurses are ineligible as the Hippocratic oath specifically forbids killing people on purpose.

Qualities employer is seeking: The willingness to kill a stranger for a few hundred dollars. (See also "Mercenary," p. 26.)

Perks: None.

Risks/drawbacks: Possibility of being haunted by your grisly deed for the rest of your days. Or worse still, by the ghost of the deceased. Also, the job is part-time only.

Overview

"People say they'd pull the trigger themselves," said Don Cabana, a former prison warden from the South who helped with four executions and carried out two personally. "That's people who haven't done it. You don't find people who have participated say they would like to do it again." Cabana was so sickened by the process that he quit the jail business altogether. He said the endeavor "scarred his soul." In New York, where the last electrocution occurred in 1963 (the death penalty was suspended and then readopted in the state), two of the last three executioners committed suicide, according to a 1995 *Daily News* article.

The entire country took a five-year hiatus when the Supreme Court banned capital punishment in 1972, declaring that the inconsistency of statutes from state to state made the death penalty arbitrary and unconstitutional. Death penalty advocates, however, wrote new laws conforming to the Court's stipulations, and state-sponsored killings resumed in 1977 when Gary Gilmore was put to death by a firing squad in Utah. Since then, the recession-proof execution business has been booming.

Credit: Jaime Rosen

Dead Man Eating: Last stop for burgers on the highway to hell.

With Texas and Missouri leading the way and other states, like Connecticut and New York, having recently adopted or readopted capital punishment, there is more work than ever for the nation's anonymous executioners.

All this activity has made it a challenge for state wardens to a keep pace. There are lots of prickly details and decisions that states must confront when instituting systematized executions. For example, some issues that Connecticut officials recently grappled with include when to move an inmate to the cell adjacent to the death chamber; how to preserve an inmate's last words (some states have a microphone in the chamber), traffic control outside the penitentiary (there can be large contingents of both protesters and advocates), how much to indulge final requests, such as special meals (Maryland won't entertain a menu more elaborate than cheeseburgers and fries; others will prepare anything within reason.)

Frank Mazzone, a former police officer and now head of Adult Detention in Atlantic County, New Jersey, is widely regarded as a guru in the field. Mazzone was recently brought in as an "execution commander" for the state of Maryland, where he was put in charge of an "execution team" of an undisclosed number to handle their first latter-day execution. "In light of the fact that it's been thirty-two years since we've done an execution, I feel it's very important to utilize his knowledge and expertise," said Richard A. Lanham Sr., chief of Maryland's prison system. Maryland paid Mazzone $500 for the two-day job, or about $31 an hour.

Since the outcome is more or less guaranteed, style counts. A surprising number of executions are botched, according to Mazzone, due to lack of planning and foresight. If the rope is not prepared correctly and the inmate's weight is not accounted for properly, a hanging can result in a decapitation. And witnesses, if not restrained, can interfere with the process, as they did in Maryland decades ago, when they stormed the deceased inmate and stole locks of his hair. Mazzone trained his execution team thoroughly to avoid any such snafus. His team rehearsed everything—including scenarios such as what to do if the needle is dropped on the ground (a new one is used—a dirty needle is not "professional"); or if a vein cannot be found to receive the injection (a so-called "cut out" procedure is used-the skin near the ankle is cut open); right down to the color-coordinated outfits worn by the team (white jumpsuits, "so it's nice and neat and clean").

Practical Information

Just as each state has its own method of killing, each state has its own hiring practices. One of the only consistent aspects is the anonymity of the executioners. Some states, such as Texas and Missouri, economize by using prison staff rather than hiring freelancers. North Carolina uses the same people over and over again, a so-called death team. "They are not known by anyone. They don't talk about it. The North Carolina team has been together about ten years—the same group of people. Once the team is put together, they keep it to themselves. They don't brag about it or talk about it," according to Peter Matos, deputy commissioner of the Corrections Department in Connecticut, who researched different states' policies recently when figuring out how to import the best practices to Connecticut. He concluded that hiring is the tricky part. "Identifying the staff members responsible for carrying out the execution is probably the hardest thing. You'll never know you're right until it's over."

"We had some fringe-type people apply, the kind you wouldn't want in a prison pulling a switch," said Vernon Bradford, a former prison spokesman in Florida, describing the screening process.

Note: Job openings are rare, especially where states use the same people repeatedly or hire from within. Yet when opportunities do arise, states often publish classified advertisements in newspapers across the state. The best time to look is just after capital punishment is adopted or readopted in your state. When applying, don't appear too eager. Unpaid volunteers are never used and the wardens and other officials responsible for the screening and hiring are put off by overzealousness.

7 Out on a Limb

Prosthetist

Body Part Model

Prosthetist

Job description: Design, create, and fit prostheses, custom-made, artificial body parts, to stand in for lost or amputated body parts. Prosthetists are often qualified additionally in orthotics, the design of braces for debilitated body parts.

Compensation: As in most fields, pay is commensurate with education and experience. Certified practitioners earn anywhere from $35,000 to $80,000 a year, and can hit $45,000 a few years out of school. Many residents earn as little as $20,000 to $25,000. Run your own clinic, though, and the sky's the limit. A below-knee prosthesis (for which the point of amputation, or "stump," is below the knee) costs the patient about $5,000. An above-knee prosthesis costs closer to $10,000.

Prerequisites: "The sad truth is, anyone can put a shingle in front of his office and say, 'I'm a prosthetist,'" explains Peter Kapelke, a (bona fide) prosthetic practitioner based in Bangor, Maine. Despite the medical nature of the profession, only four states require official licensing of prosthetists, and the industry is almost entirely unregulated. "To be a competent, certified prosthetist," Kapelke reports, "you need a bachelor's degree and a certificate, plus about 1,900 hours of residency. The certificate program takes one or two years. You can also get a bachelor's degree in prosthetics."

Qualities employer is seeking: Although prosthetics is sometimes viewed more as a trade than as a medical profession, a good prosthetist combines bedside manner with broad scientific knowledge and mechanical skills. "You have to be smart, and you have to be personable, patient with people," says Kapelke. "You have to know biomechanics, medical disease states, and anatomy. Plus you have to have hand skills to be able to put the rubber to the road."

Perks: At the heart of prosthetics are patients, usually recent amputees, who tend to be emotionally vulnerable, desiring nothing more than a limb that's as comfortable, functional, and attractive as the real thing. A prosthetist who comes through will be rewarded with warm, grateful smiles. "The real perk," says Kapelke, "is that you get to establish a relationship with the patient. In other health-care fields, you don't get to do that. I've spent twenty hours with some of my patients, whereas a normal doctor comes in, does a diagnostic, and he's out of there."

Risks/drawbacks: Prosthetists sometimes work with chemicals and other hazardous materials. Like doctors, they risk being sued for malpractice. And at the risk of their own satisfaction, lurks the worrisome prospect that a patient will be unhappy with or even further injured by the product. Other downsides to the profession include holding a title that's not only underappreciated (some consider it macabre) but also difficult to say.

Overview

Prosthetics have been used since the dawn of civilization; the earliest written accounts of artificial limbs come from the Rig Veda, an ancient Sanskrit poem dating from 3500–1800 BC, in which a warrior queen was said to have been fitted for an iron replacement leg. Most early prostheses were simple crutches or wooden and leather cups; peg legs and iron hooks were commonly used. Prosthetic technology has evolved alongside techniques used for amputation; molded legs and arms became easier to fit once brutal guillotine methods of limb removal were abandoned. Sadly, technological advances in prosthetics have typically resulted from periods of escalated amputation, such as the years after wars or during the thalidomide tragedy, where, because of an inadequately tested drug, babies were born with flippers instead of arms and legs. (To help prevent another drug mishap, volunteer your body as a human guinea pig; see p. 32.)

Whereas centuries ago, watchmakers were employed to incorporate spring-and-gear gadgetry in adding function to limbs, today robotic and computer technologies mark the cutting edge of the industry. Still, as Kapelke admits, "You're never going to get anything close to the human hand out of rubber and a motor. Making a prosthetic arm is like putting a

"You're never going to get anything close to the human hand out of rubber and a motor," says Peter Kapelke, a prosthetic practitioner based in Bangor, Maine.

Credit: CORBIS/Bettmann

wrench at the end of the arm. It looks like an arm, so it has psychological effects, but there are no nerve endings, so the person has to be watching it the whole time to tell what it's doing." Kapelke predicts that advances in genetic limb regrowth will supersede mechanical prosthetics at some point in the future. "The worst, most misshapen human hand is going to be better than a prosthesis," Kapelke asserts, "though a lower extremity prosthesis can do pretty well."

"I see a lot of unattractive feet," says prosthetist Peter Kapelke. "But they're usually attached to eighty-year-olds. . . . What we do is so obvious and tangible, so impressive to somebody's rehabilitation, that it's immediately rewarding."

To make a leg, for example, a prosthetist (and his lab of clinicians and technicians) must consider a patient's specific needs: Does the person want to run triathlons, or just stand to go to the bathroom? For most patients, it's usually the latter. "About 80 percent of the people we see are geriatric diabetics," Kapelke says. "Diabetes makes them lose feeling in their feet, so they get infections they don't even know about that don't heal, which leads to amputation." Next, a plaster wrap of the "residual limb," or stump, is made. ("*Stump*'s not politically correct," Kapelke says, "but a lot of people call it that.") From this cast, a positive model is made out of plaster, which is molded to take pressure off the patient's bones and redistribute it onto softer tissue. "Then," Kapelke reports, "you make a socket, slap a foot on it, and off they go."

Follow-up includes monitoring the limb from a biomechanical perspective (asking questions about how the limb affects the person's gait, posture, etc.), making proper adjustments, and dealing with any psychological issues that come up along the way. "You can tell if the person's really depressed," Kapelke says. "By and large, people don't know what to expect or how well they're going to do unless they have amputee friends."

Practical Information

"A good prosthetist will always find a job," says Linda Farlow, a prosthetist based in Rhode Island. Many prosthetists justly worry that the growth of managed care will lead large corporations to swallow up small practices. Currently, insiders consider the field competitive, with successful clinicians banking on frequent referrals from physicians. Some prosthetists work in clinics and make house and hospital calls; others work out of private practices. Prosthetists are versed in all limb functions, though lower-extremity limbs are especially in demand (as a result of congenital extremity deformation or diabetes).

Prosthetists may find their work in highest demand in other countries, particularly in nations where land mine explosions frequently destroy limbs.

Angola, for example, is said to have as many buried land mines as living residents; a prosthetist working there for the Red Cross reported on the Disaster Relief Web site (www.disasterrelief.org) that even without advertisement, at least fifty people wait in line each morning for his services.

An excellent Internet resource for learning more about prosthetics is www.oandp.com. Or try one of the field's few regulating organizations, the National Commission on Orthotic and Prosthetic Education (NCOPE), 1650 King St., Suite 500, Alexandria, VA 22314.

Body Part Model

Job description: Provide the hands, feet, legs, arms, hips, or lips that make bath and beauty products, shoes and hosiery, and other consumer products irresistible.

Compensation: In New York, the center of the parts-modeling business, models start out posing for magazine stories for about $150 a day, with the added benefit of working with top photographers and collecting samples, or "tear sheets," for their portfolios. Once a model has a strong portfolio, it becomes easier to land more lucrative jobs. Modeling for catalogs brings in $150 to $200 per hour, and top part models earn up to $350 an hour for advertisements. The small group of elite part models who work almost every day earn more than $100,000 a year.

Prerequisites: At least one body part must have healthy skin, regular coloring, good proportions, and when relevant, nicely shaped nails.

Qualities employer is seeking: Blemish-free beauty and the ability to stay still in awkward positions for long periods of time.

Perks: Body part models find limited fame, and in some cases, fortune, with no risk of having their private lives disturbed by fans who recognize them on the street. Hand models can also claim a no-fail excuse for getting out of washing the dishes.

Risks/drawbacks: Part models live in constant fear that something will happen to make their prized appendages unpresentable. Model Liza O'Keefe, whose hands inspire women everywhere to buy Revlon nail products, captures the fears of her fellows by describing her worst nightmare: "Satan sneaks up and rips off all my fingernails."

Overview

The most distinctive aspect of working as a body part model is organizing your life around preserving the attractiveness of one piece of your body. The maintenance regimen varies with the body part, and the extent to which it disturbs the model's daily life depends on his or her philosophy. For example, Ellen Sirot, who got her break doing foot work for Dr. Scholl's, spends every night with her feet slathered in cream, wrapped in plastic, and propped up on pillows. And that's only for her second-most lucrative set of digits. Ellen's work as a top hand model keeps her from cooking, cleaning, digging in the garden, and engaging in pastimes that involve strenuous hand action or possible collisions (such as playing a musical instrument or a sport).

Other models aren't quite so extreme. "My motto is use them or lose them,'" says body part model Linda Rose, who recommends a less strenuous regimen than Sirot's: "Stay out of the sun or wear sunscreen on your hands. Use a hand cream at least every night. Get regular manicures—but don't ever cut the cuticles. For a special occasion, coat your hands with cream and sleep with cotton gloves on. And for God's sake, use your hands. Exercise is good for them."

Beth Ann Richards, whose hands have appeared in ads for Mr. Coffee and Matrix Essentials, echoes this user-friendly approach: "I start wearing gloves as soon as the weather turns cool, like September. And I'm good about using cuticle cream and topcoat, and keeping my hands soft with lotion. But I also downhill ski and play basketball with my husband." (What would happen if one of these ladies had a mishap with, say, a thresher and lost their livelihood? She might visit a prosthetist, p. 107.)

The serious part models cluster in New York, but only about 200 people make a living on this work. Of those,

Credit: Courtesy of Parts Modeling Agency

Your livelihood is in your hands as a body part model.

Sirot estimates that possibly four or five have full-time work modeling with their hands. "It's a fun job, but it's a hard and serious job. There's a lot of running around going to auditions," says Sirot. "It's very competitive, and when you're there, if you're doing a print job and they're photographing you, you have to sit very still for a long time. You sit on the floor and get a little dirty. It's not too glamorous." Sirot believes the current level of competition, for hand modeling in particular, came with the small buzz of media attention the business has been attracting since about 1992, and she recognizes her luck in getting established just a couple of years before this change.

Practical Information

At a basic level, you either have it or you don't. If your gams aren't straight or don't come together at the ankles, you're unlikely to find work in leg modeling, and Chapstick isn't looking for a fresh new mouth with no upper lip. "I'm just lucky in that my hair and nails grow really fast," says Beth Ann Richards. "You can take as many vitamins as you want or try all that stuff, but it seems to be a metabolism thing."

If you think you have a gift in the form of hips, hands, or hamstrings, the first thing you should do is get serious about preserving your asset and cleaning up any unsightly ill-effects caused by years of unwitting neglect. Get a pedicure, have your hands peeled, or start a serious moisturizer habit. Ellen Sirot spent months getting her hands in tip-top shape before getting her first job as a hand model, so there may be hope if you think your parts are borderline picture-perfect.

"People are always surprised to discover that I'm not a dog," says body part model Linda Rose, whose hands stayed smooth down to the last dish while standing in for the mitts of Palmolive's Madge. "They figure if I'm a hand model, there must be something wrong with the rest of me."

Then, spend what it takes to have a good set of professional pictures taken and take the photos and your features to major modeling agencies in your area. Agents don't like to talk about an aspiring model's potential without seeing pictures, and without an agent, you won't find out about the best auditions. The big names in the general modeling market are Ford, Elite, Next, Folio, and Metropolitan, and the firm Parts Models (212-744-6123) specializes in, you guessed it, parts models. (If you live in an area where a local agency is your best bet, avoid any company that tries to charge you up-front fees above and beyond the cost of having pictures taken.)

8 In the Flesh

Plastic Surgeon

Body Piercer

Taxidermist

Funeral Home Cosmetologist

Tattoo Artist

Plastic Surgeon

Job description: Improve the physical appearance of people through surgery.

Compensation: First-year incomes range from $90,000 to $225,000. The median income floats around a quarter of a million dollars a year. A select group of cosmetic surgeons earn in the seven figures.

Prerequisites: "I think I can take any reasonably intelligent and agile person and teach him surgery," claims Dr. Harvey Zaerem, who spent twenty-five years as the head of the UCLA's Department of Plastic Surgery. That said, the profession requires four years of college, including nearly two years of coursework in biology, chemistry, and physics; four years of medical school; one year of internship; three years of internship in general surgery; and an additional three years of internship in plastic surgery. A year of practice as a plastic surgeon is required to sit for the oral portion of the board examination, and some surgeons spend an additional year or two doing extra training in a fellowship.

Qualities employer is seeking: Acquiring an internship is a competitive process. In choosing applicants for the program at UCLA, Dr. Zaerem sought out "bright, capable, and honest people." Research in the field is commonly used as an indicator of general inquisitiveness and avid interest in the profession. Dr. Brian J. Michelow, clinical assistant professor at Case Western Reserve University says that interns are also selected for being well-rounded individuals—people with interests beyond the scope of the profession.

Perks: Plastic surgeons can readily see the changes they effect. Dr. Michelow offers a couple of examples: "Someone comes in with a big nose that has a hump in it, and you shave down the nose, and give them a nice little one, and the patient is very happy. Or a baby is born with a harelip, and the mother and father are horrified, and they think the baby looks like an alien from outer space; he looks like a monster. The plastic surgeon comes along, he takes their child, they operate, they bring the child back a few hours later, and the monster has been transformed into a cute little baby. You're essentially taking a child that would have gone through life shunned by other people, and they can integrate and have a completely normal life." Plastic surgeons see their work as helping people by repairing self-worth and self-esteem.

Risks/drawbacks: Plastic surgeons spend $3,000 a month or more on malpractice insurance. The possibility of getting sued by a dissatisfied customer is very real.

Overview

Historically, surgeons are the descendants of barbers, who were looked down upon by the medical profession. Over the late eighteenth and nineteenth centuries, the two groups melded (though the melding only ran one direction—it

is the rare doctor today who enjoys performing haircuts and tints). The incredible expansion of medical knowledge and research forced the medical profession to specialize in the twentieth century. Plastic surgery is the second smallest medical specialty, preceded only by brain surgery.

Surgeries can be divided into two groupings: reconstructive, which consists of emergency procedures on trauma victims, and elective or cosmetic surgery. Both divisions have benefited enormously from wars. Says Dr. Michelow, "Plastic surgeons did a lot of facial and dental work around World War I and World War II. The soldiers would pop their heads out of the trenches and have their jaw shot off. In the Korean War, land mines were a big problem, so it became more of a full body thing, [involving] moving bone from one part of a body to another.

"As long as there are cars with car accidents, and bikes with bike accidents, and people with vicious tempers who beat each other up, people will need to bring in plastic surgeons," Michelow reports. Meanwhile, most plastic surgeons are desperately trying to move

BEFORE

Credit (before): AP

AFTER

Credit (after): Hans Zwez

Objects in mirror may be older than they appear.

out of reconstructive surgery because of insurance companies' involvement in most reconstructive surgeries. While antitrust laws prevent doctors from price-fixing, they do not prevent insurance companies from limiting patients to only those doctors who agree to their cut-rate prices.

"I think I can take any reasonably intelligent and agile person and teach him surgery," claims Dr. Harvey Zaerem, who spent twenty-five years as head of UCLA's Department of Plastic Surgery.

The most popular cosmetic procedures are breast augmentations and liposuction. Rhinoplasty (nose jobs) and facial surgeries (face-lifts, brow lifts, eyelid tucks) follow close behind. The stereotyped cosmetic surgery patient is the idle rich woman trying to vainly maintain her youth. But because of increased public awareness and acceptance, today's cosmetic surgeons see more men, and a primarily upper middle class clientele. California, New York, Florida, and Texas are the states where cosmetic surgery is most prevalent.

Practical Information

Fifteen years ago, a graduating intern could look forward to a position as a junior partner at an established firm. Today's recent grads are more likely to freelance at the emergency rooms of various hospitals, hoping to slowly build a private practice. A recent study indicated that 22 percent of plastic surgeons didn't have a job lined up at the time of graduation from their internship. While all of these doctors found work within a year, academic programs continue to disgorge more plastic surgeons than are necessary to mold the faces, breasts, and buttocks of the American public. This, combined with the choke-hold insurance companies maintain on payments and increased competition from non-plastic surgeons moving into cosmetic surgery, means that incomes may very well drop for at least the next fifteen years. Competition for cosmetic clients is already fierce. Business and marketing skills have become as important to income as proficiency with the scalpel.

For more info on plastic surgery and surgeons, check out the American Society of Plastic and Reconstructive Surgeons' Web site (www.asprs.com).

(You won't deal with the likes of Ivana Trump, unless she has a run-in with a combine, but you can help people regain normalcy and self-esteem through reconstruction of limbs. See "Prosthetist," p. 107.)

Body Piercer

Job description: Pierce all parts of the human body, and affix jewelry such as studs, chains, "barbells," and "u-rings." The piercing process includes carefully sterilizing the necessary utensils, as well as guiding patients through the aftercare period.

Compensation: Pay rates vary widely, depending on the location and popularity of the piercing shop. An experienced body piercer with a stable of regular customers in a busy city can make up to $1,000 a week.

Prerequisites: Local legislation is increasingly requiring that would-be piercers have some formal training, although this is still the exception rather than the rule. "Right now, you could open a store and start piercing tomorrow," says Michaela Grey, of the Association of Professional Piercers.

Qualities employer is seeking: A thorough understanding of piercing techniques, the ability to recognize the signs of infectious inflammation, a fair knowledge of anatomy, a good bedside manner, and a steady hand.

Perks: The opportunity to coach first-time patients through their first piercing or guide advanced piercees through more ambitious and complex piercings, getting to sleep until noon, since most piercing shops keep late hours, and very little paperwork.

Risks/drawbacks: A poorly executed piercing can cause painful swelling and a nasty infection. For someone interested in currying favor with elderly relatives (for whatever reason), choosing to become a body piercer may serve as a hindrance.

Overview

Body piercing, once championed only by fringe crowds, is all the rage these days. "Members of the young and trendy set—sons and daughters of the elite, for goodness' sake—are sporting nose studs and navel bangles," writes Paul Galloway of the *Chicago Tribune.* This is undeniably a quickly growing business: Tattoo and piercing parlors were recently rated as the country's sixth-fastest-growing business, after Internet and paging services and bagel, computer, and cellular phone shops. Says Elayne "Angel" Binnine, a professional piercer in New Orleans: "When I started, piercing was something done underground and only by gay guys in leather. Not anymore. I've done lawyers, accountants, hotel managers. Policemen for some reason like to have their nipples pierced. One of them asked me if it would interfere with his wearing a bulletproof vest."

Actual piercing incisions, which are rarely done with any anesthetic, last about a second and are accompanied by "a hot, heat, burning sensation, like a little sting or electric shock," according to Gahdi Elias, owner of Mastodon, a piercing shop in San Diego, and president of the Association of Professional Piercers. A responsible piercer will attempt to ascertain whether someone who's young and

interested in an ambitious pierce is getting pressured into it—either by peers or by a boyfriend or girlfriend who may have heard of the increased sexual sensitivity that genital piercings can offer. "If we think someone is getting talked into something by their peers," says Joe Scapin, owner of Fat Joe's Jade Dragon in Chicago, the world's largest tattoo and body piercing studio, "we'll give 'em a twenty-four hour cooling-off period; we'll tell them to go home and come back tomorrow. We try to give piercing a 100 percent positive look, you know, nothing negative."

One of the most popular parts of the body to pierce these days is the tongue. To do this, the piercer (wearing plastic gloves for safety reasons) will hold the tongue in a pair of forceps with one hand, while, with the other hand, marking the incision spot with a marker and then quickly making the incision with a sterile hollow-point needle and slipping in the jewelry. The initial piercing will cause immediate swelling, so a good piercing practitioner will use a longer barbell shank and ask the piercee to come back after the tongue has healed a bit to get a slightly shorter shank. Because of the tongue's vascular nature, this kind of piercing tends to heal quickly—usually within four to six weeks. Navel pierces are also on the rise, particularly among teenagers, because they are hidden, but this area of the body can in fact be one of the most problematic from a healing standpoint as tight-fitting clothes and moisture buildup encourage infection.

"We've all been in a situation where the guy is behind the female 'rodgering' her senseless, and his fingers are round the front giving her clitoris a tickle. Just as she's about to orgasm, someone moves a bit unexpectedly, and he loses his place at the critical moment. A Vertical Hood piercing with a barbell helps to reduce the problem, because its like a big neon sign saying, 'Here I am, come play with me.'"

—From promotional material for *Perforations,* a piercing studio in Brighton, England

Body piercers these days need to be capable of doing work not only "above the belt," with piercings in the ear, nose, nipple, tongue, and lip (the "Madonna," with a labret in the upper lip, is extremely popular), but also in the genital region. For women, clitoral hood piercings are currently in vogue; this kind of piercing, best suited for a woman with a large and loose hood, heals quickly with little discomfort and is easy to look after. Also popular are inner and outer labia piercings; the former brings a slightly lower risk of infection and takes about half as much time (two to three months) as the latter to heal. For men, scrotum pierces

are slightly less common than head-of-the-penis pierces. In an "ampallang," the head of the penis is pierced through from one side to the other, and finished off with a barbell. There is also the Prince Albert, sometimes called the "P.A.," which is named after the nineteenth-century consort of Queen Victoria; the prince apparently had this pierce, in which a circular ring goes into the urethra of the penis and emerges underneath. ("It keeps his member smelling sweet," the queen is rumored to have said.) In the chaste Victorian era, this pierce, installed by a haberdashery, was used to tie the penis to the leg to prevent untimely bulges in a gentleman's trousers.

Body piercing is, of course, nothing new, and those who make it their profession will find themselves part of a broad geographical and historical continuum. Egyptian pharaohs pierced their navels; Mayans pierced their tongues; Roman centurions pierced their nipples in demonstration of their heroic valor; and aristocratic French and English women in the 1800s wore specially designed bodices to show off their pierced nipples. (If you're interested in less-invasive accessories, see "Accessories Designer," p. 159.)

Most piercing shops are open only during evening hours—the shops start bustling each night around sundown—and foster an easygoing collegiality. Ambitious body piercers, generally laden with jewelry in conspicuous places, who have chosen to make this passion their profession will have the chance to work in an environment where their pierces inspire the admiration, rather than the disapproving glances, of their co-workers. "The piercing community is very tight-knit," says Gahdi Elias, "because this is a fairly exclusive type of career choice; people with a lot of pierces are still heavily judged around the world. This helps people bond, because they need to support one another." Several major chain stores, including Blockbuster and Starbucks, have policies barring their front-line personnel from prolific body piercing. (The ACLU, incidentally, doesn't mind company dress or jewelry codes as long as they don't discriminate based on race and sex.)

Practical Information

As a result of the increasing popularity of piercing (and the infections that accompany careless piercing) regulation has been popping up, much of it welcomed by professional piercers, who are eager to see amateurs prevented from doing underground and unsanitary work. In 1997, Quincy, Massachusetts, became the first community in that state to require piercers to take a fifteen-week anatomy course, serve a one-year apprenticeship under a certified piercer, and only pierce minors with parental presence. (Earlobe piercing is exempt from the majority of those rules.) Regulations such as these, along with the increasing frequency of complicated piercings, make it an absolute prerequisite that someone interested in the field gain necessary training.

The best way to learn how to pierce is to become an apprentice. This requires finding someone who has the time and the interest to impart the skills required to be a good, professional body piercer. A good mentor will be able to teach the appropriate kinds of metal jewelry to use in different parts of the body (stainless steel and 14K gold are best, and silver platings or finishes are recipes for infection) and the safest and most effective aftercare cleaning fluids (alcohol, which causes dryness, and hydrogen peroxide, which may kill new and needed body cells, are frequently poor substitutes for household soap or gentle salt water rinses). And only a first-hand apprenticeship can provide the kind of knowledge needed to differentiate typical post-piercing swelling from an infection in need of a doctor's attention.

Although it is a poor substitute for the individual and sustained attention one can get from a mentor, traditional courses in body piercing are offered by many large piercing studios. Jade Dragon Tattoo and Body Piercing, in Chicago, for example, has a beginner's course for $3,800 that teaches some of the basics (call 312-409-3352). Finally, browsing through the Web sites of some of the larger piercing studios can serve to acquaint the beginner with the more basic issues involved in the craft. Perforations (www.perforations.com), in Brighton, England, has an exhaustive site with pages of detailed prose and pictures describing even the most obscure and painful piercings. The Association of Professional Piercers Web site (www.piercing.org/app) has details about local and national conferences, as well as an online version of the body-piercing magazine, *The Point*.

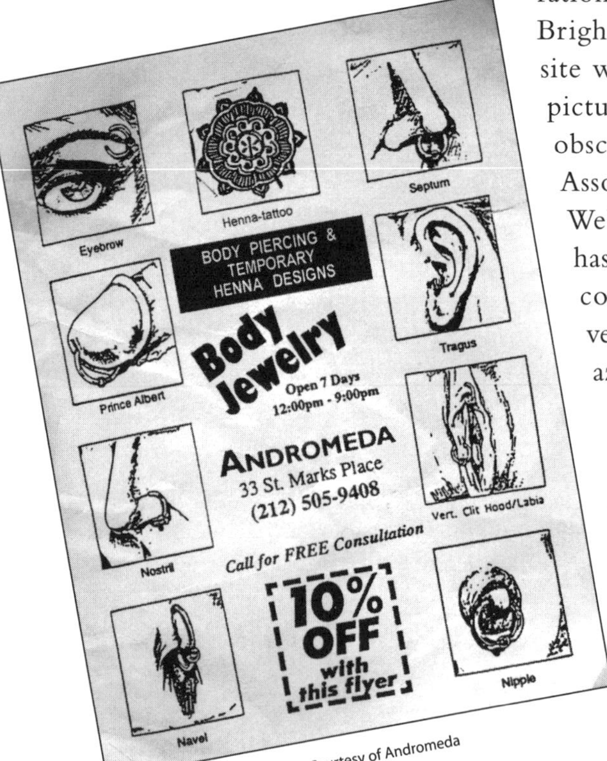

Credit: Courtesy of Andromeda

"It keeps his member smelling sweet," Queen Victoria is rumored to have said of the Prince Albert body pierce.

Taxidermist

Job description: Prepare, stuff, and mount dead animals for exhibition in a lifelike state.

Compensation: A highly regarded taxidermist can charge handsomely for his services. Russell O'Neal, a taxidermist in Pennsylvania, offers the following quotes (the first price is for a life-size mount, the second is just for shoulder and head): elk, $3,800/$600; African bushpig, $1,900/$500; and lion, $3,600/$850. A life-size mount of a duck is $175, a turkey is $375, and freshwater fish run $10 an inch.

Prerequisites: All you need is a craftsman's love of working with tools coupled with a predilection for hunting and skinning animals; the work involves handling an organism's eyes, flesh, heart, lungs, etc., so squeamishness is a significant handicap.

Qualities employer is seeking: Taxidermy, like many other arts and crafts activities, is frequently done by individuals who work alone out of their own shops. This is far from a traditional desk job; taxidermists don't really have employers.

Perks: Most taxidermists have vast amounts of personal freedom, to work whenever and wherever they choose. All that is required to get started, according to Russell Tinsley's *Taxidermy Guide*, is a workbench and the following tools: a saw, brush, hammer, knife, drill, and screwdriver.

Risks/drawbacks: Having to confront animal rights activists, who have in the past crashed taxidermy conventions to splash fake blood on some of the exhibits. Because taxidermists work in tight quarters with dead, wild animals, they may also face the possibility of acquiring an infection or sickness from a decaying (and possibly diseased) organism.

Overview

For hunting and fishing enthusiasts, killing the game is only half the battle. Following the rush of successfully slaying a wild animal or reeling in a prized fish is the long and complicated task of bringing the cooling body back to civilization intact, freezing the corpse (it is considered poor etiquette to bring an animal to a taxidermist unfrozen), and getting it properly mounted to display for one's friends and family.

The taxidermist's job is to take the animal's body and make it not only presentable but to clean and cure it so that it will hold its lifelike form for decades. This process begins by completely skinning the animal and removing and discarding all of its innards. Kory Kamps, a Wisconsin taxidermist, says that this step comes as a surprise to lay citizens. "Most people think that the inside of the mounted animals is really the animal," says Kamps.

Once the animal's outer skin layer has been cleaned of all muscle, potentially rotting flesh, and cartilage, the taxidermist will essentially have to attach the animal—whether it is the entire

body or just the head—around a carefully constructed mold. Perhaps the biggest advance in the field of taxidermy has been the widespread availability of ready-made mannequin forms that serve as the shape-holder for the animal. Taxidermists, who previously had to create these shape-keeping mannequins with combinations of wood, wire, clay, and papier mâché can now mail-order mass-produced urethane forms. While using one of these devices can save time, it may lessen the realism and quality of the final product. Chris Streetman, a taxidermist in Austin, Texas, says, "A Texas deer has characteristics that differ from the northern deer. But if I ordered a mannequin for a Texas deer, it will most likely have the shape and size of a northern deer. As a result, my finished mount won't look right."

Creating a finished mount requires myriad other procedural steps, including selecting and placing the appropriate glass eyes (as well as fitting them with cotton and beeswax in the sockets). For hairy animals, the fur will need to be deodorized—sometimes several times—and made mothproof. Mounting fish requires painting the organism. "With animals and birds, the realism originates with the creature's eyes and ears," Russell Tinsley writes in *Taxidermy Guide*. "With a fish the realistic appearance is derived chiefly from the coloration. A poor mount with a first-class paint job will be more realistic than a quality mount haphazardly painted."

Although some master taxidermists may be equally comfortable mounting all kinds of animals, the majority eventually settle on one area of expertise—be it large mammals from the African plains, small birds, fish or sharks, or whatever. Kevin Hynes, of Slidell, Louisiana, settled on his specific area definitively and from an early age. "I have been hunting wood ducks all my life," says Hynes. "I grew up in east New Orleans in a duck hunting family, and while I will mount anything, I consider the wood duck my specialty."

Mounted much lately? Remove a duck's guts, squeeze glass eyes into the head of a dead African bushpig, then break for lunch.

Credit: Courtesy of John Phillipps

Practical Information

For many years, taxidermy was a rarely discussed profession, whose practitioners preferred to protect their hard-earned trade secrets than to share them with potential competitors. In those days, the only way one might get involved in taxidermy was through trial-and-error or through an apprenticeship. This has changed substantially in the past quarter century, as state and national organizations have begun promoting the craft, offering classes and seminars in it, and selling books and magazines focusing on taxidermy techniques and equipment.

One of the best resources for the budding taxidermist is the Web site Taxidermy.net (www.taxidermy.net). This site includes up-to-date information about local weekend workshops. Ambitious students who want to invest in a more rigorous curriculum will also find information on this site about a number of formal taxidermy schools, with classes that range from a few weeks to several months. The Northwood School of Taxidermy in Pennsylvania, for example, has a thirteen-week hands-on course, which is roughly broken down into three categories: fish (four weeks), birds (three weeks), and fur (six weeks). The course also includes information on establishing one's own taxidermy business; tuition is approximately $4,995, in addition to the cost of the specimens (around $3,000, although students may bring their own animals). At the end of the course, students are graded on their abilities with fish, game birds, waterfowl, mammals, heads, and rugs.

"If you do bad taxidermy, you no longer have a fond memory; you have a permanent nightmare," says Gary Lowery, a taxidermist from Ontario. "I take pride in what I do. I want a quality mount."

A number of books and magazines exist on the subject. Gerald Grantz's *Home Book of Taxidermy and Tanning*, available for $16.95 from Stackpole Books, is a good primer. *American Taxidermist Magazine* (800-411-2154) and *North American Taxidermy News* (800-833-2699) are the leading news sources for the taxidermy industry; they cover new procedures and supplies, and taxidermy conventions and contests.

Finally, the large majority of professional taxidermists start out as hobbyists before making it their full-time job. Gary Lowery, a lifelong angler, started pursuing taxidermy as a career only after being downsized at age forty-two from his job at Canada Student Loans. Although he is now an accomplished taxidermist with several awards under his belt, Lowery acknowledges that the learning curve for this kind of work is steep: "It takes hundreds of mounts before you can get good enough to charge a fee for it."

(Although there is no skinning or stuffing involved, you can preserve human beings as a cryonicist, putting people into a deep freeze until they can be thawed and reanimated. See p. 174.)

Funeral Home Cosmetologist

Job description: A cosmetologist's range of duties varies depending on the size of the establishment. In smaller funeral homes, it's actually the funeral director, or mortician, who acts as cosmetologist, embalmer, and funeral coordinator. At larger homes, cosmetologists deal exclusively with preparing the deceased for open-casket wakes and funerals: anything up to and including perms, manicures, makeup, and clothing.

Compensation: The pay is in the low twenties to start. Funeral directors make more.

Prerequisites: Morticians need a two-year degree in mortuary science from an accredited school and a one-year apprenticeship. They also must pass an embalmer licensing exam. As far as hair and makeup are concerned, you don't need a license to work on the deceased. Increasingly, hair and makeup workers come into the field from a cosmetological, rather than a mortuary, background. While around 85 percent of licensed cosmetologists work at salons, a growing number of them are finding work in providing services for the sick, the elderly, and the deceased.

Qualities employer is seeking: Funeral homes look for empathetic people who don't spook easily. A background in chemistry can be more helpful than you think if you're doing cosmetic work—perms and hair coloring are sciences unto themselves. If you're more interested in the other aspects of being a small-parlor mortician, you'll need well-developed administrative skills. Aspiring embalmers should have sturdy stomachs (the smell of the chemicals alone can nauseate you).

Perks: Most people in any mortuary trade will tell you that the real satisfaction comes from helping the families of the deceased. One mortician estimates that he spends "about 90 percent of my time with the living. I spend very little time with the dead." Cosmetologists have the satisfaction of performing the same jobs they would perform on the living, only they also feel like they're doing a favor to society as well as helping people to improve their appearance. The work is stress-free and strictly nine to five.

Risks/drawbacks: In America's death-denying society, people give morticians about as warm a reception as they give the Grim Reaper himself. Funeral directors place the blame at least partly on their own shoulders: "People expect us to look and act like, well, like morticians," says one, "and a lot of us do." For mortuary cosmetologists, a major drawback is the lack of artistic freedom. Hairdressers and makeup artists in salons can consult with their clients on creative new looks and push the artistic envelope as far as they want. In funeral homes, they have to respect the wishes of grieving relatives who'd rather not see a sexy bilevel cut on the deceased.

Overview

Unlike more up-and-down industries, the mortuary trade is recession proof and here to stay. This isn't to say that there isn't some fluctuation in the business of individual funeral homes. If a home starts doing bad work, the clientele will often flock to a local competitor. "Bad work" can mean bungled transportation attempts, poor makeup jobs, or just "a feeling like the funeral director doesn't really care." Poor work doesn't vanish at the time of burial if the family of the deceased remembers it.

"Whenever I walk out of the funeral home, I get a terrific high because I know I took care of the grieving family," notes mortuary hairdresser Noella Charest-Papagno. "Every hairdresser should do this at least once."

Recently, the funeral industry has leaped from mostly mom-and-pop operations (where one funeral director could bury three generations of a family) to large-scale, multinational funeral chains who buy out the little guy and proffer overpriced impersonal "grief therapy" for bereaved families—or so cynics would say. Jessica Mitford's *The American Way of Death Revisited* paints a gruesome portrait of an industry overrun with ruthless, grasping, euphemism-spouting, and unctuous undertakers who leach a living from funeral prepayments ("Pay Now—Die Poorer" advises one chapter) and collusion with shady members of the clergy.

While most of the mortuary profession is service-oriented, it has its retail component as well. Morticians often have showrooms of caskets, catalogs, and brochures for various models. Funeral preplanning is a growing trend. It's not unusual for a future customer to climb into a casket to give it a "test run."

Practical Information

You can take two routes to end up in mortuary cosmetology: Either you want to be a mortician or you want to be a cosmetologist. If you are interested in being a mortician, the University of California at Irvine has a Web site with listings of mortuary science schools across the nation (www.com.uci.edu/~anatomy/willed_body/schools.htm). You can also try contacting the National Funeral Directors Association in Brookfield, Wisconsin at 800-228-6332. Their Web site (www.nfda.org) has information on careers, education, and even has a "virtual trade show."

If you're more interested in the cosmetic aspects of the mortuary profession, a great place to start is with the National Accrediting Commission of Cosmetology Arts and Sciences (www.naccas.org) for a list of accredited schools, job listings, and related sites.

Once you've gotten the education you need, entry into the field is fairly seamless. Many morticians just inherit the family business. (As with many businesses involving emotional clients and sometimes gory and gruesome situations—like prosthetist, p. 107—the mortuary business seems less appealing to entrepreneurs casting about for a business opportunity.) Others find jobs with the funeral parlor they apprenticed at. Classified ads and all of the Web sites listed on the previous page also offer up an abundance of diverse opportunities. Of course, if you're feeling adventurous, you can always strike out on your own. Freelance mortuary cosmetologists are rare, but not unheard of. But for those who want to ply the hair-and-makeup trade on the otherwise neglected, hospitals and nursing homes are full of prospective clients.

Tattoo Artist

Job description: Decorate human skin with designs, symbols, and lettering using a needle and permanent dyes.

Compensation: Tattooing is a full-time job for most tattoo artists, or "tattooists," and salaries can vary widely, depending on the individual's experience and reputation. A typical tattoo artist makes from $500 to $1,000 a week.

Prerequisites: No formal training or background is necessary, but reputable tattoo artists recommend that beginners apprentice for at least two years with an established artist before striking out on their own.

Qualities employer is seeking: Large tattoos can take several hours of work, sometimes in multiple sessions, and even small tattoos can take thirty minutes of concentration, creativity, and precision, requiring artistic ability, patience, unsqueamish reaction to blood, and a steady hand.

Perks: For many tattoo artists, the thrill of the job is knowing that people carry their artwork around for the rest of their lives. "I like the fact that my art is organic and alive," says Sunday (her professional name), of New York's Sacred Tattoo. "People get a tattoo that changes their lives, and they love it." Night owls take note: Tattoo parlors (now more politely known as "tattoo studios") keep very late hours and rarely open before noon.

Risks/drawbacks: Tattooing is legal in most states (only Massachusetts, Oklahoma, South Carolina, and Vermont ban it altogether), so the risks involved with tattooing are usually not legal ones. Because tattooing involves needles that puncture the skin, unsanitary conditions or equipment create a risk of spreading hepatitis or HIV infection. Unfortunately, just about anyone can get their hands on a tattooing machine and set up shop out of their home, with predictable results. Tattoo artists sometimes refer to these poorly trained amateurs as "scratchers"—so called because they often dig the needle too deep below the skin and raise scar tissue. A good tattoo artist uses disposable needles, keeps an autoclave (a sterilizer) on hand, and wears rubber gloves while working.

Overview

Tattooing has been around for thousands of years, and in some societies—particularly in Japan, the Pacific Islands, and among the Maori of New Zealand—body art has traditionally held great religious and cultural significance. (The word *tattoo* itself comes from the Tahitian word *tatau*, thought to derive from the sound of the tattooing instrument on the skin.) In the United States, however, tattoos long carried a seedy reputation, derived from the fact that they could usually be found only on sailors, felons, and bikers. In the last few years, though, tattoos have become a growing industry: the Alliance of Professional Tattooists, founded in 1992, now has members in all fifty states. Tattoo styles are changing, too, and reflect the long history of the art form: Serpents, hearts, and women's names are still popular, but the biggest trend nowadays is toward "traditional" body art, utilizing motifs from Celtic, Tahitian, or other cultures. Particularly popular are kanji, Japanese calligraphic characters that represent a word or phrase. (*Girl Power*, for example, can be tattooed using the Japanese characters for *woman* and *strength*).

It used to be that people could wake up after a blurry night of carousing to find they had a piece of permanent art to commemorate the evening. Artists now

Would you really want to stick a needle in this guy?

Credit: Joe Rife/Index Stock Photography

ask customers to sign a consent form (required in some states) and insist that their clients be sober before the work begins. Tattoos can also be removed, although the removal process, which involves repeated laser treatments to the skin, is quite painful and often not completely effective.

Just as tattoos were once the province of extreme macho types and sailors on leave, until recently, tattoo artists themselves have been almost exclusively male. Women now make up about a third of the industry. Studios can be found in just about every city in America. Even in states that ban it, tattoo artists practice their trade, albeit illegally. New York, for example, banned tattooing in the 1960s but maintained an underground tattoo industry until it was legalized again in 1997. Los Angeles and San Francisco have always been the unofficial tattooing capitals of America, but New York City is poised to overtake them.

Practical Information

Becoming a tattoo artist is no easy task, and the toughest part of the job may be in convincing an established artist to take you on as an apprentice. "Check out the portfolios and know the work and reputation of the people you want to have teach you," advises Eric Rignall, a tattoo artist in New York. Ideally, you'll want to assemble your own portfolio of illustrations to show your prospective mentor. Tattooing, once a low-key business that was often illegal, has become much more competitive recently. And says Sunday, "Like any other industry that involves artists, there's a lot of ego."

"A good tattoo is not cheap, and a cheap tattoo is not good," says Eric Rignall, of Inkstop Tattoo in New York. "We get a lot of people in here who think they can haggle over the price."

While some states regulate tattooing, and a few ban it, most states don't regulate tattooing at all. That means that it's very easy to become a bad tattoo artist but harder to do it the right way. Once you've set yourself up with a good mentor, though, tattooing can be a very satisfying career if you're artistically inclined and open-minded. Not only is the job low on stress, but best of all, as Eric Rignall puts it, "You get to do artwork for a living."

Many underground bookshops and large music stores carry books and magazines on body art. Two useful Web sites run by the nonprofit Alliance of Professional Tattooists are http://home.safetattoos.com/safetattoos and www.redgenie.com/apt.htm/.

9 Cool Jobs

Zamboni Driver

Polar Meteorologist

Dog Musher

Ice Sculptor

Good Humor Man

Christmas Tree Farmer

Zamboni Driver

Now ever since I was young
it's been my dream
That I might drive a Zamboni machine.
I'd get the ice just as slick as could be
And all the kids would look up to me.

—THE GEAR DADDIES,
"The Zamboni Song"

Job description: Drive a Zamboni ice resurfacer to restore "skateability" (sheen and smoothness) to ice and hockey rinks.

Compensation: Drivers at small rinks earn as little as $5 per hour. Drivers for city arenas and other large-scale hockey and ice-skating venues earn about $18 to $20 per hour, though such wages usually require membership in labor unions.

Prerequisites: Not even a driver's license.

Qualities employer is seeking: Nobody makes a career out of driving a Zamboni; the task is usually part of a larger job, something along the lines of rink maintenance, which demands various fix-'em-up tasks and heavy hauling jobs. Thus, rink managers typically look for strong workers with technical know-how. It also helps if you know a thing or two about ice sports and have contacts at rinks.

Perks: Free access to hockey games and ice shows; hot coffee served during periods of play; legions of cultish fans; and the thrill of driving such an awkwardly graceful vehicle.

Risks/drawbacks: Any time a job entails fixing and maneuvering a huge, unwieldy machine, injury looms near. Rarely have drivers been injured at the helm, however, though a few have been said to contract "Zamboni Disease" (also called "ice-hockey lung"), sickness resulting from inhaling too much propane from poorly ventilated machines. Other unique dangers to Zamboni driving come the way of belligerent fans. John Grzelcyk drove during the Boston Bruins' playoff games: "Any game with Montreal in the playoffs, the fans would be yelling at you, 'Hurry up, we want to get the game going!' Or if the Bruins were losing at the beginning of the first period, they'd say, 'The ice is terrible!' They don't realize there's two teams out there!" Says Paul Chambers, a former driver for Boston Garden: "You get kind of nervous out there, with all those people watching you. I almost got hit with a bottle one night. The bottle just missed my head. A friend of mine ducked, and it flew right by me." Still, physical harm aside, most drivers agree that the greatest danger of their job is loss of pride from screwing up: "The worst that could happen is if you crash, and you can't finish the ice. Then everybody gets mad," explains Tim Stay, a nineteen-year-old driver for Harvard University. "If you forget to take the conditioner up, you can rip the back of the whole Zamboni off. I've heard stories that it's happened."

Overview

The driver of a Zamboni ice resurfacer makes little money, needs even less education, and works scattered hours within a limited job market (in about 1,700 ice rinks in the United States). Still, hockey and ice-skating fans worldwide have developed a cultish lust to commandeer the vehicle, creating tribute songs (see the previous page), Web sites, and assorted paraphernalia emblazoned with that say-it-again name. So why is it the unsated dream of so many to drive what looks like a dumpster on wheels?

Mostly, because the Zamboni seems so darn fun to drive. It's a clunky beast of a machine that somehow cruises gracefully across the ice. It appears to require a good deal of child-level manipulation of levers and buttons, but isn't as intimidating as, say, an airplane. And the Zamboni's job has as defined a purpose as any product: between periods in hockey games or skating sessions at an ice rink, an ice resurfacer paints the ice with water, restoring the chewed up surface with a mirror-like sheen. For skaters and hockey fans, who have nothing to do but watch as the Zamboni spins its magic, the machine's slow pace mesmerizes, providing a thrill similar to watching someone apply color to the final bare section on a newly painted house.

Zamboni: There is no substitute

Credit: Courtesy of Frank J. Zamboni & Co. Inc.

Practical Information

Zamboni is a trademark for the world's largest producer of ice resurfacers, named after the machine's inventor, Frank Zamboni, who invented his product in 1942 by converting an old tractor. Innovations yielded new models through the years, but the basic principle remained the same: The modern Zamboni scrapes the ice surface, gathers the shavings, squeegees out a layer of water, vacuums it up, and finally lays another layer of clean, hot water. The Zamboni company sells about 200 machines a year; today, a top-of-the-line machine costs about $50,000.

Zamboni driving is hardly a full-time job. Most drivers work on the rink maintenance crew, which performs various repair and upkeep tasks when not nurturing the ice. Tim Stay first fell into his job by sheer proxy. "I played hockey, and I was looking for a summer job. So I knew who to talk to." Many drivers belong to unions; joining the right one might give you an edge over other candidates—of which there might be many. "Last summer I saw a lot of applications for the job," says Stay. "A few people are always looking to do it."

The demand for Zamboni drivers depends on the number of rinks and the popularity of ice skating and hockey. A single driver's hours depend on his or her rink. "Most of the guys at my rink work on the ice maintenance crew between 7 A.M. to 10 P.M.," says Stay. "Or they'll be two guys doing eight-hour shifts." For Zamboni drivers, the ultimate gig is to resurface the ice for the National Hockey League. So what's it take to get to the big leagues? Most drivers humbly claim their job requires little skill, that luck (or union affiliation) is more likely to land a sweet job. John Grzelcyk has driven Zamboni for the Bruins for fifteen to twenty years: "It's about cutting the ice, not putting the brake down too much, not putting too much water down. The guys in Detroit, Chicago, at the universities, any of those guys could do this."

"It is satisfying and endorphin-raising to produce a decent sheet of ice," writes Theresa Loong on *Charged.com*, an online magazine. "It scares people. It scares and empowers me. I'm on a turntable that keeps going. I'm on a big toy. Resurfacing seems like becoming a synthesis of half man, half machine. The Zamboni is taking on a life of its own."

But through all their self-effacement, one senses a deeper Zen of Zamboni. "It's patience, it's experience," Stay explains of driving the nine-mile-per-hour vehicle. "It's a little about covering the ice in few passes, but it's more about how much water you put down and how you move the conditioner, which is a pretty sharp blade that you move by mil-

limeters. It's not easy driving on ice, especially if it's wet, but once you know how, it's habit." Drivers need to accommodate both hockey players and figure skaters, who prefer the ice to be harder or softer; despite every Zamboni driver's best efforts, skaters commonly complain about the quality of the ice. Chambers concurs: "Once you get the hang of it, a Zamboni's easy to drive. But it takes a few months before you know what you're doing." General consensus among drivers is that Zamboni driving is as much a "nice job" as an "ice job." Just don't expect to make a full career out of it without learning a thing or two about general rink maintenance, or you'll be left driving on thin ice.

Polar Meteorologist

Job description: Track and forecast weather for a U.S. Air Force base in extreme northwestern Thule, Greenland, latitude 76°N.

Compensation: Meteorologists at Thule earn about $50,000 a year tax-free and cheap food at the chow hall. Most forecasters get thirty days' paid vacation and free transportation back to the sub-Arctic latitude of their choice. Health insurance is not included, but emergency medical care is available free at the small on-base hospital, and a dentist comes through every few weeks.

Prerequisites: A degree in meteorology or equivalent military training. Active-duty experience is not a must, but it certainly makes a candidate more attractive, and veterans have the advantage of knowing the military language and customs. A successful and well-adjusted polar meteorologist will have excellent forecasting skills and also a stoic self-sufficiency. The range of activities is limited, and boredom and lonesomeness can get to people. As Thule meteorologist Roger Ashley puts it, "If you don't read and go to the gym, chances are you're drinking." All applicants must have complete physical exams and prove they're in good medical and dental health.

Qualities employer is seeking: Employers want well-trained, thoroughly experienced meteorologists who can bear to be away from their families, live in the dark for four months at a stretch (and in the summer, sleep in daylight, which can be just as difficult), and be sane and congenial colleagues to a small crew in close quarters. No Arctic experience is required.

Perks: Ashley has been a Thule meteorologist for three years, and he rates his degree of job satisfaction a perfect ten: "If you make a good forecast in an Arctic storm, you've probably saved a lot of lives."

Risks/drawbacks: People have died within sight of Thule's buildings, in moderate Arctic storms, so all personnel are restricted to the base in winter. Perhaps a greater risk than the weather is the lure of alcohol. "There are some real professional drinkers here," says Ashley, "and some gifted amateurs." The only person to be fired in Ashley's memory was a forecaster who habitually showed up for work drunk. (For a considerably less taxing weather-related job, read about working as a TV weathercaster, p. 208.)

Overview

Thule (pronounced "TOO-lee") was transformed from a Danish fishing village to a top-secret American air force base soon after World War II, to provide a refueling stop for bombers on their way to the Soviet Union. Since the end of the Cold War, though, Thule's mission has become comparatively more benign; nowadays, it's primarily a radar site, a communications facility, and an emergency airfield for planes crossing over the North Pole. (Asked if Thule meteorologists still participate in any classified activities, Ashley replied, "Hello?") Researchers from the Danish Meteorological Service do climate studies there, and the Greenland Peregrine Falcon Survey uses it as home base when counting nests each summer. Thule is a cluster of low buildings on a plain next to North Star Bay. Employees live in one- or two-room apartments with communal kitchens, bathrooms, and TV lounges.

About 800 people live on the base, most of them civilian, male, and Danish (although English is the base's official language). A staff of eight operates the weather station. The U.S. airmen, who comprise about a quarter of the Thule population, tend to stay just a year or two, while some of the civilians stick it out for two or three decades. Base residents have infrequent contact with the native Greenlanders, who sometimes dogsled to Thule to shop. The nearest Inuit village is forty minutes away by helicopter.

Polar meteorologists collect all sorts of useful and fascinating cold-weather lore. For instance, human nose hairs freeze at about minus seventy-seven degrees Fahrenheit. Icebergs can flip over with little warning, since the top accumulates ice in the cold air as the bottom melts away in the warmer water.

And at forty below zero, the slightest breeze creates a windchill that freezes exposed flesh instantly.

"Do not mess with the polar bears," says Chief Master Sergeant Roger Ashley, USAF (retired). "They may look cuddly, but I saw one punch through three feet of sea ice, scoop up a 250-pound seal with one paw, and bite its head off in one smooth motion. No, do not mess with the polar bears."

"All that being said, though, Greenland's cold is a dry cold, and people don't walk around chilled and miserable all the time. And there are fun things to do outdoors in the summer—bird-watching, kayaking among the ice floes, hiking to the ice caves, and mountain biking over the pack ice. As every Greenlander will tell you, "It takes three months, and you can do it all in one day." (Greenland is a one-joke landmass. Come early spring, when the sun rises for about a minute and a half, people ask each other, "What did you do today?" Answer: "I smoked a cigarette" or "I flossed." In mid-October, when the sun begins to set, they ask each other, "What did you do today?" Answer: "Oh, I read *War and Peace*.")

Practical Information

The standard work schedule is twenty hours off, then eleven hours in the station, then thirteen hours "on call." Weather staff do not wear beepers: "If you're really doing your job, you'll know when to be at work," says Ashley. A typical workday begins at 5:45 A.M. with a review of the previous night's weather-mainly via satellite data and computer-relayed reports from the National Weather Service. Forecasters then extrapolate from that information, factor in current observations, and devise briefings for incoming and outgoing pilots. Only about one plane per day takes off or lands at Thule, compared with 125 to 150 sorties at a more typical base.

"Plenty of free time" is an oft-noted Thule perk. Recreation possibilities include a bowling alley, a good gym, a well-stocked library, a small casino and nightclub, and now Internet connections. A supply plane comes in once or twice a week with letters, fresh produce, and mail-ordered goodies. (With $50,000 a year and almost no expenses, people build up considerable CD libraries, camera collections, etc.) Except for fish, pets are not allowed—there's a fear dogs would get loose and violate the local huskies.

It is probably not surprising that no online job listing exists for aspiring polar meteorologists and no industry newsletter. People discover these jobs by word of mouth, usually from folks in the air force. The agency that runs the weather

station is Greenland Contractors, 1 Kristianiagade, P.O. Box 2669, DK-2100, Copenhagen, Denmark.

Those seeking *really* southern exposure might consider applying at McMurdo Station on Ross Island in Antarctic (winter pop. 150) or the Amundsen-Scott South Pole Station, settled atop two miles of solid ice (winter pop. 28). Colorado-based Antarctic Support Associates, a firm that supplies all kinds of personnel to "The Ice," holds a job fair each year. For information, call 303-790-8606 or check out its website, www.asa.org—particularly the poorly named "Hot Jobs" page. While Antarctic research stations tend to be multinational affairs, Arctic ones are more often mono- or bi-national. For instance, there's the Russians' Murmansk Branch of the Arctic and Antarctic Scientific Research Institue (011-7-8152-574053) and the Canadians' Eureka, Resolute Bay and Alert High Arctic Weather Stations (the former being on the northernmost point of land in North America).

Dog Musher

Job description: Beyond the thrills and rigors of coaxing a speedy dog team across vast wintry expanses, a dog driver must spend time caring for the team, making training runs, and doing maintenance and fund-raising work.

Compensation: The Iditarod, grandpa of all dogsled races, carries a $450,000 purse for the first-place winner, down to about $34,000 for fifth place. Smaller races like the Copper Basin 300 bestow $7,500 upon the winner. Corporations and local businesses have deep sponsorship pockets, which take time and fame to pick.

Prerequisites: Though there's no formal educational requirement to race, it takes at least five years of training and race experience to be realistically competitive. The Iditarod requires 500 miles of racing experience to enter, and only those finishing in the top ten can hope to garner a good chunk of sponsorships.

Qualities employer is seeking: Ability to mush from a speeding sled in the freezing cold for days at a time with no rest.

Perks: Sponsorships can yield anything from free lodging in Anchorage to a new truck every year to complimentary dental work. Beyond material benefits, there's no understating the chance to spend almost every day racing through some of the most beautiful, desolate, soul-searing country on Earth.

Risks/drawbacks: Dog drivers don't get a lot of sleep, especially during the wintertime. Racing and caring for the dogs are extremely taxing, both emotionally and physically. In addition, despite the possible prize earnings, very few drivers make enough money to sustain themselves year-round.

Overview

The use of sleds pulled by dog teams ("mushing") has a long and proud history in the icier portions of North America. For many towns isolated in the Alaskan bush, mushing still provides one of the only overland means of outside contact and commerce during the long, dark winters. In 1925, a group of heroic mushers and their trusty dog teams speedily hauled thousands of vials of life-saving diphtheria serum from Fairbanks to Nome, staving off a nearly disastrous epidemic. The 1,150-mile Iditarod race from Anchorage to Nome, held annually in early March, commemorates that great event in dog driving and public health. Since its founding in 1973, the Iditarod has provided the premier forum for serious dog drivers to test their skill and earn their keep. The best mushers finish in about nine and a half days, enduring temperatures of twenty below with only about ten total hours of sleep. About seventy mushers compete each year, though far fewer run the race to completion, and those who make the top times enjoy prize money, lucrative sponsorships, national recognition, and statewide adulation.

Credit: Courtesy of the Nome Visitors Center

Forget the rat race—join the dog race! Winners of the Iditarod take home a $450,000 purse. That's a lot of Alpo.

"For us in Alaska, when winters can be long and cold and dreary, it's a really thrilling thing," says Janine Seavey, of Ididaride Sled Dog Tours.

Of the 300-odd dog racers in Alaska, perhaps 100 mush as an occupation, bolstered by some sort of summer job. There are five or fewer mushers who can afford to drive dogs exclusively year-round. Mitch Seavey, fifth-place finisher in the 1998 Iditarod, supports his family and his dogs through the summer by giving tours and rides to tourists. With team maintenance costing around $30,000 per year, however, it's the Iditarod that makes career mushing possible, even profitable. Seavey says he is "totally happy" with his career, sailing across lands where there is "room for the soul to just drift." Despite the lack of steady money that a coat-and-tie job might provide, he still enjoys a stable and pleasant family life—and it helps that his wife and sons are all mushing fanciers, as well.

A typical winter day in the life of a dog driver might begin with a big breakfast, followed by cleaning the grounds and feeding the dogs. There's plenty of maintenance work to do while the dogs rest and digest. Through the winter, a team will progress from short hauls to full-day voyages: forty miles out, four hours' rest, and forty miles back, up to five times per week. Any multiday race presents an enormous logistical challenge, especially the Iditarod. Food caches must be prepared carefully and far in advance, and proper packing becomes an issue not just of winning or losing, but of survival. Any serious musher must master canine psychology, always anticipating the needs of the team and keeping the dogs healthy and happy. The better the coach, the more likely a victory; the more wins, the easier it is to attract sponsorships.

Practical Information

Dog driving is a pluralistic sport, where maleness and youth are not important prerequisites. Some of the finest mushers are female; Libby Riddles was the first woman to win the Iditarod, and Susan Butcher has won four times. Mushing takes extreme patience and the ability to make quick decisions, and winners are most often in their thirties or forties, with plenty of experience—both general and dog-specific—under their belts. While professional dog driving is concentrated in Alaska and neighboring Canadian locales, opportunities also exist in Montana, Wyoming, Michigan, and Maine.

A number of organizations that can provide the prospective musher with more information. The Iditarod Trail Committee (907-376-5155; www.iditarod.com) has the scoop on the big race. *Mushing Magazine* (907-479-0454; www.mushing.com) publishes every other month. Mush with Pride (800-50-PRIDE) prints booklets on sled dog care and equipment, plus a quarterly newsletter.

Ice Sculptor

Job description: Transform blocks of ice into majestic, albeit short-lived, works of art.

Compensation: According to Jerome Shea of Atlantic Ice Sculptors in Weymouth, Massachusetts, "Most sculptors who work from single blocks earn between $50 and $100 per sculpture. One block takes me no more than three hours; I'm good for eight to fifteen sculptures each week." That works out to about $45,000 to $50,000 per year. Sculptors can also earn income (and travel) through competition prize money.

Prerequisites: Many ice sculptors start out their careers as chefs; top kitchens often train staff to sculpt for large events. Freelance sculptors generally have backgrounds in cooking, or in some cases, sculpture and visual arts. Among sculpting media, ice particularly demands fitness, dexterity, and speed.

Qualities employer is seeking: The ability to produce high-quality work at a quick pace will secure a sculptor's career. As with any artistic endeavor, a good eye and talent are important, but sculptors claim anyone can learn their trade with enough time and dedication.

Perks: "The best part of my job is that when it's very hot in the summertime, I don't even know about it. It's cool year-round," says Eric Foncecchio, who's been sculpting ice for fifteen years. "Plus I make my own hours, and I get paid by the piece, so if I'm fast, I can take advantage of that." Top sculptors in power centers can rub elbows with celebrities; iceman Duncan Hamilton, according to the *London Independent*, has met Margaret Thatcher, Clint Eastwood, Elton John, Steven Spielberg, Richard Branson, and other bigwigs while carving out pretty meltables.

Risks/drawbacks: Ice sculptors work with chainsaws. They must learn to wield big, buzzing death machines over their heads while in awkward positions. They also use chisels and sharp instruments to chip at the ice. Then they have to move their heavy product around, which presents the usual dangers of high-load moving. Beyond that, it's a relatively safe job.

Overview

Most artists dream of leaving a legacy, but for sculptors of ice—as well as sand and snow—history forgets quickly, usually within four to six hours after a piece's unveiling. Still, the frozen-water medium has risen to unprecedented popularity in recent years, so that no modern wedding or banquet spread seems complete without a glimmering statue growing steadily blobbish at table's center. (See "Wedding Cake Chef," p. 220, for other short-lived wedding art.)

Of course, serious sculptors don't use ice, and ice sculptors make no pretense to high art; their subjects are usually

angels, birds, boats, punch bowls, and other low-concept forms. Tournaments, held at winter carnivals across the country, bring out more thoughtful large-scale designs, but an ice sculptor's bread-and-butter remains banal bar mitzvah–type figures. *Honeymoon on a Harley*, from one sculptor's catalog, depicting a happy couple poised on a hog, sells for $1,100. An *Aloha Girl* sells for a mere $350. Some can fetch more than $3,000. Most commercial sculptors' pieces range from $150–1,000 each; cost includes setup, drains, and lights.

"It doesn't bother me that my sculptures melt," says ice sculptor Eric Foncecchio. "If they didn't melt, I'd be out of a job. If I like the piece, I take pictures of it. Everything's temporary in life."

Larger ice sculptures are shown at outdoor winter events, smaller, more popular figurines at weddings, graduations, holidays, corporate events, grand openings, bar mitzvahs, christenings, and similar occasions. "I recently had to make a piece for a funeral," Foncecchio says. "An angel, with long, elegant wings. It was kind of sad."

The day in the life of an ice sculptor varies by demand. Foncecchio describes the process of creation: "I dress up in a ski suit, hat, winter boots, and gloves, then I head into the freezer, which is set to about twenty-six to twenty-eight degrees. The ice blocks are usually about 300 to 500 pounds, and I start by drawing my image out with a magic marker. Then I rough it out with a chainsaw before proceeding with the ice-sculpting chisels to form the ice. I have artistic license, usually." Many sculptures are made from a template form; the most difficult designs, Foncecchio says, are portraits, where the artist is given a picture and told to carve out an actual person. "If I make a mistake on a portrait, I have to start over. You have to take your time; a single mistake can change the whole appearance. The biggest challenge for a sculptor is contorting and capturing the human body." Like stone, ice requires "subtractive sculpture," where a piece is made not by putting together, but by taking away matter from a central block.

The biggest drawback for artists interested in carving ice is the ephemeral nature of the medium. But as Jerome Shea rationalizes, "As a chef, you watch your food disappear when you put it out. With ice, you put it out, it melts, and then they want more."

Practical Information

Ice sculptors offer mixed opinions about what it takes to get into their frigid field. Some say artistic training is a must; others insist that anyone can do it. The industry has no known center, though sculptors in cold climates are more likely to land gigs at larger, outdoor events. "We offer lessons," says Jerome Shea. "We have it

down to a science. We provide you with a template, and just as you paint by numbers, you can sculpt by numbers." If local ice sculpting companies (found in many Yellow Pages) don't offer instruction to the general public, check with glitzy hotel restaurants. "If you're working as a chef, it's best to practice with free sculpture for Sunday brunches," Shea says. Styrofoam and clay are said to provide comparable training material for beginners. "It's the same with any craft: practice makes perfect," says Shea. "There's a learning process. It comes with years and years; not to make it sound complex, but experience pays off."

Good Humor Man

Job description: Cruise local streets during the summer months in a beat-up truck, hawking Good Humor popsicles and ice cream bars—Choco Tacos, King Cones, and the inimitable Toasted Almonds and Chocolate Eclairs.

Compensation: Drivers work on a commission basis with local distributors, frequently keeping one-quarter of the gross sales; a sultry weekend day can gross around $400, leaving the Good Humor man a cool $100.

Prerequisites: Aside from a valid driver's license, basic command of English, and a familiarity with U.S. currency, there really aren't any formal prerequisites for this job. It is in the best interest of distributors to ensure that all of the trucks remain on the street throughout the summer, so detailed, needling interviews are a rarity.

Qualities employer is seeking: In the golden era of Good Humor—before supermarkets made getting ice cream a cinch—requirements for this job were rather particular. An early manual from the company, *Making Good with Good Humor*, stated: "Customers will not patronize you if your hands are dirty, your face unshaven, or if you are careless about such things as haircuts and trimmed nails. Body odor, unclean teeth, bad

breath, and the like are, of course, inexcusable. For your own welfare, you will be wise if you are careful of your diet. On hot days eat very little; avoid fried foods and fats."

Perks: The mere sound of your truck can send eager ice cream–eating tykes into a veritable frenzy. "It's the best when you come down the street and a little kid sees you," says Yoni Fine, of Mt. Kisco, New York, "and they actually start jumping up and down, and then to make sure you stop they put their hand up and then they run, run, run inside to get money 'cause they don't want you to leave. Then they come back, and then—it's just so much fun."

Risks/drawbacks: Many of the trucks are rickety and offer poor visibility. As kids sometimes sprint toward the moving trucks with reckless abandon, drivers need to be careful not to injure any small, eager customers.

Overview

For decades, the Good Humor man has been an indelible part of the American landscape—cruising around town in a shiny vehicle wearing a crisp, white uniform, bringing merriment and inspiring the kind of childhood excitement generally reserved for Santa Claus. Although the fleet of trucks may be aging slightly (most are Fords and Chevys from the sixties and seventies) and the frozen dessert industry has been swamped by competitors, the Good Humor man remains the most well-known and revered of the street vendors. As *Boston Globe* reporter Joseph Kahn once asked, rhetorically: "Has there ever been a more wholesome ambassador of American enterprise than this mobile emperor of ice cream?"

Drivers generally settle into particular routes, which offer maximum exposure at popular gathering points; a well-timed trip will hit the little league fields just as practice is ending, the local community pool during midafternoon peak periods, and residential streets after most families have just completed dinner. The most entrepreneurial drivers know that attempting to constantly refine one's driving route can be less ultimately successful than adhering to a relatively fixed schedule. Predictability breeds loyalty from Good Humor patrons: Parents and kids will wait at fixed points for the arrival of the ice cream truck, if it sticks to a well-known route.

Drivers need to be prepared for a young clientele. Most Good Humor men have a bucket of gum aboard, which can forestall tears and sobs when a kid shows up for a snack but is unaware that there's a cost involved. (Drivers must also be prepared to receive payment in handfuls of pennies.)

Heat spells can be a mixed blessing: While ice cream demand peaks on days when the weather is unbearably hot, few Good Humor trucks are air-conditioned. It is a widely acknowledged truism among vendors that ice cream trucks are like furnaces, except for the freezers. Many of the vehicles are frail

after jingling several hundred thousand miles—to say nothing of their interiors. "I don't think the seatbelt really works," says Good Humor man Yoni Fine, "and the chair is kind of falling apart, so when I make a big sharp turn, I have to fight to stay in my chair."

One of the most enjoyable aspects of the job is that Good Humor drivers still command divine respect and slack-jaw gazes from admirers. "Over the years, you build a relationship with the kids," says Omar Sillah, twenty-nine, who purchased his 1979 Chevy truck for $10,000 in 1989 and works daily from noon to 10 P.M. during the summer months. "They know you. They have a lot of things to tell you. Even if you are in traffic, they shout your name. They will be on the school bus and they will all be cheering, 'Omar! Omar!' Like that, you know? That keeps you going."

Practical Information

The Good Humor company, headquartered in Green Bay, Wisconsin, licenses out the use of its name to approximately 500 drivers nationally. (This is up from twelve trucks in 1920, when Ohio candy maker Harry Burt invented the "ice cream on a stick"—patented shortly thereafter—and began selling the frozen treats from chauffeur-driven trucks decorated with his son's sleigh bells.) The Washington, D.C., area, one of the oldest Good Humor stomping grounds, has the

Credit: AP

"Has there ever been a more wholesome ambassador of American enterprise than this mobile emperor of ice cream?" asked the ***Boston Globe.***

largest fleet, with approximately 150 trucks; the entire New England area, by comparison, has about 40. Most of the trucks, which may get as little as nine miles to the gallon, need to be plugged into household electricity overnight to recharge the on-board freezers.

"Everyone knows to wave to you 'cause you're the ice cream man," says Good Humor man Yoni Fine, "and even if they don't want to buy ice cream, they'll just wave. That's just nice."

As many of the Good Humor distributors are highly autonomous, becoming a Good Humor man may require a bit of intrepid research. The first step should be to contact Good Humor at 920-499-5151. Beyond that, one might try to locate a Good Humor distributor in your area. This can most easily be accomplished by simply asking one of the local Good Humor men. Don't be too obvious about your intentions, as some drivers may be protective of their turf. In general, the ice cream delivery season lasts from around April through September; as some drivers may be actively looking for partners to split up part of the week, it's best to make inquiries in early spring.

As of now, distributors may not have a rigorous application process. This may gradually be changing, however, as a few embarrassing incidences may cause Good Humor (now Good Humor-Breyers) to review hiring procedures. Two men in Brooklyn, New York, were arrested in August 1998, for selling hashish and marijuana from their ice cream truck—a "different kind of good humor," a reporter for *Newsday* wrote at the time. The men were charged after undercover detectives simply requested "two" from the vendors, who immediately proffered a couple of $10 bags of hash. (The men had apparently obtained the appropriate Good Humor decals and ice cream for their truck, although local police say they may not have been the legitimate drivers of the vehicle.) The previous summer, a fifty-five-year-old Good Humor driver in the Boston area was accused of sexually assaulting two younger women in his truck.

Christmas Tree Farmer

Job description: Christmas tree farmers are first and foremost farmers, though trees are a much different crop than corn or tomatoes. Christmas tree farming is a demanding and exacting profession, requiring equal doses of green thumb, business savvy, and salesmanship.

Compensation: Some Christmas tree math: Most tree species grow comfortably at a density of about a thousand an acre; with Leyland cypress trees, for example, each acre produces about 950 salable trees, with a five-year span between when you plant the trees and when they are harvestable. At a sale price of $35 a tree, gross income on that acre is $33,250. Costs per acre run $1,200 a year. After the costs of replanting new trees, management costs such as fertilizing, watering, and insect control, and sales and marketing expenses, net income is roughly $20,000 an acre, for a net income of $4,000 a year, per acre. A fifteen-acre Christmas tree farm could provide enough income for a comfortable living. (OK, now calculate the net present value of the amortized investment using a 6 percent discount rate.)

Qualities employer is seeking: Patience, since trees take anywhere from five to fifteen years to grow to full size, is most important. You also must be prepared to duke it out in a cutthroat, cyclical, commodified industry. Marketing skills go a long way toward success in this business; farmers who can lure consumers to cut their own trees save on distribution costs and have an almost guaranteed sale for every minivan that pulls into the parking lot. Finally, ten or fifteen acres of farmland is key.

Perks: Christmas tree farms demand less work than other types of farms and provide a comfortable living. They are also pretty (trees of different ages are typically planted together, so the farm never looks clear-cut); and provide shelter for wildlife.

Risks/drawbacks: As with most other kinds of farming, bankruptcy is a looming threat. Tree farmers forecast that the Christmas tree surplus will actually dry up in the next decade, as the Christmas tree industry's environmental marketing messages take away the stigma usually associated with the timber industry. Fighting insects, fungus, and other tree diseases is an ongoing battle. Insects and disease can decimate as many as 40 percent of less-resistant species, such as Virginia pine. Battling the public perception that Christmas trees harm the environment is in itself a full-time job.

Overview

Live Christmas trees have only been in American homes since the 1850s. It is thought that German immigrants brought the tradition of the *Tannenbaum* to America; what was once a Teutonic tree-worshipping ceremony has grown to become one of most promising crops of the twenty-first century. Christmas tree farms only began to spring up in the 1950s; before then, families typically chopped down a tree in the forest (or from the side of the road). Today, roughly 2,000 Christmas tree farms slay helpless firs, pines, and cypresses for our holiday amusement; 98 percent of today's American Christmas trees grew up on a farm or plantation.

"Christmas tree plantations in the United States produce enough oxygen to supply the needs of 18,000,000 people, over 7 percent of our population."

—The Louisiana-Mississippi Christmas Tree Association

Some farms are just that, a few acres that provide supplemental income to a farmer grateful to have planted a relatively low-maintenance crop. Because Christmas trees can grow on barren slopes and under power lines, they are sometimes planted as a second crop where other crops will not grow. However, Christmas has become big business on tree plantations, where economies of scale really kick in. These well-equipped fir fiefdoms have large greenhouses for cultivating planting stock. Most Christmas trees begin life in a nursery where superior seed is planted and grown to two-year-old seedlings. Farms that have to purchase their seedlings from a nursery are at a cost disadvantage.

Thirty-three million Christmas trees were sold in 1997, at a retail cost per foot ranging from $3.10 to $5.65, according to the National Christmas Tree Association. Christmas tree prices have held steady for most of the decade, which means that prices have actually declined in inflation-adjusted dollars. The challenge for Christmas tree farmers, then, is to sell "premium" trees, those that sell for $5 or more per foot. Farmers often boost tree prices, save on distribution costs, and add value to their trees by allowing customers to choose and cut their own trees. While it is true that Christmas trees are an emotional purchase, consumers are also intelligent enough to realize that they will typically throw the tree away in less than a month.

State university agriculture departments are some of the biggest boosters of the many benefits of Christmas tree farming. Many farmers claim that academics are responsible for the current tree glut by spreading many myths about how easy it is to grow premium Christmas trees. A truly optimistic projection would be 90 percent salable trees out of 1,000 per acre planted, depending on the species of tree planted; a more realistic projection would be between 50 percent and 70 percent of trees planted actually making it through their entire growth cycle to harvest time.

Practical Information

Most states have their own Christmas tree associations, which work with the state board of agriculture to coordinate Christmas tree production. These Christmas cartels coordinate marketing, pricing, and distribution, and are especially active in November and December; for example, they often set up toll-free hotlines so that consumers can find the Christmas tree farm closest to their home.

The National Christmas Tree Association (314-205-0944; www.christree.org) can put you in touch with your state's Christmas tree farmer association and sponsors tree research and educational programs for the tree industry. It also publishes the quarterly *American Christmas Tree Journal.*

An excellent primer on the economics of Christmas tree farming is at www.southerntrees.com/cforest. The site covers species selection, fertilizing, insect control, pruning techniques, harvesting, and marketing.

Choosing the most economically viable tree species for your particular region and acreage will be the most important decision you will make as a Christmas tree farmer. Tree farmers urge you to carefully weigh climate conditions, costs per acre, number of years for a tree to reach harvest size, and other factors. Michael Dirr wrote the 1,000-page bible of Christmas tree farmers, the exhaustive *Manual of Woody Landscape Plants.* You should have a copy on your nightstand.

10

God Is in the Details

Crossword Puzzle Writer/Editor

Product Name Developer

Pooper Scooper

Accessories Designer

Baby Proofer

Mohel

Crossword Puzzle Writer/Editor

Job description: Write and edit crossword puzzles. Most crossword constructors, or "cruciverbalists," the term used by those in the know, work on puzzles as a sideline. Freelancers are self-motivated and driven by an interest in puzzles, not paychecks. For those lucky enough to get jobs as editors, the most regular gig in the field, the work consists mostly of checking puzzles submitted by freelance constructors. Will Shortz of the *New York Times*, arguably the most envied man in puzzledom, spends fifty to fifty-five hours a week, trying out eight to ten crosswords for every one he uses in the newspaper.

Compensation: The standard rate for a daily newspaper crossword, usually a puzzle with fifteen rows of fifteen squares, known as a "fifteen," is $30 to $50. An experienced constructor can produce one of these in four to six hours. A Sunday-sized puzzle, known as a "twenty-one" for obvious reasons, generally takes six to twenty hours to create. The *New York Times* pays the best in the business at $75 for a daily puzzle and $300 for the Sunday stumper.

Prerequisites: A cruciverbalist must have an exceptional vocabulary and perfect spelling as well as a blinding interest in obscure words and esoteric facts. An organized, analytical mind doesn't hurt either.

Qualities employer is seeking: Shortz says he's "always striving to come up with a new idea for a theme" and picks puzzles with "original themes and fresh, colorful vocabulary."

Perks: Freelance constructors work at home and make their own hours, and everyone in the business appreciates spending their days thinking about puzzles. Shortz says, "It's a fun field. You're playing games all day. It's always a challenge, and crossword people tend to be intelligent, colorful, and opinionated characters." As an editor, Shortz also enjoys reader mail. "It's like a performer getting feedback from an audience, but on a more delayed basis."

Risks/drawbacks: Mistakes can be embarrassing and occasion an avalanche of negative reader mail at larger publications. "For every good letter, there's a bad one," says Shortz. Freelancers also suffer with the unfortunately low rates paid for their work. Very few constructors make a good living from their puzzle-making efforts.

Overview

The hard and fast requirements for becoming a successful puzzle constructor are obvious: good spelling skills, a large vocabulary, and a love of words. Beyond these basics, it helps to be self-motivated. People who enjoy a structured office environment may find freelance puzzle work lonely or difficult. Most people get into the business because they find puzzles stimulating and keep their involvement down to a

Interview with Will Shortz, puzzle editor for the New York Times

Job description: "I'm responsible for the daily and Sunday puzzles in the *New York Times*. That means I look at submissions from contributors, edit, and proofread. There are three people who test the puzzles, which are submitted by both regulars and lots of others. I try out eight to ten for every one accepted."

Why he's the person for the job: "I have the world's only college degree in enigmatology. I went to Indiana University, and they let students make up degrees. So I made up a degree in puzzles."

What he meant to do for a living: "My plan was to practice law for ten years, make a lot of money, and then retire to do what I really wanted, which was puzzles. But after a year of law school, I knew I couldn't go through with it. I finished though."

Why he loves his work: "I don't think it's a job you ever get bored with. Crosswords lead you into every field of human endeavor and every field of thought, and so you're always learning something."

The worst thing that can happen on the job: "Having a mistake in a puzzle. After I edit the puzzles, three people test them. Then one of the three rechecks every word again. It's extremely rare for an error of any consequence to appear in the *New York Times*."

The best thing that can happen on the job: "A really good letter from a reader."

How he got his last big break: Predecessor Eugene T. Maleska died in 1993.

Whether he plans to stay at the *New York Times* for the foreseeable future: "Oh, longer than that."

His advice to aspiring crossword constructors: "You have to be prolific, if you want to make a living. Have fun with it though. Be persistent."

pastime. (For more stimulating and less contemplative work, read up on a job as a porn star, p. 87.) As you might imagine, crossword constructors tend to be avid readers, and many are analytical thinkers who enjoy computers, math, and music. "I've got at least eight things going on in my head at the same time," says Raymond Hamel, a crossword puzzle editor living in Wisconsin who claims this "eight-track" function is integral to his ability to draw up creative puzzles. Though the field escapes the dangers of gender bias by being based almost entirely on mailed-in submissions, surveys show that there are twice as many male constructors as female ones. Most editing work is found in the New York metropolitan area.

Though few outlets distribute explicit guidelines for constructors to follow, beyond conventions of size, some rules have developed among editors and accomplished puzzle makers. (The *New York Times* distributes a sheet of specifications for submissions, which can be found on the newspaper's Web site.) For example, it takes four related clues to make a theme puzzle, and regular constructors like Hamel often set their personal limits higher. Hamel says he shoots for six. Other limitations have grown out of editors' knowledge of their audience. Editors frown upon disease-related clues because crosswords are such a common pastime for hospital patients, and as Hamel explains, no one likes a puzzle full of "downer" words.

Practical Information

There are few full-time jobs for constructors, but freelance work abounds. Shortz estimates the number of daily crossword markets at twelve to fifteen, and the number of puzzles needed to fill the many magazines and books on the market is almost limitless. "The first thing is to create puzzles and sell them to different markets," says Shortz, putting it simply. Making a living is a matter of turning out as many puzzles as you can manage. Though the field is competitive, the large number of puzzle markets makes it relatively easy to break in.

"Crosswords are all about free association and humorous takes on things," said Raymond Hamel, a librarian at the University of Wisconsin at Madison and a successful freelance crossword constructor. "The trick is to come up with uncommon definitions for common words."

Budding constructors don't have to look far to find detailed advice from their more experienced fellows. The *Random House Puzzlemaker's Handbook*, by Mel Rosen and Stan Kurzban, is one of many books that can help you get started. It includes systematic advice on creating puzzles and extensive tips

on selling your work, but it has a wider focus than some of the other books on the market. The Internet has opened up additional avenues for communication between crossword solvers and constructors. To get an idea of the breadth of crossword culture and the number of puzzles on the Web, stop in at Ray Hamel's site (www.primate.wisc.edu/people/hamel/cp.html). Prospective constructors should check out www.cruciverb.com to get in on dialogue with other crossword writers, including occasional comments from Will Shortz. Many sites, such as www.crosswordkit.com, include downloadable software and templates to help budding constructors get the hang of structuring puzzles.

The American Crossword Puzzle Tournament brings together the nation's top cruciverbalists each year in Stamford, Connecticut. More information can be found at www.crosswordtournament.com, or by writing to American Crossword Tournament, 55 Great Oak Lane, Pleasantville, NY 10570. Another helpful resource is the National Puzzlers' League. Established in 1883, the league is the world's oldest puzzler's organization, and its annual convention is called Enigma.

Product Name Developer

Job description: Brainstorm and generate lists of names for new products or companies.

Compensation: Freelance namers, who work as contractors for naming companies, get paid approximately $1 per name and are usually asked to produce a list of between fifty and a few hundred names per project. Full-time namers, who have a track record in the business and might work for a high-level naming firm, can earn in the six figures.

Prerequisites: Being a namer requires no prerequisite background or set of skills; in general, employers may look for familiarity with foreign languages, a predilection for linguistics, or a breadth of knowledge in an arcane subject area—like botany, aviation, or music.

Qualities employer is seeking: Many namers work off-site on a part-time basis; if you can do good work in a timely fashion, that is all that counts. Freewheeling "creative" types who don't produce reliably aren't welcome; adhering to deadlines is paramount.

Perks: Cuddle up with an evening liqueur, let your mind wander, and record the results on a sheet of paper; do work while bathing, cycling, or having sex.

Risks/drawbacks: Product namers may generate a long list of suggestions, winnow down the finalists, conduct thorough trademark registry searches, only to find that their best candidate is entirely unusable. "There is a famous story about a marketing director who presented a new product with a new name to his worldwide board of directors, only to be told that the name was a term for female genitalia in Yiddish," says Jonathan Mercer, managing director of Brand Guardians.

Overview

Picking a name for a product is generally considered the single biggest marketing decision a company can make. A successful one, like Procter & Gamble's Ivory Soap, Gillette's Sensor, or Sony's Walkman, can help boost a product's visibility and success; a poor one (Ford's Edsel is the industry's favorite flop) can be ruinous. Product namers need to be experts in producing long lists of suggestions; techniques might include "anything from looking out the window and doing blue-sky thinking to throwing Scrabble tiles up in the air and seeing what comes down," according to David Burd, founder of the Naming Company.

Most companies have a particular image they want to promote, and hence will ask for names that suit their preferences. Jeff Crerie, who works as a freelance namer in San Francisco, recalls one project in which a retirement village in Australia wanted their newly built complex to sound expensive, maybe a little European, with certainly nothing suggestive of aging. Among Crerie's suggestions were New Phoenix, Dominion Links, Trinity Springs, Lago del Sol, Hopefair Landing, Crystal Cove, Lake Fontaine, Jackrabbit Run, and Centurian Square. (The company eventually went with Waterford Valley, another namer's suggestion.)

"I would to God thou and I knew where a commodity of good names were to be bought."

—Falstaff, Shakespeare's *King Henry IV, Part I*

Some namers may adopt particular methods to gradually settle into a state of mind in which names flow more easily. "One woman that works for me curls up with some brandy and turns up loud music," says Chris DeMassa, founder of Name-It. "I spread out with books, maps, and a nice strong light. One way or another, you sort of get into a groove—almost like in golf or tennis—and when you're there, you can basically do any industry, whether it's crab food or antifreeze."

One of the major hurdles that product namers face is the exponentially growing list of already trademarked names. "You can come up with fabulous names, or at least what they think are fabulous, but some obscure company in Ohio may have that name, knocking it out of the ring," says Art Medici, senior vice president for sales and marketing for Thomson & Thomson, a trademark database and research firm in Washington.

Partly in response to the near impossibility of using a common word to name a product (there are roughly five times as many trademarked names in the federal registry as there are words in a standard English dictionary), a good namer will have to entertain the possibility—particularly for high-tech companies—of using numbers along with letters: Examples include 3Com Corp., C2B Technologies, 24/7 Media, and N2K, Inc. Another possibility, as David Burd suggests, is to stick with traditional letters but to invent a word, which might still describe the product or allude to its benefits. "If you were naming a cookie," says Burd, "you might want to call it *giggles*, which could imply a quality or attribute you're gonna get when you eat these cookies. But then, since *giggles* is already trademarked, you might turn it into something fanciful, a made-up word, like *Googles*, and then you'd be on your way to finding a product name."

For companies that are interested in using the same product name in more than one country, time must also be spent researching if the name will be viable in other languages. "Finding the right name for an international brand is expensive, time-consuming, and fraught with difficulty," says Bridgett Ruffel, a director of The Brand Naming Company. The Chevy Nova was a laughingstock in Central and South America (*no va* means "doesn't go" in Spanish). The naming industry is strewn with examples of such name-translation problems, including foreign products that are well-nigh useless to bring to America—Krapp toilet tissue and Skum sweetener in Sweden, Pschitt lemonade in France, a popular Turkish biscuit called Bum, and a yellowish drink from Japan named Calpis (say it out loud).

Practical Information

Companies that do only naming are relatively new in the marketing industry. Product names, for many years, were under the sole domain of large advertising agencies, which packaged the slogans and the names together. Many naming companies tend to be small so as not to

be left with a large overhead and little income when business is slow. Among the handful of full-time employees may be a few highly prolific and proven brainstormers, as well as individuals who are versed in the field of trademark research.

The best way to find work in the business is to send an intelligent, personal letter (impersonal "To Whom It May Concern" letters will be frowned upon by companies that prize creative thinking) to any number of naming companies. Chris DeMassa of Name-It has upwards of thirty regular namers. David Burd, who says he'll almost always give someone who contacts him a chance to be a namer by asking the person to try to generate a couple of sample lists, has a similarly sized group of freelancers.

Companies to contact:
The Naming Company (e-mail: dburd@thenamingcompany.com),
Name Trade (www.nametrade.com),
Name-It (www.nameit.com),and
Namebase (www.namebase.com).

Pooper Scooper

Job description: Clean up animal excrement in public parks, at parades, and in the yards of wealthy families.

Compensation: Matthew Osborn, of Columbus, Ohio, is unequivocally America's doo-doo guru. After founding a pet waste removal service of his own, Osborn wrote a book, *The Professional Pooper Scooper: How to Start Your Own Low-Cost High-Profit Dog Waste Removal Service*, considered by many pooper scoopers to be the bible of their trade. Osborn suggests that a scooper charge $6.50 per week for one dog, $3.50 for each additional dog; or about $25 per hour for larger areas. From there, total income depends on market size. Osborn's business boasts more than 600 customers per week; a company in Colorado claims more than 2,000 clients. Many customers tip around the holiday season.

Prerequisites: Officially none, though experience with animals (and a certain familiarity with their excrement) can definitely give you an edge. A driver's license and a car can broaden your business, but even those are not required.

Qualities employer is seeking: "What do I look for in a good turd herder? Someone who has a lot of knowledge about dogs and animals, especially about their behavior," says Debbie Levy, a self-proclaimed "entremanure" and eight-year owner of Yucko's, a St. Louis based pooper-scooper

Going to the Dogs

Contrary to popular conception, a dogcatcher doesn't just drive around scooping up stray dogs and piling them into the back of a truck. In fact, "animal control officers" deal with a range of problems. "The term *dogcatcher* is very outmoded," explains Sgt. Rudack of Boston Animal Control. "We deal with everything from domesticated puppies to animals that've been bred and raised to be used as lethal weapons. I just had one case that was attempted murder: The girl didn't come across with the money, so they threw her in the room where four dogs were expected to eat her."

Leslie Strahl, twenty-three, works as an animal ambulance driver, a job more in line with the traditional view of a dogcatcher. Strahl rescues cats stuck in trees, helps birds with broken wings, and has even had to net and tranquilize a cow trapped in a ditch. Strahl works nine to ten hours per day.

"Of course everybody wants to be paid more," she admits, "but it's great that everyone works less for the money than for other things." Strahl responds to five to twenty calls per week, working more heavily on weekends: "That's when people go outside, and they notice things, stranded animals, that kind of thing." Drawbacks to the job include occasional harassment from bystanders. "I'll get some vocalization," she says. "Rescuing a bird in a crowded place, I'll hear things like, 'Hey baby, I'm an animal, wanna come pick me up?'"

Still, animal ambulance drivers enjoy constantly seeing results from their work, and the job is a perfect step toward becoming a veterinarian. What does it take to become an animal ambulance driver? "A high-school diploma," says Strahl, "and intelligence and compassion. You always wish you could do more, and it can take a lot out of you. You have to be motivated, willing to get your hands dirty, and able to understand why we do euthanasia, that not every single animal can be treated."

business. (Yes, she said "turd herder.") Most professional pooper-scoopers neglect to mention the job's major requirement: a serious tolerance for nastiness. Matthew Osborn lists self-direction, initiative, and self-discipline among qualities that lead to scooping success. "You don't have any supervision, and you have to keep moving through the day, so you need organizational skills and attention to details." While one needn't have expertise in dogs, Osborn recommends some familiarity with animals. "You have to be comfortable with them, and know when a dog is just barking and when it's warning you not to come closer."

Perks: Replenished demand and large potential for market growth. Most scoopers like that their jobs are unsupervised and that they can work outdoors, according to their own schedule, often in the backyards of beautiful homes.

Risks/drawbacks: A pooper scooper's job is to walk through minefields of excrement; occasional blow-ups (or at least "step-ins") are inevitable. Some scoopers have been bitten by dogs, and scoopers must maintain excellent hygiene to avoid feces-borne diseases. Even in the face of countless hazardous heaps, however, Osborn says the job's greatest dangers spring up outside the field. "The biggest risk is associated with driving," he says. "Half the actual working hours are driving from one place to the next."

Overview

The pooper-scooper industry emerged about fifteen years ago in Denver, Colorado, according to Osborn. Since then, more than 100 poop-gathering companies have cropped up around the country, (usually) home-based businesses with names like Doody Calls, Turd Busters, Dr. Doo Litter, Scoopy Doo, or Poop de la Scoop. Despite the industry's surge in recent years, most Yellow Pages still hesitate to list pooper scoopers in their desired category: pet waste removal.

Osborn says pet owners usually hire out their dirty work for one of three reasons: "Lack of personal time; physical infirmity or disability; and the big one, which I call 'the Repugnance Factor.'" Why it's necessary to scoop poop, explains Levy, is to reduce risk of transmitting parasites, particularly to dogs and children. "Puppies get worms from it early on. Kids put it in their mouths; a child will run up with some in their hands and say, 'Look, mommy! A chocolate Easter egg!'"

"There's a dirty little secret behind some of the nicest homes," says doo-doo guru Osborn. "Changing a baby's diaper is a lot worse than picking up dog poop," says Levy.

While the job offers notable benefits, including the chance to work outdoors at a self-determined pace, poop scooping obviously has its gruesome aspects. "It's strange, to think you're making a living picking up after hundreds of animals each week," Osborn admits. "And the conversations you have with other people in the business can be strange. We discuss the best ways to scoop different consistencies of poop, or what you can tell about a dog's health from the poop's color and content." Osborn says it's important to inspect his crops of crap and to notify owners when something suspicious appears. One of the hidden factors affecting the pooper scoopers' market is legislation about dog curbing; expect growth where laws are strict. Many politicians feel strongly

about the subject. Said Joe LeFevre, chairman of the selectmen of Adams, Massachusetts, regarding new laws: "My feeling is if dog curbing laws aren't working, make them put pants on their animals. You may think I'm a nut, but I feel this is the only way it's going to work."

Practical Information

Unquestionably, the first place to begin is with Osborn's book; also check out his Web site at www.pooper-scooper.com. While online, be sure to read your dog's "poop-a-scope" at www.thepoop.com. Osborn encourages would-be dung collectors to advertise their services in local papers and to send out press releases to bait the occasional "human interest" story. In advertising, remember not to limit yourself to doggy doo: "We've done pigeon poop, pot-bellied pigs, and we were even in a Mardi Gras parade, picking up for the Anheuser-Busch horses," boasts Levy.

The task itself is simple, especially using one of the many tools custom-made for picking up doo, usually a combination plastic-lined dust bin and metal shovel for sweeping. Levy uses a special rake, pan, and bag combination that she frequently disinfects. Weapons in hand, simply prowl the territory, scanning more astutely near areas used for bedding by the dog (under trees, in flowerbeds) and in children's play areas. Osborn finishes between four and seven yards per hour, generating between $30 to $50 per hour.

Many companies also serve larger areas: public parks and apartment complexes, for example. "A yard can take anywhere from fifteen minutes to eight hours, depending on the size," explains Levy. Come winter, a crap harvester's work is hardly done. "Dogs keep doing their thing, even on top of snow," Osborn asserts. "If we didn't keep up with it through winter, things would get awfully foul by spring." Levy says winter scooping poses sticky problems. "Sometimes dogs think their poop is a toy, because it's frozen and hard. They'll bring it into the house."

Some scoopers don't haul away their doo once the deed is done; they leave it for clients' disposal. Others bring waste to a dumpster, where it's whisked away by private haulers.

Overall, today's pooper scooper is optimistic and proud to fill a clearly defined need-based niche. And unlike many markets, there's still plenty of room for the can-doo newcomer. "A person can do very well, if they're willing to crawl before they walk," says Levy. "You have to do the best that you can do. You can't do a half-assed job."

Accessories Designer

Job description: Anticipate trends in the world of straps, laces, and buckles and apply these insights to all the extras—handbags, shoes, barrettes, etc. Once a designer conceives and produces a new item (for example, a satin-padded fanny pack), he or she must market the item to department stores and boutiques, which in turn sell it to the public.

Compensation: The vast majority of designers lose money starting up their businesses. Some take jobs with larger design firms and make $25,000 and up. If you're wildly successful (like Miuccia Prada, whose bags decorate ladies' shoulders worldwide), the sky's the limit.

Prerequisites: Technically, all that's needed is good design sense, a massive dose of luck, and the confidence to launch yourself in a competitive business. Many designers, however, have degrees from places like Parsons School of Design and the Fashion Institute of Technology (FIT), both in New York City. Practical skills—like drawing and sewing—are a big plus.

Qualities employer is seeking: Creativity, a good sense of style, and the ability to present and execute your ideas. Also, the fashion world is political, so be prepared to schmooze.

Perks: If you work for yourself, the most obvious perk is autonomy. You won't find any successful designers trapped in jobs they don't like. It's a struggle to make a name for yourself, but once you do, you run the show and produce your own designs. Ultimately, there's nothing like seeing someone on the street wearing the leopard-print scrunchie you designed. Plus, the fashion world can be fun, for those who like to party with models.

Risks/drawbacks: Most designers never make it—their work never gets to the showroom floor (that's where prospective buyers for stores check out the merchandise), much less to the cash register.

Overview

Fashion is one of the most successful businesses of the nineties. Designers like Ralph Lauren and Tommy Hilfiger have slapped their names on everything from sneakers to sheets to perfume and made billions of dollars in the process. Over

Credit: Courtesy of Novick Designs

Papa's Got a Brand New Bag! Express your creativity in the form of handbags, shoes, barrettes, and earrings. The collection pictured is from a series called Lolita with Leather.

the last decade, the industry has also seen an explosion of mini brands. Everyone, from magazine editors to retailers to big-name designers, is on the lookout for someone who can come up with the next big thing. (For instance, when handbag maker Paige Novick designed a line of handbags using a vintage fabric, her retro-style purses were copied everywhere. "People knocked them off so fast," she says.)

Paige Novick, the woman behind Frou, a successful line of handbags and accessories she began five years ago, says that an entrepreneurial designer should be able to do an infinite number of things at the same time: "It's really all about putting out fires." She adds, "You have to be positive when bad things happen and not get complacent when things go well."

There's no real path through the tricky maze of fashion, and Paige Novick is a good example of how tortuous the road can be: She got her start in retail. She loved fashion, and while a student at New York University (she studied French), Novick made money by working in some of lower Manhattan's coolest style venues. After college, she worked for Cotton, Inc., a not-for-profit organization that promotes the fabric (you know: "the fabric of our lives..."). As a "trend forecaster," Novick tried to divine what colors, shapes, and items would be hot the next season, but she quickly learned that the rarefied ways of the fashion industry were a mystery to most consumers. "Most people don't think in those terms. They buy something because they like it."

Most designers get their start in accessories working for a larger company. Novick did, and through a combination of luck and determination, she became the head designer for hair accessories at a design firm called Riviera. She admits that, at the time, she had the ideas but not the know-how. "I had to learn the technical things backwards."

Frou was born when Novick struck out on her own, with only $5,000 and an idea that she could offer people cool hair accessories not available anywhere else. Working out of the warehouse of her father's fabric company, she experimented before coming up with a series of hardware-inspired barrettes and clips. A friend helped her put together her first independent line of hair accessories and another friend photographed the collection. She then sent promotional material to places she thought might be interested in her designs. Several stores bought her work, and she began expanding her inventory. When Barney's, the New York–based department store, placed a huge order for her handbags, Novick's fate was sealed. Today Frou is a multimillion-dollar operation with handbags, makeup cases, and a limited clothing line. (To reach Novick, call her showroom at 212-633-2066.)

Practical Information

The best way to get on track as a designer is to study fashion design, but ask yourself first if you really want to do the work required to break into such a competitive and uneven business. Make sure it isn't your latent desire to shop that's talking when you make this career move.

If you are indeed the next Calvin Klein, it's a good idea to study. While Novick didn't, she is an anomaly. Most designers know how to conceive of a design on paper and execute a prototype using their chosen materials. Business school can also be useful. Novick started out gluing nuts and bolts to hair clips and now runs a business, complete with suppliers, factories, distributors, and publicists. Her business is successful because she convinced buyers for stores all over the world that people would carry her bags and wear her headbands. A little knowledge of how to structure a company, hire and fire people, and produce a product can go a long way.

Ultimately, however, none of this is about getting an A in a marketing class or a sketching seminar. Launching yourself as a designer takes money, contacts, talent, luck, and tremendous doses of self-confidence. If you have all those things, the fashion world is yours to conquer, darling. (To find out more about the heads and hands that bring Paige Novick's work to life in ads, see "Body Part Model," p. 110.)

Baby Proofer

Job description: Inspect the homes of new parents for potential sources of harm to a child and install safety devices that will prevent the child from being seriously injured.

Compensation: Weekly pay for an employee is $400 to $700, usually derived from a base wage and a commission; company owners can earn far more. A typical house can be baby-proofed in a single day, at a cost of $1,000 to the parents. Twenty-five percent of that is spent on purchasing the safety mechanisms. Inspections and estimates, which typically take an hour and a half, are done for free. Many proofers own their own companies and work alone; some also run stores that sell safety mechanisms to parents who prefer to install them on their own.

Prerequisites: Familiarity with the habits of toddlers (most easily acquired by parenting one yourself), a presentable and trustworthy demeanor, and skill with construction tools.

Qualities employer is seeking: Richard Palmer, owner and founder of Family First, one of the largest baby-proofing companies in the United States, says, "I look for married, middle-aged to older people, who are more secure and who are personable and have sales experience and are able to close the estimates." Parents will be expecting a proofer with an

excellent knowledge of typical accident risks of children, and someone who can be trusted to install the safety mechanisms without damaging their house or furniture.

Perks: More children today end up at the emergency room as a result of accidents than as a result of illness. Mike Radel, co-partner of Safer Baby, says, "If I go through a house, and I help prevent a baby from getting hurt, I'm doing good. Unless the parent completely ignores everything I say, I'm helping them. It really is a feel-good business. And the people that use your services are happy to get the work done." Radel notes that some people might enjoy proofing the homes of the rich and famous, but that this novelty usually wears away quickly.

Risks/drawbacks: Bankruptcy. Radel, whose business operates out of the San Fernando Valley in California, says, "In four years, we've seen ten or twelve companies come and go." There are 100 to 150 baby-proofing companies in the United States. While baby proofing is becoming increasingly de rigueur for upper- and upper-middle-class families, some geographical areas are already surfeited. Lawsuits from the parents of a child that is injured after your services have been rendered are another potential risk.

Overview

The first baby-proofing companies were started in Southern California around 1984. The largest companies may have a half dozen proofers who are consistently booked two to three weeks in advance. The success of these businesses is predicated by the baby boomers' baby boom. Today's middle-income parent is typically older, more worldly, more wealthy, and more likely to plunk out two or three grand for proofing than parents of the seventies, sixties, or fifties. More families have two parents working full time and are somewhat insecure about the quality of their hired help. Pediatricians and Mommy and Me classes now recommend house proofing. Still, resistance to the profession continues: "I can't tell you how many people think it's absolutely ridiculous: 'I grew up without it and I didn't get hurt. My brothers and sisters grew up without it and didn't get hurt.' And then there are some parents who want their kids to learn by trial and error," Radel explains.

Baby proofing is intended for kids six months to two years. Says Radel, "At six months they start developing their motor instincts but don't realize the consequences of what they're doing. And they're putting a lot of things in their mouths." Most safety products are only guaranteed to protect a child up to the age of two, though many products will successfully prevent children of four or five years of age from slamming doors on fingers, finding electrical outlets, falling down steps, and jumping into pools.

To the baby proofer, an average house looks like one big baby booby trap. Any hard floor or corner is potentially dangerous, but proofers focus on

the items that can cause permanent damage or death. "We look for how to prevent children from getting shocked, from getting into toxic chemicals, to keep them from falling down stairs, to keep them from pulling on cords attached to heavy objects, keeping them away from any standing water, keeping them out of appliances that could harm them, like stoves or refrigerators. Refrigerators used to be a big problem. Kids used to get stuck in them." Other big risks to children are posed by second-story windows, electrical appliances, marbles, and big pieces of dog food.

"You have no way of knowing if anything you've ever done has helped. A child may never go near electricity. We can never claim for certain that we prevented children from getting hurt. But statistically speaking, we can lower the chance of a serious accident happening by 70 to 90 percent," claims Mike Radel of Safer Baby.

Practical Information

Learning the business can be accomplished by working for a successful baby proofer. Proofers estimate that installation techniques can be learned in three months, and a working knowledge of the perils of the common household can be acquired in about six months. A quicker route is to take a course in baby proofing, which can cost anywhere from $1,500 to $5,000 dollars. Says Richard Palmer, who teaches a proofing class, "I try to do a complete job. I help them get tools and teach them how to install. I give out breakdown sheets and teach them how to do estimates."

The International Association of Child Safety (888-677-IACS), which has over seventy members, became a nonprofit corporation in 1997. The association meets annually in Dallas at the Juvenile Product Manufacturers of America Show (JPMA), which usually takes place in October. Most of the manufacturers of home safety equipment attend to show off new advances in the field, and most baby proofers go to check out and buy the new gear. The KidsSafe Web site (www.kidssafe.com) contains good general information on child safety.

Mohel

Job description: A mohel (pronounced "moyel") presides over the most sacred ceremonies in the Jewish faith, while slicing off the foreskin of an eight-day-old boy's penis.

Compensation: Mohels make $200 to $300 per circumcision, depending where they perform it. (For the record, a nonreligious hospital circumcision goes for between $300 and $500.) Dr. Ruvin Fraser, an internist and certified mohel who works at Boston's Jewish Memorial Hospital, estimates that he performs one circumcision every ten days.

Prerequisites: A clear understanding of the religious significance, the related texts, and the mechanical process involved in performing the Bris Milah (covenant circumcision) ceremony, commonly referred to as a Bris. You must be Jewish and a man to be a mohel—but not necessarily a doctor.

Qualities employer is seeking: The unwavering divine command that the Bris be performed on a child's eighth day means that scheduling flexibility is a must for a mohel. It's also good to have something of a flair for performance. Not everyone feels comfortable leading strangers in prayer or snipping a penis in a room full of onlookers.

Perks: Taking part in an extremely significant ceremony within the Jewish faith. Immense gratitude of the parents for not screwing up.

Risks/drawbacks: All joking about amputation aside (it's virtually unheard of), there is some risk of hurting the baby—though a wriggling infant is more dangerous than an unsteady mohel. For the baby, more common risks include unusual swelling or bleeding. (The side effects of circumcision are much like those a body piercer, p. 117, hopes to avoid.)

Overview

Serving as a mohel is a sideline for specially trained doctors or the role of a designated member of a temple's congregation. However, the responsibility for the service rests traditionally with the father of the child. If the father is not able to circumcise his son himself—and most of today's men feel unequipped to handle this responsibility—he must designate a mohel to do it in his stead. Out of this transference of responsibility, a tradition has grown up, and most congregations count among their members a man who has taken on the role of performing the Bris Milah.

A mohel makes a difference that lasts a lifetime, but the act itself is over in one excruciating moment (excruciating for the onlookers; the boy is said to feel no pain as the nerve endings have not developed). The exact procedure may vary with the practitioner, but most often a Bris begins with some introductory words from the mohel, to explain the significance of the ceremony and the act that will take place. This is sometimes followed by traditional readings from the Torah. The process of preparing

the child for the circumcision takes only about a minute and may include giving him Tylenol, wine, and if the parents aren't feeling too ascetic on their child's behalf, novocaine. The ten-second snip is made almost foolproof by the use of a clamp, or a person (often a grandfather) leaning over the boy and pinning his legs down in what looks like a grossly mismatched wrestling bout; this immobilization prevents the mohel from doing the boy lasting harm. After the cut, the mohel would traditionally take the baby's penis into his mouth and suck off the excess blood, a potentially alarming practice called *metzitzah b'peh*; gauze or tubing is used to remove the blood in most ceremonies today. The disagreement between more and less conservative Jews over this final detail of the service illustrates the importance of the Bris tradition and its proper observance within the Jewish faith.

The baby's reaction to this unexpected intrusion comes in a few stages. "The baby will fuss for about ten minutes, feed, fuss for another ten minutes, and fall asleep for three hours," explains Dr. Fraser matter-of-factly. "At this age, babies just don't deal with pain the same way adults do. Their nerves aren't fully developed, so they know something is wrong, but they can't localize it." As men get older, the discomfort they feel from circumcision and the time involved in recovering from the procedure increase. However, thanks to the serious nature of the Bris tradition in Jewish culture, no mohel is ever going to find himself working on an unsedated thirty-year-old.

Credit: Rabbi David Kelmi

"Take a little off the top."

"You have to be willing to do a surgical procedure in front of a group of people and pass it off as a meaningful religious experience," says Dr. Ruvin Fraser, a certified mohel in Boston.

Bris is the Hebrew word for covenant, and the Bris Milah is considered a central part of the agreement between God and the Jewish people. The commandment is given in the book of Genesis (17:12) that, on the eighth day of a young boy's life, he must be circumcised. While there are several theories about the origin of the rule, the significance of the Bris Milah derives simply from the Biblical verse, and the ceremony takes precedence over all other Jewish holidays and ceremonies (i.e., if your son is born eight days before Yom Kippur, he will still be circumcised on the eighth day, atonement notwithstanding).

Practical Information

The one hard and fast requirement for mohel-dom is that you be a practicing member of the Jewish faith. The job is usually performed by an adult male whose father, grandfather, great grandfather, and so on before him were also mohelim.

However, if you are interested in taking on this responsibility (and extra income), ask your rabbi about the need for mohelim in your area. As older mohelim age and fewer young Jews step into the breach, some communities are finding themselves in search of men who will sustain the tradition. Dr. Fraser began his service as a mohel in response to such a shortage. Rabbis in his area appealed to doctors in the temple to sign up for a training course. After four months of study, Dr. Fraser became certified to practice the Bris for members of Reform and Conservative temples.

11 Weird Science

Bigfoot Research Director

SETI Researcher

Cryonicist

Atomic Clock Timekeeper

Hypnotist

Cryptographer

Demolition Contractor

Telephone Psychic

Bigfoot Research Director

Job description: Direct research in the study of the mythical creature Bigfoot (also known as "Sasquatch"). There are only a few full-time directorships already in existence, with duties including public relations, newsletter writing, educational programming, personnel management, fund-raising, and actual field research.

Compensation: "We'll call it marginal," says Tod Deery of the North American Science Institute (NASI). His salary in 1992 was $12,500.

Prerequisites: Any combination of scientific expertise and outdoor savvy is appropriate. Some background in anthropology, primatology, field biology, and business management can't possibly hurt. Mobility, flexibility, and a keen interest in Bigfoot research are major musts. "The best investigators are those who've seen them," says Ray Crowe of the Western Bigfoot Society. "They want to do it again!"

Qualities employer is seeking: Leaders in Bigfoot research must be able to deal with a wide range of personalities, some of them bordering on fanatical (both non-believers and believers). Directors receive sharply barbed criticism from both sides and need to be both diplomatic and thick-skinned.

Perks: Plenty of travel and outdoor activity, plus a great degree of personal freedom, and the satisfaction of studying something both controversial and beloved.

Risks/drawbacks: There are no medical benefits or retirement plans, and those who take responsibility for field research find themselves on call at all times, making any sort of stability or family life a major challenge.

Overview

According to the latest research, the Bigfoot (or "Sasquatch") is a seven-foot-tall, omnivorous, forest-dwelling primate of as-yet-unproven existence. The foundation of modern Bigfoot research rests squarely on the pivotal Patterson-Gimlin film of 1967—the one with the large, furry humanoid running across a gravel bar into the forest. Experts affectionately call this particular Bigfoot "Patty," much as they affectionately bestow the label "Bigfootitis" on those all-too-vigilant enthusiasts who claim to spot four or more Sasquatch per month skulking through their backyards. Reports of "Bigfootlets"—little baby Sasquatches, often seen with their mothers—have been drawn from more reliable sources.

The task of the Bigfoot researcher is to investigate and coordinate reports of this cryptic beast, in an effort to learn as much as possible from available evidence. Each directorship is a rare position that involves a unique set of goals and tactics. The North American Science Institute is the only Bigfoot-related organization

Interview with J. Richard Greenwell, Secretary, International Society of Cryptozoology

Job description: Greenwall is the head administrator and the only paid employee of the ISC.

What the ISC is: "The International Society of Cryptozoology was founded in 1982 at the U.S. National Museum, for the purpose of creating a sensible forum for analysis of zoologically 'unexpected' animals, as yet unexplored by mainstream science. There is an international board of fifteen active scientists, three of whom are officers. We publish a standard, peer-reviewed scientific journal, *Cryptozoology*, and a more newsy sort of newsletter, *The ISC Newsletter*. We're funded by the dues from 900 members worldwide, two U.S. nonprofits, and a German industrial firm."

On being the only employee: "I am retained half time by the board, but I end up working more, whether at night, weekends, or through expeditions. We have several volunteers, and there may be another salaried employee position soon."

How he got started: "I made a name for myself as a boy back in Britain; I enjoyed catching strange animals, and the snakes I caught were the first live snakes ever exhibited in any British museum. Once I caught a rare melanistic adder—you know, a "black adder"—and people were terribly afraid that it was more poisonous and dangerous. That's when I began to realize the power of the unknown in people's minds."

On the ISC's success: "Well, in the fifteen years of the ISC's existence, there haven't been that many confirmations. Recently, we published a description of a new snake species from Vietnam, though the type specimen was lost; this has caused some controversy among herpetologists. There have been many more confirmations of smaller animals, but what does the public care? It's the same problem in conservation biology."

On charismatic megafauna: "To science, an unknown rodent may be as important as a Bigfoot, but the lay public doesn't realize this."

On his job satisfaction: "Well, the disadvantage is that our research can be ignored, even derided, which means very little funding. It's too controversial, and I can understand that. But the job is intellectually very positive, very stimulating. We're doing something that conventional zoology really should do, but doesn't."

International Society of Cryptozoology
P.O. Box 43070
Tucson, AZ 85733
520-884-8369
iscz@azstarnet.com

with salaried employees, though a handful of other directors, at the helm of volunteer networks, manage to survive on meager earnings drawn from membership fees, private donations, and creative fund-raising. Nobody is in the Bigfoot biz for big bucks, and Tod Deery, of NASI, recognizes how nice it is to be one of the only people in the world paid for this sort of research. As he describes it, this is "definitely not a career you'd be raising a family with."

"It has fulfilled a personal niche for me," says Bigfoot watcher Tod Deery.

Despite the pay, job satisfaction runs high. The job offers a constant stream of challenges and plenty of room for personal creativity. Tod Deery has derived great satisfaction from steering the North American Science Institute toward greater methodological rigor, raising the level of respect accorded the research "from that of a tabloid to a more professional and academically acceptable approach." All directors, whatever their angle, work with a wide variety of interested parties on a daily basis, from professional geneticists to technological consultants to amateur Bigfoot trackers.

Bigfoot research directors enjoy the position of big fish in a small pond—small in terms of leadership, not interest or geographical influence. While NASI hypothesizes that the Bigfoot may live only in the Cascade Range of the Pacific Northwest, Bigfoot organizations span North America, and sightings have been reported in every state except Hawaii and Rhode Island. Allied organizations across the globe investigate potential Bigfoot relatives like the Tibetan yeti or the "Russian wildman." Research directors attempt to coordinate these far-flung activities through frequent communication and regular publications. An average day will be spent largely on maintaining correspondence with volunteer groups, fielding media queries, organizing fund-raising initiatives, keeping the organization's books, preparing newsletters, and traveling to nearby hotspots. The exact nature of each directorship is up to the individual director, based on his or her priorities and vision.

Practical Information

The number of full-time directorships out there could be counted on one enormous, hairy foot. While there isn't an inordinate amount of money earmarked for Sasquatch research, that isn't to say that the well is dry. Many directors are self-starters, creating nonprofit organizations from scratch. Once a Bigfoot-related organization is established and achieves respectability, openings can inspire a great deal of competition. When Tod Deery first applied for a job with NASI, the applicant pool numbered well into 400 hopefuls. Whether applying for a preexisting post or organizing a new group, prerequisites need not present a specific barrier. The most

renowned Bigfoot research directors came into the field from occupations as diverse as civil engineering and professional game hunting. Note that Ray Crowe, director of the 250-member Western Bigfoot Society, is looking for a replacement by the time he hits seventy, ten years from now.

For more information, contact one of the major research organizations. The North American Science Institute (541-387-4300; e-mail: nasi@gorge.net; www.nasinet.org), publishes the *NASI News*. The Western Bigfoot Society (503-640-6581; e-mail: raycrowe@aol.com; www.teleport.com/~caveman/newwbs.html) publishes *The Track Record*. The Bigfoot Field Researcher's Organization (www.moneymaker.org/bfrr) maintains a network of volunteer field researchers. (Skeptics who might be considering donning big, furry suits and making trouble for Tod Deery and the rest, should turn their energies toward becoming sports mascots, p. 196.)

SETI Researcher

Job description: You don't have to be the scientist sitting by the satellite dish gazing dreamily into the night sky, à la Jodie Foster in *Contact,* to qualify as a SETI researcher. Engineers, radio astronomers, and physicists all contribute to the search for extraterrestrial intelligence. Tasks range from designing and building the equipment for a particular experiment to sitting at the computer and listening (actually, it's more of making sure the computer is listening) for faint radio signals from alien civilizations—errant signals from some oldies station from across the galaxy, perhaps? Paleo- and microbiologists—the people who look for evidence of ancient microbiological life using rock samples from Mars, for example—have a lot in common with SETI researchers, although they're looking for evidence of extinct life, rather than living, radio-broadcasting alien life. SETI researchers are also not to be confused with UFO hounds; Seth Shostak of the SETI Institute points out that SETI researchers look for "aliens in situ" rather than aliens on vacation.

Compensation: People with the education and training to do SETI research could make twice as much doing similar work in Silicon Valley. Shostak cites the "psychic income" from his mind-bending endeavors as more than compensatory. Because a lot of SETI research is funded by grants from educational institutions,

salaries are determined by whatever is in the grant budget. Don't expect a lot. (Science-fiction type? There are more fringe-science jobs in cryonics, p. 174, where you'll pioneer the future working side by side with enlightened romantics like yourself. You'll make less than your skeptical, mainstream counterparts, but will they ever bring Granny back from the dead? Not likely.)

Prerequisites: For scientists, a Ph.D. in astronomy or physics is the norm. Engineers, who do less conceptual and more hands-on work, often lack a degree beyond a B.S., "but they're all hotshots." A background in computer science is also helpful.

Qualities employer is seeking: The SETI endeavor is one that could take years, or decades, before it yields any tangible results, and therefore it requires imagination, technical abilities, and a forward-thinking mentality. "It's a bit like building a cathedral in the Middle Ages; you may not see the project through to completion," says Shostak.

Perks: SETI research facilities usually rent a few weeks' worth of time every year from a variety of radio telescopes around the globe, from England to Puerto Rico to Australia, so travel is definitely a perk. Since research is privately funded and not-for-profit, researchers don't have angry stockholders or Congress members to deal with. And points out Shostak, "When you're at a party and somebody asks you what you do, you get to tell them."

Risks/drawbacks: Those telescoping junkets usually involve round-the-clock monitoring. Then there's the money problem. Government funding is nonexistent, and the survival of the entire SETI effort is dependent on the generosity of private contributors. The twentieth century has seen the first time in history that humans have actually had the capability to perform serious extraterrestrial research. To be held back by a lack of funding can be extremely frustrating. "Imagine it's 1492," says Shostak. "You finally have ships that can cross an ocean, and instead of doing it you just sit in a bar and talk about it. That's what it's like."

Overview

Due in part to the success of movies like *Contact*, *Species* (and *Species II!*), and the *Alien* series, public awareness and appreciation of extraterrestrial intelligence research has blossomed. While this may appear to be a good thing, it also has its downside: Shostak cites as a major source of frustration the "lack of criticality" in the way the public thinks of science. It's not that people don't appreciate what SETI researchers do; it's that the public's scientific illiteracy makes it difficult for SETI to explain what it does. "People are often unable to distinguish between wacky anecdotes and real science," says Shostak.

And SETI researchers aren't just misunderstood, they're also underfunded. Originally a NASA project, the American search for extraterrestrial intelligence is now entirely privately bankrolled.

(Congress withdrew all government funding in 1993.) This means that there are thousands of people who want to join in the search for ET, "but alas, we can't hire any of them," Shostak laments. The majority of the funds for any research project go to salaries, and not to equipment. A telescope you pay for once and have forever; it's the people whom you have to keep paying. Consequently, the job market is woefully small.

The positive side of this somewhat grim equation is that SETI researchers, almost without exception, love their work and their co-workers (although there's probably the same chance of finding Mr. or Ms. Right on the job than there is of finding life on Jupiter). The work atmosphere is intense but collegial. Most people happily work over forty hours a week, although "the engineers usually manage to get their work done" in a normal amount of time. Scientists tend to have a longer workday commitment, since they also write articles for scientific journals and give talks at conferences.

Practical Information

Visit one of the myriad SETI pages on the Web for (admittedly sparse) employment opportunities and a taste of the life of the average researcher. Try www.seti.org/jobs.html (jobs at the SETI Institute), www.aip.org/aip/careers/careers.html (information on careers in physics), www.nasa.gov(guess who), or www.aas.org/jobregister/aasjobs.html (jobs in astronomy). Don't bother with the SETI Institute newsletter (www.seti.org/seti-news.html) unless you want a lot of technospeak. They don't publish help-wanted ads. Your best bet breaking into SETI circles is to get a Ph.D. in astronomy or physics, get a job in academia, and then wait for ET to phone you. One university professor notes that "it's best to get tenure first before you start looking for little green men." Getting a job at a place like the SETI Institute, where research is focused solely on extraterrestrial searches, is even less likely than landing a professorship.

"We like to figure [aliens are] emotionless, because men in particular figure that indicates a higher level of advancement," says SETI researcher Seth Shostak."

However, if you just want to help without making a career out of it, you can start by joining the ingeniously ambitious SETI@home program. The clever folks at SETI are recruiting people to donate the otherwise unutilized computing power of their Internet-connected PCs by running a special screen saver that helps analyze data collected by the world's largest radio telescope. See their Web site at setiathome.ssl.berkeley.edu.

Cryonicist

Job description: Freeze people (or in some cases, just their heads) at the time of death in hope that doctors in the future can "reanimate" the frozen person/head. Specifically, the job entails injecting a corpse with an anticoagulant, securing transport of the corpse to a deep-freezing facility, freezing the corpse—at temperatures as low as minus 196 Celsius—and finally, storing the corpse indefinitely in a stainless steel pod.

Compensation: Generally, this industry pays people less than they could earn with similar technical positions in mainstream science, from $20,000 to $40,000 a year, and up to $100,000 for Ph.D.-level researchers.

Prerequisites: At Alcor, an industry leader, a veterinarian performs medical procedures. A general scientific education helps, though no specific training is required (the president of Alcor used to be a librarian). There are opportunities here for pure science research that simply would not be available to people without Ph.D.s anywhere else. At the American Cryonics Society, Ph.D.s work alongside self-taught researchers. As a testament to their belief in their vision, workers at these companies aren't just employees, they're almost always full-fledged members, having committed themselves to a frozen fate alongside their customers.

Qualities employer is seeking: Though most of the time nothing much happens on the job, there are brief moments of frenetic activity when a client dies and a "cryo team" suddenly springs into action. Employers therefore seek people who can think quickly on their feet, improvise when necessary, and quickly perform such grisly tasks as drilling holes in a dead person's skull to inject glycerol into his or her brain (or lopping off someone's head with a scalpel and surgical saw in the case of head-only customers).

Perks: Pioneer immortality. Also, your own office, flexible hours, and an easy-going relationship with management—according to one cryonicist, an "almost hippie environment."

Risks/drawbacks: Potentially dealing with disoriented, cranky patients as they emerge from their suspended state, especially the "neurosuspension patients" (the head-only clients), demanding to be fitted with a new body.

Overview

Entering this field has some clear pros and cons. On the one hand, having cryonics on your resume may put off certain closed-minded future employers, though one firm reports that people leaving their company have not had problems finding jobs outside this industry. Also, the job entails some health risks, since the patients occasionally have contagious diseases (e.g., AIDS, tuberculosis, hepatitis).

On the other hand, this may be your chance to get in on the ground floor of a blossoming new industry. Millenarian anxiety has been a boon to business as baby boomers rush to sign over their insurance policies and their bodies to the cryonics companies. Alcor has over 30 people/heads on ice already and 400 more "members," i.e., clients who haven't died yet. A "whole body freeze" can run $120,000 and "neuros," the head-only option, $50,000, though prices vary from firm to firm. For each full-body patient, Alcor takes approximately $70,000 and invests it to support ongoing operations. "We invest in real estate, mutual funds, and a spread-out series of investments," according to Steve Bridge, Alcor's president.

Besides the potential financial upside, there is also the possibility that cyronics is the fountain of youth, the true path to immortality (or at least a second go-round). As medical technology improves, reviving people from the dead may seem less and less implausible. In recent experiments, living hamsters have been frozen solid and reanimated. ("You could pick 'em up and pound 'em against a desktop, they're as hard as a rock, and we can revive them," according to Jim Yount, COO of the American Cryonics Society.) The seminal case of Miles the beagle demonstrated that suspended animation is possible for larger mammals as well.

"Just because we can't revive them in 1998 doesn't mean we can't ever revive them," Yount says. One "immortalist," science-fiction author Charles Platt writes, "Visionary? Crackpot? I can't answer that.... Gene splicing and molecular manipulation via scanning tunneling electron microscopes would have seemed impossible a century ago. We simply cannot predict the technical advances that may be made in centuries to come." With scientists now cloning sheep, and soon humans, you have to admit: He's got a point.

Practical Information

To break into this field, the people at Alcor suggest that you volunteer for a while, demonstrate that you are trustworthy, have skills, and are willing to

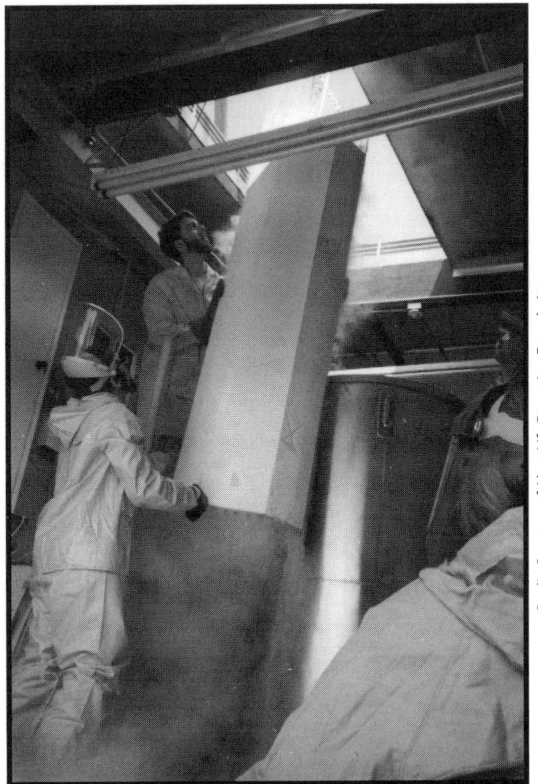

Freeze him and ship him. Cryonicists guide another happy customer into the tranquil world of suspended animation.

Credit: Courtesy of Alcor Life Extension Foundation

put in the time. If it works out, they will hire you, if they have the funds. They are looking for optimistic, science fiction–oriented people. A spokesman for the firm sums up the employees at his company as "nerds whose dream came true."

(Science or science fiction? The same could be asked of SETI researchers; see p. 171.)

While the job can be laid back, this is not a sedate industry. The so-called "freezer wars" of 1995 led to a defection of some employees from the Alcor company to a new venture, CryoCare. For one of these defectors, Saul Kent, the split meant that his mother is on ice with Alcor, while he supports CryoCare.

"It's weird because when someone's dead, they're dead," Mrs. Epstein, the widow of a recent patient, told the *New York Observer*. "But when they're frozen you still worry about things like whether their tank is going to run out of liquid nitrogen. I'm in sort of an emotional limbo."

Alcor Life Extension Foundation (800-367-2228; www.alcor.org) publishes *Cryonics* magazine ($15, free to members). Note: At Alcor, as a service to their members, clients can suspend their pets on an at-cost basis. Bodies are stored four to a tank with assorted frozen dogs, cats, and rabbits shoved down the middle. Other organizations include the American Cryonics Society (800-523-2001; www.jps.net/cryonics) and the CryoCare Foundation (800-TOP-CARE; www.cryocare.org).

"Immortality on Ice," a one-hour video of a program that aired on the Discovery Channel presents supporters and skeptics discussing cryonics and shows the process. The tape costs $20, and you can order it by calling 800-994-3131.

Atomic Clock Timekeeper

Job description: Watching and maintaining atomic clocks, thereby controlling time as we know it.

Compensation: Starting out, $30,000 to $40,000.

Prerequisites: You'll need a doctorate in physics or electrical engineering just to get your foot in the door—many researchers moonlight as timekeepers while working on their postdoctorates. The good news is, once you're in, you don't need any special background to manage the atomic clocks. NIST (the National Institute of Standards and Technology, in Boulder, Colorado) and other timekeeping institutions expect that applicants will arrive with little experience in this relatively obscure technology. They don't hire often, however; "It's a big investment to train people," says a source at NIST.

Qualities employer is seeking: Punctuality, naturally, but you'll also need engineering skills. One of NIST's current timekeepers describes himself as a "handyman at heart." While the timepieces themselves are extremely precise instruments, the entire network of clocks is magnetically shielded within temperature-controlled enclosures that can get out of whack. It takes a real fix-it type to track down the problem and patch it up on the fly. The job also requires people who are sincerely devoted to their profession—on the operations level, employees carry beepers and are on call in order to keep things running continuously. "It's a high-tech monster that requires constant babying," laments an employee.

Perks: No other arbitrary standards—temperatures, distances, or weights, for example—come close to the precision of the atomic clock. You will be responsible for making the most exact measurements on Earth; the world's economic markets, religions, and all of TV and radio programming are adrift without accurate timekeeping. Being at the helm of such a powerful device can lead to mischievous speculation about how much fun it would be to tamper with the fourth dimension. Slow things down, say, and extend a first kiss or a professional massage. Make everyone early for work. Your birthday could last weeks. On the other hand, you might speed up time, buy municipal bonds and have them mature overnight. Or let dinner with your mother-in-law last just seconds. On a less grandiose note, the job has its small pleasures. As a NIST timekeeper reflects, "I suppose I can set my watch before I go home."

Risks/drawbacks: You'd think it would be a high-pressure job: Everyone's relying on you to make sure the time is correct, and if you don't, the bigwigs in Washington could get upset because it's a political embarrassment for the United States to lose track of time. Actually, timekeepers are able to keep a good

perspective on this kind of responsibility. Nothing in the universe really runs like clockwork; the earth's rotation isn't constant, comets are sometimes fashionably late. If it weren't for leap seconds—additional seconds thrown into our calibration of time to account for celestial inconsistency—in 10,000 years, the sun would be rising at noon. On the other hand, it lightens the load a bit to know that even Mother Nature sometimes oversleeps.

Overview

Atomic clocks compute time based on the physical characteristics of radiation from a cesium atom; it's not quite as simple as just counting the number of times an electron rotates around the nucleus of the atom, although that's a common misconception. Atomic clock timekeepers monitor several atomic clocks and compute the average. The result is the standard timescale. If a clock's performance seems to be slipping, the timekeeper can instruct the computer that takes the average to give that clock less weight when calculating time. In the world of timekeeping, there's more to do than just look after the clocks: You can also perform research, analysis, or actually build the clocks that keep the time.

Atomic clocks are made and maintained by a number of institutions around the globe. The government runs some of them, most notably NIST and the U.S. Naval Observatory, but there are plenty of businesses that need to keep careful track of time (most notably the telecommunications industry) and purchase their own commercially made atomic clocks. Retail businesses need to have a uniform source of time to track points of sale; stockbrokers have to time-stamp all their transactions to within three seconds; the electric power industry needs to know how long the power's been on; and so forth through a myriad of businesses. Currently, most of these businesses simply log into NIST's server to periodically check and recalibrate their clocks, rather than purchase their own. The price of $70,000 a pop for a commercially manufactured atomic clock may finally prove that time is in fact money.

People assume the only atomic clock in the world is at NIST and that if it were destroyed then mayhem would ensue. Not so. A source at NIST says that the world timekeeping network "is sufficiently redundant that our building could burn down and time would continue."

A common misconception about timekeeping is that the primary goal of high-level timekeepers is accuracy. While this is true to a certain extent, it's also true that another large concern is stability. The atomic clocks that people set their watches by don't necessarily say when it is definitively midnight, for example, but they can say definitively when a second

has elapsed. UTC, or "coordinated universal time" (the mismatch between phrase and acronym was due to a compromise between speakers of French and English), signifies the conversion of timekeeping from an astronomical to a physical standard of timekeeping. While people once based their timescale on the Earth's rotation, they now base it on measurable physical standards (like cesium atoms). As a result, there's a slight discrepancy between UTI (the old astronomical timescale) and UTC. Leap seconds solve the problem by keeping atomic time in sync with the earth's rotation. The most recent leap second occurred between 1998 and 1999, when the time went from 11:59:59 to 11:59:60 to 12:00:00, according to a plan set forth by Dennis McCarthy at the U.S. Naval Observatory, who has one of the best titles around: Director of the Directorate of Time.

Despite this, the clock-keepers still tend to be blamed when things go wrong. A NIST source recounts the New Year's Eve a few years back when, due to a mechanical error, the famous dropping ball in Times Square was off by a few seconds by the time it got to the bottom. A spokesperson in Times Square, when asked by reporters about the inaccuracy of the ball, shrugged and said, "I don't know, we got our time from NIST." A flurry of calls resulted.

Never be late again when you're in charge of the world's master clock.

Credit: AP/Wide World Photos

Practical Information

The most cutting-edge technologies and opportunities are generally available at scientific institutions like NIST, who can build their own clocks. *Primary frequency standards*, as they're known, are built for very high accuracy and can cost upwards of $1,000,000 just to duplicate. Outside the United States, one of the nations most feverishly involved in the pursuit of accurate time is, shockingly enough, the one best known for wine, love, and joie de vivre: France.

Breaking in to a career as an atomic timekeeper is hard to do. You can check on the Web for information from the U.S. Naval Observatory (www.usno.navy.mil) or try the Directorate of Time's Web site at tycho.usno.navy.mil, where they post everything from information on the coming leap second to job openings. (They also have one of the least riveting broadcasts anywhere: a man's voice announcing the exact time, over and over again, ad infinitum, at http://tycho.usno.navy.mil/what.html; you'll need RealAudio to hear it.) NIST (www.nist.gov) is another good resource for information on both timekeeping and ways to find a job in the field. As with most rare scientific careers, you'll learn more from looking on the Web than from making phone calls or looking in the help-wanted ads.

One final tip: If you get an interview, don't be late.

Hypnotist (Hypnotherapist)

Job description: Ameliorate suffering—or amuse crowds at county fairs—by guiding people into narcotic states.

Compensation: Varies with the two branches of the job. A run-of-the-mill hypnotherapist in the St. Louis area makes between $50,000 and $60,000 a year, according to a local hypnotherapy teacher. Paul McKenna, the media-savvy hypnotist from the United Kingdom, inked a deal worth roughly $1.1 million with ABC for a series of shows last year.

Prerequisites: A hypnotherapist must get certification, via 100 hours of training from an accredited school. For entertainment, less formal training is demanded—though stage hypnotists should know therapeutic decorum and avoid stringing along subjects who may later resent being made to act like a duck on stage.

Qualities employer is seeking: Optimism, friendliness, and "inner caring" help subjects to trust their therapists.

Perks: A sense of pleasure derived from making people do silly things. For therapists, contracts to work on corporate wellness programs and the occasional gig on a team of police detectives.

Risks/drawbacks: Litigation is one possibility. Paul McKenna had to settle for

roughly $1.6 million with Christopher Gates, a Briton who claimed McKenna forced him to develop schizophrenia in a trance that had him thinking he was Mick Jagger, among other things. The plaintiff got backing from the Campaign Against Stage Hypnotists. Hypnotic trances can spell trouble for people with heart conditions or asthma. Some studies have found that 20 percent to 33 percent of stage-hypnosis subjects can experience ill effects from headaches to suicidal urges.

Overview

Hypnotists say they get a bum rap. They're always suspected of breaking out a gold watch and telling subjects to get sleepy; some religious groups brand their expertise "the work of the devil," and even those who choose to be hypnotherapy subjects tend to be embarrassed by it.

Records of modern-day hypnosis date back to eighteenth-century Vienna, where a doctor named Franz Mesmer first experimented with the healing powers of what he mistakenly judged to be a supernatural "animal magnetism." Mesmer did give us the word *mesmerize*, a boon to generations of movie critics, but his hocus-pocus was soon debunked and still embarrasses hypnotherapists. The next wave of research came in the late 1800s, when rural French doctor Ambroise-Auguste Liebeault turned a young Sigmund Freud on to the powers of the technique. Freud, however, dropped it when some subjects resisted induction.

Today, hypnotherapists are humbler about their magnetism. "All forms of hypnosis are self-hypnosis," said one respected teacher. That is, nobody goes under totally against his or her will; a hypnotic trance (of which there are different kinds) is simply a "state of heightened suggestibility" in which the hypnotist is a "facilitator." Hypnotherapy has also emerged as an above-board science: One researcher notes that hypnotherapy can correct pseudoseizures, which cause involuntary spasms. Psychiatrists sometimes use hypnosis to induce restfulness or help patients recover memories. Therapists may use hypnosis to help people conquer obesity, nicotine addiction, or bedwetting and thumb sucking

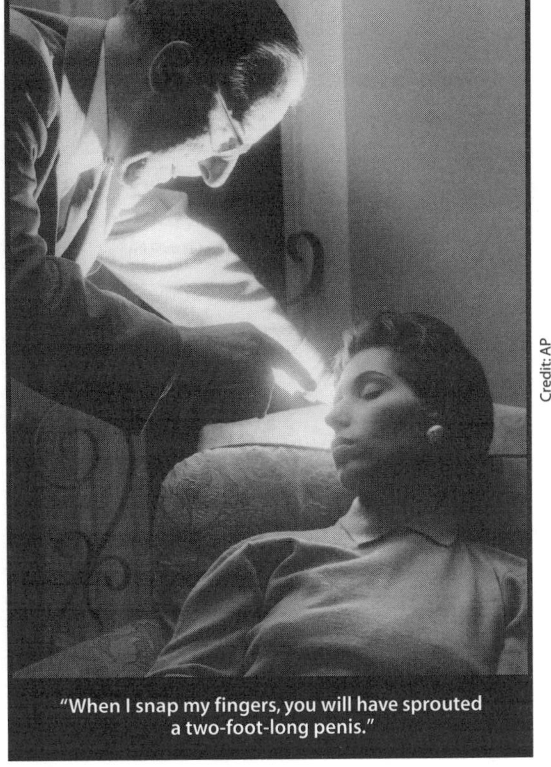

Credit: AP

"When I snap my fingers, you will have sprouted a two-foot-long penis."

(most common with juvenile subjects). Studies have also shown hypnosis to be an effective agent in the battle against warts. While many hypnotherapists try to keep themselves separate from the world of R-rated, comedy club hypnotists, there is some crossover. Stage hypnotists like McKenna may provide services to corporations or associations, and therapists may make extra money on the performance circuit.

Practical Information

One can be a sole hypnotherapist, a member of a hypnotherapy clinic, or a hypnotherapist on call to a corporate health program. To hang a shingle (whether or not that shingle swings suggestively back and forth), you first have to survive 100 hours of training at an accredited school. The National Guild of Hypnotists, which accredits programs from its headquarters in Merrimack, New Hampshire, maintains a database of schools through chapters in thirty states, as well as France and Italy. The schools are regulated in some states and more autonomous in others. They teach operators how to chart a subject's response and use voice, timing, tone, and signals to help a subject into "hypnosleep," a "hypnotic coma," or one of five other recognized states.

A one-on-one session begins with a "pre-talk," then moves through "induction" and "deepening." While the pendulum watch hasn't entirely fallen from favor (see sidebar), many hypnotists rely on audio and kinesthetic paths as well as visual ones to reach the hypnotic state. During regression, a subject may mentally revert to an earlier time in his or her life. The whole process takes about forty-five minutes on average; a typical therapist might see six to eight subjects a day. Therapists often write out an "induction plan" involving topics, voice techniques, signals, and movements, and then adjust it during a session. A disciplined approach can yield gladdening results; 85 percent of graduates from one antismoking hypnotherapy program stayed off tobacco for ninety days. Of course, says hypnotherapist Don Mottin, these people volunteered for hypnosis, so they were predisposed to quit. Wiseacres don't get very far. On the other extreme, when subjects are predisposed toward confusion, chaos can take root.

"I can sit down with you and teach you in three hours to induce a hypnotic state. But what are we going to do with the person?" challenges Don Mottin, a teacher/hypnotherapist/retired cop who says he's entranced some 38,000 people.

Another danger that might arise: An unscrupulous therapist can plant a false memory of child abuse or humiliation in the mind of a susceptible or imaginative subject. While it's relatively rare for

Now You're Getting Sleepy...

So what's the deal with the watch? Hypnotherapist Don Mottin blames television for fostering this stubborn image of hypnotherapists as jewel-swinging manipulators with *basso profundo* voices. In fact, among the three categories of response—visual, auditory, and kinesthetic—kinesthetic (i.e., movement) seems to be the least prevalent. The "sleepy, sleepy" trope does have some resonance, though. Hal Goldberg, who hypnotizes focus group members to elicit information about consumer products, is on record in the *New York Times Magazine* as saying, "I want to take you back, back—back to the last time you bought sandwich-spread-type products." Goldberg is a purist when it comes to the audio induction, eschewing music or waves in favor of his own voice. He manipulates it to become deeper, softer, more authoritarian—or otherwise more likely to exact the desired effect on a given subject.

It may alarm you to realize how little it can take to induce hypnosis—or the fear thereof. "The state can be entered and left in seconds," David Spiegel writes in the September 1998 *Harvard Mental Health Letter*. "Long-winded inductions and dangling watches are not necessary." TV commercial director Barnaby Jackson learned the hard way how scared some are of hypnotic powers. He had to obtain an endorsement from a licensed hypnotherapist before ABC would broadcast his ad featuring a mesmerizing golf ball. The hypnotist who provided the sign-off, Ann Elkin, decries the "Svengali" image that leads to such heebie-jeebies.

the hypnotherapist to indulge in such hijinks, Mottin admits, "Since there is a very strong rapport, someone unethical could manipulate it."

A hypnotist needn't practice strict therapy: Irvine, California, market researcher Hal Goldberg hypnotizes his focus groups to get them to remember the last time they went shopping or the way they respond to certain brands of cologne; Mottin, in his police days, used hypnosis in interviews to glean telling identification about perps.

When one becomes a hypnotist, one volunteers to do a lot of cheerful self-promotion in the face of stiff resistance. Your corporate clients may not want you to publicize your association with their brand. You may be refused advertising space in a local newspaper that refuses to promote "black magic and witchcraft." Thanks to the efforts of the National Guild and a growing cadre of psychiatrists, this cloud is lifting. But hypnotism remains an awfully young science; it only got the Catholic Church's seal of approval in 1957. As the science evolves, so do its champions. The National Federation of Hypnotists is a union of about 500 members designed in part to combat restrictive legislation like a Missouri statute that would have criminalized counselors who "changed the perceptions" of their subjects. Hypnotherapists argue that they aren't counselors but facilitators, since they don't have the power to inject thoughts. Nonetheless, they acknowledge the science's mysterious power. One man who has been inducting and deepening since 1973 warns: "I tried it with my children once as a kick, but hypnotizing one's own family isn't something I would recommend."

The National Guild of Hypnotists (603-429-9438; www.ngh.net) publishes the *Journal of Hypnosis* and *Hypno-Gram* and provides links to its members on its Web site.

Cryptographer

Job description: Write and break codes. Cryptographers create or maintain computer software systems that allow two or more parties to exchange secret messages. Most professional cryptographers work in the computer industry, protecting information from prowling hackers, while others work in academia or behind very closed doors in government intelligence work.

Compensation: Companies can't walk into a software supermarket and purchase an "off-the-shelf" solution; there's no such thing as a bargain basement price for encryption, and a poorly designed code is almost as useless as no code at all. Consequently, many companies are willing to pay top dollar for a high-quality product. Experienced cryptographers can command salaries of $100,000 or more. In contrast, entry-level cryptographers can make below $30,000, despite their highly marketable computer savvy. According to *Computer World* magazine, the pay rate for managers in the industry has risen 20 percent in the past two years, whereas entry-level salaries have dropped 10 to 15 percent. Just like in any other industry, working for a larger company means bigger bucks, but also less opportunity for advancement. Working in academia (even in computer-related academia) means earning an academic salary.

Prerequisites: Surprisingly, successful cryptographers do not require fancy computer science degrees. However, a high level of experience with computer programming is essential. A strong background in electrical engineering—with expertise in signal processing and digital architecture—is particularly helpful. To compute the algorithms that provide the building blocks of any cryptosystem, expertise in applied mathematics is also necessary.

Qualities employer is seeking: If you can't keep a secret, you shouldn't apply; cryptography is all about protecting information. Ironically, an effective security expert also needs to be skilled at code cracking. A "hacker's mentality" is essential to anticipating and solving weaknesses in a security system. In other words, you must understand how someone might break into a system to effectively keep them out. "Classical cryptanalysis involves an interesting combination of analytical reasoning, application of mathematical tools, pattern-finding, patience, determination, and luck," writes the moderator of sci.crypt, a crypto newsgroup. Perfectionists should beware: A meticulous nature may be wasted in this industry, since factors are unpredictable and clear-cut solutions are rare.

Perks: Cryptography is not a foot-in-the-door, work-your-way-up-the-corporate-ladder kind of industry. It's just plain difficult to become an industry "insider." However, once you've gained a reputation for quality work, you can be afforded a great deal of trust and responsibility at a relatively young age. Paul Kocher, the founder of Cryptography Research, was courted by the likes of Microsoft and Netscape at the age of twenty-five.

Risks/drawbacks: Cryptographers and cryptanalysts (better known as "hackers") are often tempted to "turn to the dark side." But this is more often for the excitement than for the money. "You can make more money fixing the programs for the good guys than you can working for the bad guys," explains Ben Jun, a cryptographic engineer at Cryptography Research.

Overview

Although cryptography has existed since the time of Julius Caesar, the field has recently enjoyed a renaissance with the emergence of the Internet. The rapid growth of electronic commerce and e-mail has created an insatiable demand for a method of securing online transactions and communications.

Despite the presence of encryption in our everyday lives, there's a reason why *cryptography* is not a household word. Many people use ordinary products, such as mobile phones and ATM machines, without actually knowing that they contain encryption devices. "Everybody knows they need security, but not many people know what that means," says Jun. "Usually people don't go around saying 'I want cryptography.' They say, 'Can you make it safe?' "

"Cryptography requires a broad knowledge of the computer industry. It's kind of like securing your house. You can put a lock on the door, but that's only going to make someone go through the window," says cryptographer Ben Jun. "Nothing is a hundred percent secure. It's about providing just the right level of security so that they'll give up."

Creating an encryption system is about more than assembling computer chips. The multilayered process begins with a client meeting, at which cryptographers thoroughly examine the company's business model, products, and customers. They try to determine the vulnerability of the system, in part by assessing who might want the information or products the company is offering. (For example, the latest version of DOOM is considered more valuable to a hacker—and therefore, more vulnerable—than a lab report written for a limited audience.) Like any other service provider, cryptographers also consider the client's priorities: Does it value brand name? Does it want to protect intellectual property? After these tough philosophical issues are settled, the cryptographers may also be responsible for the nitty-gritty of building the encryption software. However, the actual construction of the system is often regarded as a secondary concern that can be delegated to engineers.

RSA, a leading information security company, owns patents on encryption algorithms that are set to expire in 1999. This development is bound to alter the playing field for the entry-level cryptographer. With the removal of patent restrictions, more companies will be using encryption software, leading to more jobs for cryptographers.

Practical Information

Cryptographers can choose among several career tracks: the young, dynamic atmosphere of a start-up; the more structured ranks of a software corporation; the intellectual milieu of academia; or the airtight secrecy of government work. ValiCert, a company implementing certificate technology, has expe-rienced a hiring frenzy in recent years. System administrators, who maintain and protect a company's network, are in particular demand. Information security is a hot item on everyone's list, includ-ing computer industry bigwigs like Microsoft and Cisco; most companies need security experts. On the academic track, research areas range from number theory to a broad range of computational issues. And, of course, the supersecret National Security Agency (www.nsa.gov) and other intelligence agencies are always looking for a few good math geeks. Those interested in studying protocols should point their browsers to www.iacr.org, to explore an active community of implementers.

Becoming a cryptographer epitomizes the recent college grad's catch-22: You need experience to get a job; to get experience, you need a job. The ingenious have been known to design their own cryptosystems and "get noticed" by the experts. Another route might be to conduct research for a known professor, who might introduce you to the ranks.

To learn more about the industry, subscribe to the Cypherpunks mailing list by sending a message to majordomo@algebra.com with the words "subscribe cypherpunks [your e-mail address]" in the body of the text. Also, check out the sci.crypt newsgroup for FAQs and tips for crypto beginners. Your study materials should also include Bruce Schneider's *Applied Cryptography*, the "bible" of the industry.

Demolition Contractor

Job description: Destroy all kinds of physical structures, sometimes with the use of strategically placed explosives.

Compensation: The pay scale for demolition workers, as in traditional construction, varies widely; entry-level hired hands may earn about $20,000 per year, while senior managers can earn in the low six figures.

Prerequisites: The ability to safely maneuver some of the heaviest machinery available. In many cases, experience combined with an intuitive understanding of how concrete and steel behave under pressure is valued more highly than a glossy degree from an engineering school.

Qualities employer is seeking: A certain destructive inclination in one's personality, coupled with a strong work ethic, is paramount.

Perks: Get out of bed and go to work, smash everything in sight, go home.

Risks/drawbacks: Deconstruction work, like construction work, carries inherent safety risks. For implosion specialists, there is also the ever-present, potentially emasculating concern, that the explosive mechanism will be unsuccessful—and that the building will be left standing.

Overview

The majority of demolition work is done with traditional construction equipment—bulldozers, cranes equipped with huge jaws that tear at the sides of buildings (the Komatsu PC400 "Super Long Reach" and the Cat Pulverizer are industry favorites), and of course, the archetypal symbol of destruction, the wrecking ball.

"The adrenaline is pumping like mad," says Andy Shoemaker, an explosive implosion specialist, reflecting on the moment of detonation. "Really, to say you're nervous is an understatement. It's a case of tucking your trousers in with cycle clips and just not disgracing yourself." Mr. Shoemaker got his training in the British army, where he defused terrorist bombs.

In those cases when electrical implosion is necessary—either because the height of the structure requires it or because there is a certain public relations sexiness to it—a demolition company usually calls on one of about five small implosion subcontractors. These highly specialized implosion companies undertake only the implosion—none of the preparatory exercises like emptying the building, clearing the area, and especially none of the cleanup. "The implosion guys load the site, do the shoot—boom!—and then they're gone, bye," says Michael Taylor, Executive Director of the National Association of Demolition Contractors. The leading company in the implosion business, Controlled Demolition, Inc., whose founder, Jack Loizeaux, is often credited with being the godfather of the technique, has imploded an average of one structure every two and a half days for the fifty years they've been in business.

The actual implosion mechanism involves blanketing a given building with up to 1,000 pounds of explosives. Dynamite is predominantly used in reinforced concrete; for steel structures, military-style plastic explosives called "shaped charges" are used. These plastic charges are bolted to each side of a steel column, and upon detonation, create an intense pressure (the temperature rises as high as 50,000 degrees Fahrenheit) and "cut through the steel like a hot knife through butter," according to Richard Diven, vice president of IconCo, a California demolition company.

The strategically timed explosives are set off in the middle of the building first, and over the course of a few seconds, work their way to the outer walls, so the building crumbles in upon itself. According to literature from Controlled Demolition, this "creates a controlled progressive collapse which parallels the natural failure mode of each structure." (Each implosion job allows for very little margin of error: Too many explosive devices can destroy underground sewer tunnels and power lines, while too little

Credit: AP

What goes up must come down. Demolition experts prove the old adage with a vengeance. Shown here is the Sands Hotel in Las Vegas being reduced to a 30-foot pile of rubble.

can leave a building half-collapsed and too dangerous to reenter.) It took a total of twelve seconds for the Loizeaux family to level the 356-foot-tall Landmark Hotel and Casino in Las Vegas; Tim Burton recorded the explosion for his movie, *Mars Attacks!*

As much as this line of work may inspire images of reckless and free-for-all destruction, demolition work in fact requires a great deal of preparation and management expertise. In order to get a job, a demolition company must first create a thorough proposal and bid for the project; this can take weeks of visiting and meticulously analyzing the site in question. The chosen demolition company will frequently have free reign of any salvage, some of which may be valuable. Most successful demolition contractors have workers whose job it is to comb through leftover but potentially

useful refuse from the project. Finally, projects that require the removal of asbestos and hazardous materials from buildings necessitate workers who can skillfully dismantle a structure rather than just mindlessly smash it to smithereens (although those who can do the later are certainly in demand, as well).

Practical Information

For traditional demolition work, any number of construction management or engineering classes can help one's ability to find work—particularly at the administrative level. Those interested in taking this route should be aware that there is a certain hard-hat bravado that views construction academia with skepticism, and sometimes even disdain. "Cutting metal from high in the air and getting it safely down on the ground where it has to be cut again to fit into the dumpster is not something that you learn at a trade school," Doug Iseler, president of Iseler Demolition Co., wrote in *Water Engineering and Management*.

Those interested in implosion work will likely have to penetrate one of a handful of the family-owned implosion companies to work as an apprentice. These organizations are very tight-knit. "You'll notice that none of these implosion companies are publicly held," says Mike Taylor of NADC. "If you've got a partner, it's your brother." Although not impossible, securing a position with one of these companies will require a certain degree of persistence. Those who are successful will find themselves in good standing to learn the tricks of the trade, and perhaps eventually, to form a company for themselves. Of the five organizations that do implosion work, three were created by individuals who once worked for Controlled Demolition, the leading implosion company.

The National Association of Demolition Contractors is a good general resource for the business. Write to NADC, Suite 200-B, 16 N. Franklin Street, Doylestown, PA 18901. The organization also publishes a bimonthly magazine, *Demolition*, which contains articles about the details of recent demolition projects. (A six-issue, full-year, subscription is $40.)

The February 1998 issue of *Reader's Digest* has an article, entitled "A Booming Business," on the infamous implosion family, the Loizeauxes, and their company, Controlled Demolition. The article discusses CGI's blowup of the Sands Hotel in Las Vegas. An article that focuses more closely on the electrical procedures of implosion can be found in the October 1995 issue of *Scientific American*.

Telephone Psychic

Job description: Responding to callers hungering for life's answers and a sense of direction. Acting out a script while pretending you can see into the future, read minds, and decide destinies.

Compensation: Between $10 and $15 per hour—a pittance, considering the services earn between $3 and $5 a minute.

Prerequisites: Telephone psychics need possess no psychic abilities whatsoever. "Some people come on and challenge you," one psychic reported. "They'll say, tell me how many kids I have and what their names are. You're a psychic, you should know that." Most callers don't question psychics' powers, however.

Anyone can be a phone psychic. Some psychics truly believe they possess supernatural insights. "I invoke the White Angel of God to sit with us during the reading," said a psychic during an interview for the publicnews.com Web site. Others don't take their jobs quite so seriously. One man reports working under the name "The Great Shamu," performing his job stoned drunk (after imbibing "magic psychic juice," aka tequila), and with a red towel on his head.

Qualities employer is seeking: *"For entertainment purposes only,"* the disclaimer at the bottom of every psychic advertisement, suggests what employers want in their psychics: that they entertain. That means acting out a script convincingly, and thinking quickly enough to react to what callers say. What matters most in the business is that a psychic can keep callers on the line for long periods of time.

Perks: Psychics follow their own hours, work out of their homes, earn incentive bonuses, such as vacations and cash, gain riveting insights into the human psyche, and possibly receive glimpses into the future.

Risks/drawbacks: Psychics deal with a heavy load of callers' emotional and personal problems; depression can be a severe side effect.

Overview

The Miami Herald reports that the cash generated by 1-900 phone calls for entertainment and information services will reach $1.4 billion a year by 2000, up from $670 million in 1994. A good chunk of that change comes out of the phone psychic business, in which callers typically pay between $3.99 and $4.99 per minute for fortunes, tarot readings, and other psychically elicited information. Celebrity infomercials typically lure callers.

Many psychics agree that the number of troubled souls who call make the job seem more like therapy than entertainment. While psychics are not trained in dealing with real troubles, their $3.99-a-minute rate costs two to three times more than professional therapy.

Interview with former phone psychic Lauren Hirshfield, twenty-three, a Dartmouth graduate who describes her days of purveying ESP as "the most depressing job I've ever had."

"I was a telephone psychic.

"I was living in New York, working as an intern at MTV for free. I was searching through the *Village Voice* for a paying job, and I saw an ad that said, 'Do you like to talk on the phone? Can you think of creative things on the spot? Are you a dramatic person? If so, call.'

"I had an hour interview with a guy; I was trying to figure out the whole time what I'd be doing for him. Finally, he said: 'You could be a telephone psychic for $15 an hour, working from home. You can do it tax free and do it whenever you want, we'll give you a PIN number.'

"I told him, I'm not psychic, and I was getting nervous, because I might have believed in this stuff. He said he would send me information and a script. The guy laughed when I told him I had no psychic skills; he was like, 'Oh god, you have a lot to learn!'

"The script is so ridiculous. It's a scam. For example, you're supposed to use the person's name all the time to create a bond. You say, 'Oh John, I had a feeling you were going to call me, John. So are you very close to your mother, John?' And all the questions pertain to everyone. And if the person says no, you say, 'Oh, I didn't think so." I'd ask when they were born, then say, 'Hold on a second while I shuffle my tarot cards.' But I didn't have tarot cards. The script just said for me to rustle the script pages and say, 'Tell me when to stop.' Then I'd do the cards, and it was always the same thing: 'The first card is death. But not bad death. Death as in change.'

"Each time I wanted to work, I'd have to log in by dialing in a PIN number. You'd hear a recording from the network with all sorts of announcements, things like, 'The top psychic today logged on nineteen hours!' I was paid $12 an hour, and was paid checks; I had to have a fax machine, because I had to fill out forms about everyone I talked to. The nice thing about the job was that I could call whenever I wanted. I'd go home and call for an hour. They weren't allowed to ask questions until I was done with the script, and it took twenty minutes to finish the script (roughly $80). And at the beginning it was really fun.

"But the longer I went on, the more extreme cases I got. I started out hearing teenagers asking me if they'd fall in love. But then they started to send me calls every minute. I'd be hearing about an abused wife or a cross-dresser who had no friends. Women would call, and they were broke, and their electricity had been turned off, and I'd say things to help, to keep them off the phones: 'Maybe you should get outside more' or 'Maybe you should take walks more.' People were calling who'd had the worst lives, people who'd been beaten, whose children had run away. And they'd ask, 'Will the children come back?' And I didn't have any training, but I felt so responsible, and I knew I at least had a brain, so I tried to talk these people out of staying with their abusive husbands or whatever.

"Some of these people must have been logging on huge hours. It cost them between $3.99 and $5 a minute. The average call lasted about forty minutes.

"One woman got handcuffed while I was talking to her on the phone. She said, 'I've gotta go! They're handcuffing me!' One woman asked me where her child was hiding; her child had been hiding for ten days. I said, I have have a very strong feeling that you might want to talk to the police about this."

"I wanted to tell people to hang up, but the calls were monitored. I was torn: I knew it was a big scam, but then I thought, if I don't do this, who will?

"The guy who worked for the network told me he had fraternity houses full of guys who were working the phones on a rotating basis. They'd earn bonuses, because the network gave out bonuses for whoever logged the most hours. They were making tons of money, and there are all sorts of incentive trips and bonuses offered each week. The psychic networks are a weird, big underground world.

"I'd just go into my room to work; I'd hang a little sign that said 'psychic mode.' If you're on the phone with someone who thinks you're a descendant of God, it looks bad if your little sister picks up the phone on the other end. Sometimes my sister and her friends would go into the kitchen and put the phone on speaker and mute to listen to my calls.

"But once I went out waitressing, and apparently my log off hadn't worked, because someone called, and my sister answered. She knew she had to talk to them. She was searching around my room for the script, and she wrote down the person's name, and then she listened to this woman talk for an hour about how she was going to leave her husband. My sister was fifteen years old. She came to my restaurant crying."

Practical Information

Secrets of a Telephone Psychic, by Frederick Woodruff, offers insights on all aspects of the trade. To order the book from Beyond Words Publishing, Inc., call 800-284-9673.

Woodruff also sells a book called *How to Work as a Telephone Psychic,* which you can buy for $5.95 sent to P.O. Box 15414, Seattle, WA 98115-0414. Beforehand, check out samples from the book on Woodruff's comprehensive phone psychic Web site, zenpop.home.mindspring.com. His "how to" book includes tips on what you need to begin ("A good speaking voice…, an ability to create solutions to unexpected problems…, an ability to dis-identify with other people's problems…, and "aspirin").

For more information about psychic powers in general, contact the Berkeley Psychic Institute at 510-548-8020; they offer a "kindergarten" to help beginners hone their mind reading, future seeing, and general sixth sense.

Beyond that, one way in the door could be to call a psychic hotline directly (see any infomercial, sleazy magazine ad, or alternative newspaper for guidance) and simply tell the psychic immediately that you're looking for a job. Assuming they've got their business's number close by, psychics may willingly help; after all, it's your future in their hands.

12 Your Name in Lights

Sports Mascot

THE REAL WORLD and ROAD RULES Story Editor

Performance Artist

Paranormal TV News Show Researcher

TV Weathercaster

Radio Contest Winner

Voice-over Actor

Sports Mascot

Job description: Entertain fans at sporting events by dressing as a team's mascot.

Compensation: As with any job in athletics, the pay varies considerably from the semipro and minor leagues, where mascots can be paid hourly, to the majors—NBA, NHL, NFL, and MLB—where top salaries run into the low six figures and may include revenue participation in side gigs. These special appearances can be lucrative, from $300 to $700 for a one- to two-hour appearance. "Bar mitzvahs were the most fun," says Dave Raymond, the former Phillie Phanatic.

Prerequisites: Command of the classic elements of nonverbal skit techniques, mastery of the art of comic theater, and ability to rile up thousands of rowdy, drunken fans while shadowboxing with an umpire.

Qualities employer is seeking: Stamina, physical fitness, and dedication. "You're going out there night after night, entertaining the crowd in excruciating heat," says Ted Giannoulas, the San Diego Padres' Famous Chicken. Matt Marlowe, who was recently called up to the majors to be the Tampa Bay Devil Rays' mascot after an acclaimed collegiate and semipro career, claims to lose seven to ten pounds a performance, wearing a forty-pound costume. "You can't be effective if you're not strong, healthy, and rested," he says.

Perks: Field-level views of sporting events. Also, the chance to meet celebrities. Around his house, Raymond has pictures of himself as the Phillie Phanatic with Richard Nixon, Heather Locklear, and Arnold Palmer.

Risks/drawbacks: Heat exhaustion and dehydration are common problems. Also, Tommy Lasorda. The Dodger's hall-of-fame manager was known to get agitated at mascot antics, reportedly assaulting both Giannoulas (the Famous Chicken) and Raymond (the Phillie Phanatic). One day, Lasorda had enough of the Phanatic's ridicule, stormed onto the field in the middle of the game, and started attacking the mascot, who had been parodying Lasorda by imitating his bowlegged walk and playing around with a pillow-stuffed dummy of the overweight manager. "Right in the middle of the game, he came running out of the dugout and tried to drag the dummy away from me. He was beating me over the head with it," Raymond said. "He flipped out." In another similar outburst, according to an article in the *Denver Post*, Lasorda approached Giannoulas under the grandstand, near the locker room, and started shouting, "You want to step on the Dodgers' hat? Come step on my Dodger hat! I'll kick your [expletive] ass!"

Overview

Despite the existence of mascot schools (see "Practical Information"), many pro mascots never receive any formal vocational training. Most, in fact, get their

start on some fateful day when their peers coerce them into wearing a silly costume.

In the case of Matt Marlowe, it took coaxing from his fraternity brothers at Eastern Kentucky University to prompt him to try out to be the school's mascot. "I threw up in the costume the first time I wore it," he says. But as is the case with so many successful mascots, he recognized his calling immediately. He was a natural and was later named the country's top college mascot in 1992. Marlowe even proposed to his wife during halftime at a basketball game. After graduating, he went into computer sales, but returned to his first love when a minor-league hockey team in Lexington, Kentucky, signed him up to be Lucky the Horse. Marlowe became so successful as Lucky that he was called upon to create the Tampa Bay Devil Rays' first mascot. He is now represented by Coordinating Sports Management Group, the same sports agency that represents several of the Devil Rays' baseball players.

Dave Raymond had a similarly serendipitous path to stardom. Before becoming the legendary Phillie Phanatic, he was a college intern for the Phillies, handling menial tasks in an organization known for its wacky promotions. "I was picking up the cowchips after the cowchip-throwing contests. I was watching the ostriches before the ostrich races." When the Phillies decided to test out a mascot during the 1978 off-season, they knew that Dave the intern wouldn't complain about having to wear the silly costume, so they had the new suit fitted for him. It was his ticket. "It was like a gift from heaven," Raymond says. "Here I am, just a regular guy working at a job. Then all of a sudden, I'm a mascot…I was getting paid to be a clown."

Practical Information

Believe it or not, there are professional mascot schools. Mascot Mania, Inc., in Nashville, Tennessee, offers a $795 course run by Dean Schoenewald, a mascot for the Philadelphia Eagles and the New Jersey Devils. Schoenewald's course runs the gamut of mascoting techniques: developing a signature "funny dance," appropriate use of props in on-field skits, interacting with screaming, frightened children, and

Credit: Dave Raymond

President Nixon greets the ambassador from the Philadelphia Phillies.

driving an all-terrain vehicle onto the field while inside a cumbersome polyester-and-plastic costume. "Think of the game," Schoenewald tells the class, "as an intermission from your act."

"I'm a professional idiot," says Dave Raymond, former Phillie Phanatic. "I'm forty-two and making a great living. It's the best occupation you could possibly have."

Dave Raymond, currently employed as the man inside a rotund blue creature called "Sport," is starting a rival school, Dave Raymond's Mascot Master Class, where for $800 you can learn all about the fine points of belly bumping and other essential moves from someone with twenty years' experience.

With the growing importance of merchandising in sports, mascots have taken on a more central role in the revenue equation. Job openings are rare in the big leagues, but they do surface from time to time. Prospective mascots should regularly check teams' Web sites, where these jobs are often posted. Pay particular attention to expansion teams and to teams whose mascots are in need of revitalization. The San Francisco Giants, for example, recently sought to refashion their tired mascot, Lou Seal, aka Luigi Francisco. They posted ads on their Web site as well as at local acting schools and colleges seeking someone who "understands the feel of putting on a costume." Raymond recommends getting experience in college or with minor league teams. He also notes that big-league mascots have understudies who do special appearances and substitute when the primary performer is unavailable—another good way to gain experience.

Given that you are hoping to be a goofball in front of thousands of people, you shouldn't be shy in taking a little initiative when it comes to getting a job. Raymond suggests putting together a resume that highlights athletics, dance, traditional theater, and visual arts, and then showing up at professional baseball's winter meetings. "Pass your resume out to all the sports teams that are out there," he says. "And take any and every opportunity you have to get in a costume and perform."

A useful reference ($200, but available at libraries) is *Sports Market Place*, an extensive directory of sports teams (colleges, pros, amateurs) and related organizations, published by Sportsguide, Inc., Box 1417, Princeton, NJ 08542.

Acme Mascots, a husband-wife mascot-creation team in Brooklyn, is in the process of building a Web site intended to be the ultimate Internet resource for all matters relating to professional mascots. Call 800-450-ACME for details.

THE REAL WORLD and ROAD RULES Story Editor

Job description: Create a story out of thoroughly documented lives for popular MTV shows.

Compensation: Story editors make from $500 a week to $70,000 a year, without benefits. The job is considered freelance and assigned on a contract basis.

Prerequisites: A creative mind and an eye for juicy, interesting subject matter; a background in screenwriting or television editing.

Qualities employer is seeking: Jon Murray, cocreator and executive producer of *The Real World* and *Road Rules*, sums up the unique nature of the story editing job: "It's unusual in the business. It requires someone who has a great sense of drama, but also understands the documentary form of filmmaking. Unlike a fiction writer, who's sitting there dreaming up a story, for our shows you have to watch material that exists then figure out how to pick and choose to tell a story. It involves all the same principles, but the existing material can be a trap or a help. We look to hire someone who not only has a good understanding of human behavior, but who's written some scripts and hopefully has some experience with nonfiction film. We wouldn't hire someone just out of school for this position; they'd be hired for the logging area, where they'd be logging tape, which requires similar skills: watching material and seeing if it will fit together. Our most successful strategy has been taking young people out of college then teaching them the skills required to perform the story editing job. They'd spend two or three years on various aspects before getting a story editing position."

Risks/drawbacks: The amount of time you spend watching television, especially since most of the subject matter is bratty kids at their dullest.

Perks: Advanced knowledge of what comes next (and who's sleeping with whom) in internationally renowned true-life soap operas; occasional travel (for *Road Rules*).

Overview

The Real World is a "real-life soap opera" in which a group of young, usually strong-willed strangers are brought to live together in a house for several months. The youngsters are filmed around the clock, and their lives are transformed into a multiprogram TV series. The show was devised by Mary-Ellis Bunim, who'd overseen more than 2,500 hours of soap opera programming, and Jon Murray, who had worked in news and documentary production. To date, seven *The Real World* series have

been produced by Bunim-Murray, which is owned by MTV. *Road Rules* follows a similar concept, but instead of living together in a house, cast members travel around in an RV, searching for clues and performing various missions. The shows have become mainstays for MTV and in concept were once thought to represent television's final plunge into voyeuristic filth.

"The first thing most people say to me is 'I thought it was real!'" says story editor Toni Gallagher. "'How can they have a story editor?' It's 90 percent real, I'd say, and the other 10 percent of it is how we manipulate it. To create a three-act story, sometimes, you have to jump around in time."

The story editor's job is to piece together each show (and the whole series) after the cast is done living together. He or she must watch all the footage then decide what to include for maximum excitement and drama. The main question asked of the story editor: How real is it? "*Road Rules* is restricted by chronology and location," explains Toni Gallagher, thirty-three, former senior story editor for the two shows. "Editing *The Real World* gives you more freedom to mix things up and include a better story arc." Gallagher describes the details of her job as follows: "I'd watch all the documentary footage shot, take notes, decide how to shape the show, write a detailed prose story for the editor to cut, watch and document the weekly interviews with cast members, and oversee the final editing."

Many viewers assume the cast members are shown in an unfavorable light to add to the conflict and melodrama of the show. According to Gallagher, though, the opposite is true: "In general, the people are worse than they appear. They're brattier; they complain more; and they're meaner and dumber. But the producers want them to look good. The kids themselves always think we've done them wrong."

Occasionally, in all those hours of watching the Young and the Frisky, the story editor comes across things that can't be shown in television. "We've seen some masturbation that didn't get on the show, and some audio of sexual liaisons, things like, 'Oh, I'm usually such a good girl, Puck.' Most of what you don't see is too boring. If it's good, we try to use it."

Gallagher is candid about what producers look for in the show's cast members, who are drawn from the public at large. "Each season they go in with a different idea of what they want. They want dissention, but also romance and the potential for opposites to understand each other. And the people have to be telegenic." Occasionally, the cast surprises the producers. "For *The Real World: San*

Francisco," Gallagher recounts, "we had a kid on the show who was HIV-positive. We had no intention of showing a guy die on television, but we didn't know how far along he was. Ultimately, it's one of the things I'm proudest of, too. Pedro [Zamora, the AIDS victim,] has become associated with AIDS awareness."

Practical Information

Gallagher landed her job at Bunim-Murray by contacting the company directly: "I'd been an assistant in the development department at Amblin, Steven Spielberg's company. I read and critiqued scripts. I was a fan of *The Real World*'s first season, so I wrote the production company a letter, and threw in some jokes. I never followed up, but six months later they called me. That was to be an assistant story editor for L.A.'s *Real World*." After a few years, she'd risen in rank to senior story editor and worked on both shows.

The Real World films for five and a half months, *Road Rules*, eight to ten weeks. Gallagher describes her workplace as a "fun, young office environment," but still complains that her job mostly entailed watching tapes. "We watched between 20 and 100 hours of tapes for a single 22-minute show." About four people work in the story department at *Road Rules*, three or four on *The Real World*; each show's production involves approximately thirty to forty employees. Although Gallagher got to travel to Canada and New Zealand as part of a "*Road Rules* All-Star Special," she ultimately left her job because she grew tired of living voyeuristically and vicariously. "I thought, I'm tired of watching these other people have fun. I want to go out and have those adventures myself!"

(For another job where you get paid to watch more of people's private lives than you might care to see, check out "Private Investigator," p. 71.)

For further information on working on either of the shows, contact Bunim-Murray Productions, 6007 Sepulveda Blvd., Van Nuys, CA 91411.

Performance Artist

Job description: Express yourself, preferably in an entertaining way.

Compensation: "You don't need to go to a casino if you're a performance artist. Your slot machine is built in," says Flash Rosenberg, who performs a show titled *Camping in the Bewilderness*. A ten-minute spot on Comedy Central can pay $1,500, while a two-hour show at the Public Theater in New York might not cover your cab fare. A single performance at a university or a museum can pay $5,000. A week-long seminar at the same venue might pay $10,000. A year-long tour with the National Performance Network could pay travel expenses, a per diem, and $500 a week. A handful of nationally recognized performance artists (e.g., Laurie Anderson, Eric Begosian, Spalding Gray) have gotten rich at this. Everyone else has a day job. Those who rely on day jobs tend to work in fields related to performance art—television, film, music, and publishing. "I am teaching at various universities, which is my waiter job, though I consider it richly meaningful," says Deb Margolis, performance artist and faculty member of Yale University's theater department.

Prerequisites: Ellen Hulkower, who has toured the United States with her show, *Jumping off the Fridge*, recommends a disciplined background in some aspect of theatrical or visual arts. Deb Margolis disagrees: "You can come with physics training. I believe that desire necessitates talent." The main prerequisite is perseverance. Many artists take two to five years to mold a show into material that can attract mainstream audiences. "If you keep telling the truth over and over again, people will eventually tap into it no matter what you do," says Flash.

Qualities employer is seeking: "In the sixties and seventies, it was so in-your-face to not make any sense. Today no one will stand for lava lamp art," says Flash. In addition to providing a rarefied show of self-expression, performance artists are expected to present intelligible and insightful material. The more unique your perspective, observations, and format, the more likely you are to receive regional or national attention. A sharp wit is essential as is a charismatic stage persona.

Perks: "I have the best fucking life. My life is so full of the beautiful. I have everything except money. No one tells me what to do. I cannot be censored. If I want to play the ingenue, I do. If I want to play Hamlet, I do. I've toured Europe three times," says Deb Margolis. If you have a burning desire to express yourself in a format that offers few limitations, this is it. Flexibility of schedule and travel opportunities are added perks.

Risks/drawbacks: Near-certain poverty.

Overview

The origination of performance art is a matter for debate. One viewpoint looks to the visual arts and the "moving statues" shows put on early this century in Russia. Another perspective traces performance art to the post-WWII deconstruction of traditional theatrical forms. Others see the mother form in dance, pointing to the early sixties when dancers began to speak to the audience. Deb Margolis looks later still for an inception date: "It began in the late sixties. Beat poets were the precursor to it, and it just kind of came out of that. We were disenfranchised and poor and weird and not good-looking enough to take a place in the conventional theater. It was a radical political act to take the stage. You didn't see a bunch of homely people taking the stage, and now you do."

The National Endowment for the Art's retraction of four grants administered to performance artists in the early nineties thrust the field into the national limelight. Says Deb Margolis, "Karen Finley got a lot of attention for smearing her body with chocolate and sticking a sweet potato up her rectum. The whole thing that went down with the NEA brought a lot of attention to performance art. The overall result was good." Ellen Hulkower disagrees with this assessment: "It made it seem like you had to be somewhat blasphemous to do performance art. It marred the reputation."

Taking the late sixties as an inception point, performance art is still in its first generation of existence—the original performance artists are still out in the field. The future is as obscure as the past. Some solo performers refuse to accept the title of performance artist, maintaining that they are part of the legitimate theater. The movement of performance artists into stand-up comedy blurs the distinction between the two fields. The preponderance of entertainment headhunters at venues like P.S. 122 in New York City, and the perception of television spots as a primary

"You don't need to go to a casino if you're a performance artist—your slot machine is built in," says Flash Rosenberg, who performs a show titled *Camping in the Bewilderness.*

Credit: Flash Rosenberg

Breaking In

Flash Rosenberg's background is in photography. "I got frustrated with the idea that people wanted to see the photographs when I wasn't there," says Flash. She began doing narrated slide shows. "I thought it was easy to memorize text. Just before I was supposed to go on, I couldn't remember the text. I wrote the text all over my hands, my arm, my body. So I get on and say, 'Excuse me, I have to get out my notes,' and took my clothes off. I had on this goofy camouflage underwear, just because I was wearing it at the time 'cause I thought it was funny. And people were howling with laughter. I became a performance artist by accident," chortles Flash, recollecting her first performance. Following the show, a public radio director invited Rosenberg to put one minute of her insights on the air every day. Flash combined five years of those insights into a single live piece titled *Camping in the Bewilderness*. "When I perform, I'm not doing characters. My persona isn't pathetic, it's not PC. I'm usually the weird one in an evening of performance artists. My performance is more like a live storyboard," Flash explains.

source of income, suggests the field could dissolve into a runway for mainstream entertainment. Flash terms most shows, "Theater of the lonely. The artists are maneuvering through the world alone and they give a report of their maneuverings. I don't think it's a great art that will endure." Margolis counters, "The singular nature of our lives has beauty. I really think there is always going to be a need for this forum."

Practical Information

"New York, let's face it, is the only place where I feel like I didn't drop from Mars. I think you can live this life anywhere you choose to live it. It's still easier in New York." On the other hand, all you need is a place to perform, which can be your living room, a local café or bar, or a sidewalk. Beginners may prefer to develop their show in a less competitive area and bring it to the Big Apple when they think they are ready for a long run.

"The theater belongs to whoever is demented enough to take it," says performance artist Deb Margolis .

The Foundation Library in New York City can help you find out about grants and resident artist programs. The prospect of making a living off these is dim. Flash looks elsewhere: "I think artists are the most capable people on the earth. I don't need a grant or a handout. There's things we can do." Flash, who has supplemented her income through photography, cartoon work, and by instructing in Niger on birth-control methods, suggests breaking down elements of your show into marketable skills. "I don't think my work is reduced by having to earn money in other ways. I'm going to earn a living so the thing that feeds my soul doesn't have to be compromised," says Flash.

Until you're fortunate enough to find a booking manager, you produce your own shows. The less renowned can get gigs by paying the techies themselves and giving the theater the first ten tickets. When your draw grows, you can split sales with the theater. Some bars will give you all the sales, provided that your audience does a fair amount of drinking. Fringe theatrical festivals held annually in San Francisco, New York, and Edinburgh can be a bonanza. You pay a venue fee to the festival, which in exchange provides a space, does your sales, some publicity, and provides stage management. The festival fee depends on the festival and your ticket price, but can run as low as $250 a week. Once you've built a reputation, try to book yourself on tour.

Paranormal TV News Show Researcher

Job description: Uncover breaking news in the paranormal world. Paranormal events include UFO sightings, cryptozoology (e.g., vampires, werewolves, Bigfoot, the Loch Ness monster), near- and postdeath experiences, ESP, time travel, conspiracy theories, crop circle researchers, and more. A typical day might include people telling you that a comet is about to crush the Earth and that giant squids have just washed up on the coast of New Zealand.

Compensation: Positions pay $700 to $1,000 for a five-day week. Ten-hour days are the norm.

Prerequisites: Excellent research skills, familiarity with Internet search software, the ability to recognize material that will spark public interest, and the ability to distinguish obvious shams from less obvious ones.

Qualities employer is seeking: This is not a field for dilettantes. Steve Nalepa, researcher for the high-profile daily news show *Strange Universe*, notes: "There aren't a lot of paranormal news jobs out there. The people I worked with were all serious freaks. It's a competitive field." An almost obsessional interest in the material is expected. Expertise in one or more areas of paranormal phenomena is a bonus.

Perks: For many in the field, researching paranormal events is what they would do in their free time, anyway. Getting paid to do it is a real bonus. "You get to interact with a really eccentric group of people," says Nalepa. "You become a walking encyclopedia of strange and unusual facts that you can use to be the star of any party or to woo a love interest. Every day I could call a girl that I was after and leave her a minute-long message of weird stuff. You know where all the weirdest, funniest places to go are."

"You get to interact with a really eccentric group of people," says Steve Nalepa, researcher for the daily news show *Strange Universe.* "You become a walking encyclopedia of strange and unsusual facts that you can use to be the star of any party or to woo a love interest."

Risks/drawbacks: Conspiracy theories may have some truth at their core. Believers claim that numerous paranormal researchers have been killed by various government institutions. Most of these claims are difficult to prove. To date, no television show researchers are known to have been harmed by the government. (A caveat: The government may have threatened them into not talking about it.)

Overview

Charles Fort is the grandfather of paranormal research. Born in 1873, Fort held reservations on the scientific method, noting that scientists tended to argue for theories that upheld their own belief system, and that significant pieces of data are sometimes ignored when they prove to be inexplicable. Fort's interest was in the data that couldn't be explained, which he explored in four volumes: *The Book of the Damned, New Lands, Lo!*, and *Wild Times!*

The supposed Roswell landings gave UFO research a healthy jump-start in the early fifties, and the field retains primacy among paranormal topics to this day. Roger Patterson's 1967 film of Bigfoot was a big event for the field of cryptozoology. (For more about Bigfoot, see p. 168.) The *Star Trek* series and *Time/Life's Mysteries of the Unknown* series helped to further impress the paranormal on the mass consciousness. The seventies sponsored two popular television shows: *Ripley's Believe It or Not*, and Leonard Nimoy's *In Search of*, which is still considered by many to be the greatest paranormal news program in history.

In the nineties, interest in reality-based television programming helped to sponsor a flurry of shows: *Strange Universe*, *Sightings*, *Encounter*, *Paranormal Borderline*, and *Looking Beyond*, to name the more successful. With the demise of *Strange Universe*, mass interest appears to be dropping. Says Steve Nalepa, "Airing five days a week, in a matter of two years,

they covered everything that needed to be done. New topics need to emerge to perk up the field." The turn of the millennium is expected to launch renewed interest in paranormal news.

Practical Information

Professionals advise those of us lacking the good fortune to get propelled 3,000 years into the future or to get abducted by aliens, to get on the Internet. Another starting point is Art Bell's radio program, which with over 350 syndicated markets is the largest syndicated show in the history of radio. Art's show is composed largely of interviews with people who have experienced the paranormal firsthand. At press time, Bell had just quit, but the show will probably continue in one form or another.

A half-dozen magazines are devoted to the subject matter: *Bizarre*, *Fortean Times*, *UFO Magazine*, *Science Digest*, *Omni*, and the *Mutual Unidentified Flying Object Network Newsletter*. *Communion* by Whitley Streiber and *Chariots of the Gods* by Erich Von Daniken are required readings in the book department. The Whole Life Expo is the largest traveling conference focusing on paranormal subject matter. The Expo travels from city to city and is something of a Wal-Mart for the soul—it has a little bit of everything.

Most researchers select a specific subject and go off to uncover what's going on firsthand. The limited earnest research extant in most paranormal fields insures that you can become an expert within a couple years and start marketing your own findings in videos and books.

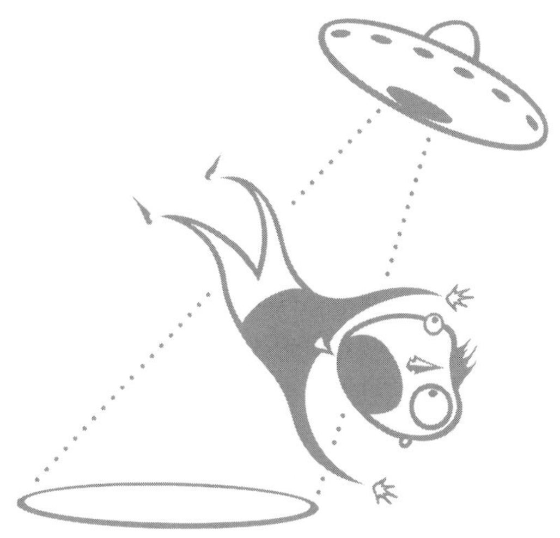

TV Weathercaster

Job description: Study and interpret weather data, deliver extemporaneous forecasts on live TV, and smile.

Compensation: Salaries vary from about $20,000 for working early mornings and weekends in a small market to $200,000 or more for prime-time work in a major city. The major factors in determining pay are time of day and size of audience. Advancement, from mornings to evenings or from small markets to large ones, comes with experience.

Prerequisites: You'll need a bachelor's degree in meteorology or atmospheric or oceanic sciences or equivalent military training to become a member of the American Meteorological Society (AMS) and get their official seal of approval. Most TV weather jobs require this training and certification, but some stations prefer to have a person with a broadcasting background simply present a prepared forecast.

Qualities employer is seeking: Like most positions in broadcasting, the weathercaster job requires an outgoing personality and strong communication skills. The weather is the only part of the news program that isn't scripted—yes, weathercasters ad-lib the entire time—so stations value people who can think on their feet. The people most suited to the job are cool under deadline pressure and practical enough to cut corners when it comes time to get the ready. (Perfectionism has led to more than a few missed cues in this business.)

Perks: In the bigger markets, a weathercaster may be given a clothing allowance and paid trips to the AMS annual meeting. Moreover, successful weathercasters often become local celebrities.

Risks/drawbacks: Broadcasting is not a stable field, and would-be weathercasters usually have to start in small markets with bad hours. Furthermore, advancement for TV meteorologists means a job change every two to three years. On a day-to-day basis, there's always the threat of a Freudian slip or other gaffe raining on the weathercaster's improvisational parade.

Overview

Of the weathermen on TV, 60 percent to 70 percent are trained meteorologists (this group represents less than 9 percent of the American Meteorological Society's members); the rest are anchor or reporter wannabes who present prepared forecasts. Meteorologists who present the weather on television create forecasts by interpreting data provided by private weather companies such as Earthwatch. While the weather information companies provide graphics, most stations like to go for a unique feel, and many meteorologists end up designing their own forecast graphics using special weather-show software.

A primetime weathercaster's day begins at about 1:30 P.M. (almost no one in TV weather gets to work nine to

five), dealing with calls about public appearances. After surveying the available data to get an idea of the weather picture, the weathercaster goes to a news department meeting to brief the news team on the forecast for the next couple of days. The detailed work comes after this meeting. As Bart Adrian, the weekend weathercaster for channel six in Milwaukee, explains it, "Weather forecasting is a two-step process. It involves analysis of the present weather and predictions for the future." The tools at a weathercaster's disposal include surface maps, upper-air maps taken from weather balloons, satellite pictures, radar readings, and the view outside the window. Computer models provided by the National Center for Environmental Prediction do most of the work in predicting what's to come. For the last hour and a half before the forecast, the weathercaster types scripts that describe for the show's director which graphics to use, the video sources to draw from, and the effects needed for the forecast.

In addition to forecasting duties, a weathercaster spends time out in the local community, talking to school groups and promoting his or her station. "It's a position of visibility and responsibility, which allows you a chance to have an impact on a community," says Adrian, who makes the most of the exposure his position affords him. Adrian teaches part-time for the University of Wisconsin, conducts educational tours of the station, and gives talks in high schools around the area. He doesn't mind talking about the weather and takes every opportunity to share his knowledge of the science behind it.

Weather is a booming industry. Looking back on about fifty years of weathercasting, National Weather Service Director Richard Hallgren con-fessed, "I never thought I would live to see a twenty-four-hour-a-day, all-weather channel." Yet, even in this weather-aware age, when people care what's going on in the air, the age-old conflict of style versus substance causes conflict over the future of TV weathercasting. One meteorologist summed up the fears of many in an anonymous Internet posting titled "Broadcasting Trends as Seen by a Mid-Market Meteorologist, or Weatherman's Lament" (found at www.tloffman.com/lament.txt):

> I see two conflicting trends in broadcast meteorology today. As the National Weather Service expands and improves, more and more information becomes available to broadcasters. New generation satellite imagery and Doppler radar data are two primary examples. Quickly, private weather vendors respond with ever more animated and detailed graphical products requiring increasingly knowledgeable on-air interpretations. Meanwhile, however, the broadcast news industry seems headed in the opposite direction—what one might call the "dumbing-down" of the news.

Miami meteorologist Bryan Norcross recalls his decision to go into weather reporting: "It was the most amount of money for the least calories expended of any job in television that I knew."

For people who have yet to start their training, this may mean that the nonmeteorologist route will be your most efficient path to success as a weathercaster. If you intend to use weathercasting as a means of breaking into broadcasting, the best first steps are getting yourself in front of a camera and finding an agent.

Practical Information

Seize every chance for camera time that comes your way. Every station will want to see your resume tape, and many keep tapes on file even when there aren't any current openings. The paradox of needing a tape to get on the air in order to be filmed can be overcome through college classes in broadcasting, which often include taped assignment pieces, and cable access channels, where you can start your own twenty-four-hour weather channel.

The American Meteorological Society Web site (www.ametsoc.org/AMS) has information on journals and newsletters, job postings (though few are related to TV work), descriptions of scholarships, grants, and prizes, and a list of the college meteorology programs across the country (though not recently updated). You can also write to the society at American Meteorological Society, 45 Beacon Street, Boston, MA 02108-3693.

For more focused guidance, check out www.tvweather.com. As the address suggests, it's one-stop shopping for relevant information for budding weathercasters, with information on weather software and educational programs and links to TV stations, Web sites, and online weather map sources.

Radio Contest Winner

Job description: Be caller number seven; win cash and prizes on promotional radio giveaways.

Compensation: During a three-year period leading up to 1992, a sixteen-year-old kid won more than $50,000 in stuff. A woman in Canada won a comparable amount in a single year. For the devoted player, it's impossible to predict winnings; income depends on what the stations are giving away. Just decide before plunging in whether you'd be satisfied earning your hard day's pay in the form of Disney vacations and Blue Oyster Cult tickets.

Prerequisites: All you need is to own a radio and live within range of a large, competitive radio market. These days, many radio stations are accessible over the Internet, making it possible to enter contests around the world. Not much need to worry about long distance charges, either; if the lines aren't busy when you call, you've probably won.

Qualities employer is seeking: Radio contest winners are self-employed. They require self-confidence, almost obsessive determination, a will to deceive, and lots of spare time. An inadequate social life is helpful—as is a telephone with a speedy automatic redial.

Perks: A random assortment of goodies handed to you at every turn: CDs and concert tickets are most common. Stations have given away Porsches, trips around the world, breast augmentation, baskets of erotic toys, and other eclectic treasures—not to mention bags of cash.

Risks/drawbacks: The biggest risk is not winning, though most players pass through the occasional dry spell. Hardcore callers can acquire an unhealthy obsession. In 1995, a computer hacker rigged telephone lines to win contests; he was sentenced to fifty-one months in prison, and had to give back the worth of his prizes: two Porsches, at least $22,000 in cash, and two trips to Hawaii.

Overview

In recent years, competition among radio stations has become fierce, and many stations bait listeners with occasional prize giveaways. Stations estimate that 10 percent to 20 percent of listeners participate in games; the *Toronto Star* reported in 1994 that only 2 percent play. But among those who participate are an elite bunch with patience and devotion sufficient to prevail repeatedly.

During the eighties, the contest frenzy reached a peak, when stations gave away cash for listeners willing to perform loony stunts. One man got hypothermia after schlepping a boat full of piglets across a reservoir in Colorado. For $95, a man in Phoenix marched into a convenience store, barked, purchased a can of dog food, and ate it. In

Denver, a station offered cash to a listener willing to change his or her name to "The New Q103 FM"; forty-nine people rose to the challenge. Two men ate a barbecued leather football to win tickets to the Super Bowl. In 1986, a soap opera actor parachuted onto the field during the infamous sixth game of the World Series; he put in a claim for a $25,000 radio contest prize, but didn't win it because he broke the law.

Too much liability brought an end to the craziness; most stations settled back into a "Be caller number X, and win now!" format, which keeps listeners tuned in until the final moment and opens the game up to anyone willing to make a phone call. A few individuals quickly found ways to improve their chances of winning, however. These "prize pigs" or "contest pigs," as radio management and disc jockeys call them, scan the dials waiting for giveaways, then use speed dial, "demon dialers" (which redial immediately after detecting a busy signal), and other devices to improve their chances of getting through.

Practical Information

The radio contest player knows two nemeses: The dreaded yet ubiquitous busy signal and contest regulations imposed by stations to prevent individuals from winning more than once during a given time period (usually thirty to ninety days).

Among prize pigs lurk a fair number of freaks, of course: obsessive, lonely people who scan several radios at once, using multiple phones to call in. But most players are simply radio listeners who play when given the chance. Even those who win big say the thrill in winning comes from, well, winning, and not from the prize itself.

"I love to hear my name on the air," says Bob Gross, winner of nearly $10,000 in radio prizes. "If you win a radio contest, you're a star for one or two minutes. You're on the air, they're asking you questions, congratulating you. You really feel good about yourself."

An article in *What! A Magazine* describes several tips for winning goodies. The piece stresses frequent but not obsessive listening. The key, instead, is always to play when a game is offered. Other tips emphasize calling fast and hard, redialing instantly upon hearing a busy signal; playing during off hours, while the competition sleeps; and teaming up with friends to use multiple phones to play. Keep stations' numbers by the phone. If it's a trivia-based game, have a set of resources nearby. James Samuel, an avid contestant from New York, tells the story about how he was lucky enough to be the "album rapper" on WPLJ—a contest where the caller would win as many album names as he could recite in ten seconds—but the DJ

suddenly hung up on him when he stumbled while thinking of names on the spot. He called back and got through, this time prepared with a long list of titles, and managed to win seventeen records.

To be the right caller, the article recommends "using the force." Assuming a standard switchboard has four incoming lines, use intuition to calculate how long it takes a DJ to tell premature callers they've lost. One semipro notes that many times the DJ takes his time getting to the winning caller and that being persistent (calling even after you're sure the DJ has found a winner) pays off.

Other experts suggest avoiding small-time prizes (which may block you from winning larger booty); offering the names of friends in case you do win more than once in the allotted time period; and keeping good track of what games regularly occur all across the dial. Also be aware of seasonal "sweeps period," certain times of the year when ratings are monitored, when promoters are most anxious to woo audiences.

With those tips in hand, anyone has a sporting chance of winning on the radio. The games are open to all (with certain age restrictions), and prizes often vary enough to sate all sorts of hungers. "I don't buy anything ever," contest pig Matt Legg told the *Chicago Tribune*. "I win everything I need." Oh, and before tucking into that sweet trip to Hawaii, remember to set aside a pool for the tax man; the IRS wins every time you do, taking a chunk of all prize winnings over $600.

Voice-over Actor

Job description: Sway public opinion and consumer preference by narrating TV and radio commercials or make a play for cult status by delivering voice mail instructions.

Compensation: As in any profession based on performance, payment varies with the artist's experience and affiliations, the requirements and location of the job, and the number of times the work is used. Members of the American Federation of Television and Radio Artists (AFTRA) can rely on minimum payment levels determined by the union. For example, solo appearances in recorded radio commercials start at $200 per session, and a solo appearance in a network television commercial for unlimited use over a thirteen-week season pays $1,215.40. Meanwhile, freelance artists starting out on their own may have to take whatever's offered. Lary Lewman, a political commercial specialist who found fame as the voice of President Carter's 1980 reelection campaign, says the select group of heavy-hitters each take in over $1 million per year doing commercial work for national markets.

Prerequisites: Beau Weaver, voice of Dr. Reed Richards, aka "Mr. Fantastic," leader of The Fantastic Four, and countless commercial spots, boils down the requirements succinctly: "To compete in this arena, you need (1) a killer demo tape, (2) representation by one of the top agents, and (3) the ability to audition well." Lewman puts things in slightly more subtle terms, saying that successful voice-over announcers need "a certain amount of equanimity, strong interpretation skills, and sensitivity to the language." Both agree that acting ability matters more than the natural beauty of one's voice. "People who have beautiful voices are not necessarily voice-over performers. I think of voice-over performers as extraordinarily skillful interpretive readers," says Lewman.

Qualities employer is seeking: Voice-over actors have to know what their clients want, even when the clients can't tell them.

Perks: Once you've made it, you can sit back and appreciate being in charge of your schedule, working without extensive preparation, and leaving your work in the studio at quitting time. "You have more leisure time than most," says Lewman, relishing his mastery of a tough business.

Risks/drawbacks: When you've made it as a voice-over actor, you've really made it. Until then, you'll risk poverty, while competing strenuously for work. "It's enormously difficult to get enough customers to make a living. It's the same problem actors have. It's hard thinking of yourself as a performer when you have trouble getting paid," Lewman laments.

Overview

From the mellifluous tones of James Earl Jones to Mr. MovieFone's zealous previews, many of the commercial ploys that demand our attention are brought to life by a group of hardworking actors who rarely see the spotlight (unless, of course, they came from the spotlight in the first place). The work takes concentration and a subtle ear for the nuances of delivery, but little preparation before the recording. While Lewman says he generally reads each piece seven or eight times, there are magic moments when the commercial is done on the second try, as well as tedious twenty-take sessions. During his busy season, August through October in election years, Lewman works as many as twelve hours a day. Voice-over announcers not fortunate enough to have in-home recording studios can clock up to fifteen hours a day with commuting—if they're lucky enough to be working on several projects at once.

In general, voice-over announcers come from acting or broadcasting. Each route has its advantages, and trying both may be the best way to get the training you need while earning enough to afford the groceries you need. "It's a lot easier for actors to make the transition than it is for broadcasters," Weaver believes. "Spoken word is not primarily about having a good voice. It's storytelling with a point of view. It has more to do with attitude and emotion than voice quality." On the other hand, Lewman explains, "Radio and TV are good places to be, because the work is regular."

Despite their lower recognition factor, voice-over spots can be as difficult to win as on-screen parts. As a voice-over actor, you'll compete against Broadway actors who do it as a money-making sideline, celebrities who take much of the lucrative work because of their familiar voices, and any other struggling actor who's decided that making money without having to look like a Barbie doll would be a good thing. "What's seductive about my profession is that a voice-over actor can make a living on a couple projects a week. However, it's hard to get a couple projects a week. There are a lot of people soliciting the work, and everybody wants to find the high end," explains Lewman, who teaches a workshop for AFTRA and Screen Actors Guild (SAG) members on voice-over announcing and sees the large numbers of actors who want to broaden their range of potential parts.

Practical Information

For tips on developing your skills, check out *Word of Mouth: A Guide to Commercial Voice-over Excellence*, by Susan Blu and Molly Ann Mullin (Pomegranate Press). There are also acting teachers who specialize in coaching voice-over talent. Weaver highly recommends that "you do whatever it takes to get yourself into a seminar taught by nationally renowned coach Marice Tobias.... Though her waiting list is sometimes long, she also produces some of the best voice-over demos in the country. She is expensive,

and worth it."You can request a schedule of Tobias's classes by writing to Tobias Communications, P.O. Box 15396, Beverly Hills, CA 90209-1396.

"It's the best job in America if you can get it," voice-over actor Lary Lewman once told the *Wall Street Journal*. "Hell, man, it's like taking candy from babies."

Don't be discouraged by the competitive nature of the business. If you think voice-over work is for you, there are steps you can take to give yourself a leg up in the business. If you're really serious, moving to one of the major voice-over markets—New York, Los Angeles, or Chicago—will increase your chance of making a living as a voice-over actor. People do build careers in other markets, but they depend heavily on particular local industries, such as the political work found in the Washington, D.C. area.

Next, you'll need to make a demo tape and find yourself an agent. "On a demo tape, I'd tell people to give examples of about six different things they can do. Send the tape with a cover note, not a resume. And don't send a picture. If you do, you'll be typed by your appearance even though it's what you can do with your voice that should count," advises voice-over artist Barbara Rosenblatt. Most of the major talent agencies in New York and Los Angeles represent voice talent. Ironically, finding an agent to represent you usually requires finding someone else to represent you to the agent. You'll need to get your demo tape noticed by a commercial producer to get in the door, and that means finding any work you can to amass samples and gather contacts. Work that will qualify you for membership in the unions is especially helpful. Check out the Web sites of SAG (www.sag.com) and AFTRA (www.aftra.org/home.html) for details on qualifying for membership. AFTRA, an affiliate of the AFL-CIO, is particularly strong within this subset of the acting trade, especially for actors looking to do commercial announcing.

13 Food for Thought

Ice Cream Flavor Developer

Wedding Cake Chef

Army Food Technologist

Brewmaster

Restaurant Critic

Sommelier

Professor at Hamburger University

Ice Cream Flavor Developer

Job description: Taste and evaluate lots and lots of ice cream. Lots.

Compensation: According to a representative of the University of Wisconsin's Center for Dairy Research, first-year "research specialists" earn between $25,000 and $35,000; senior specialists earn more than $50,000. Experienced flavor developers at larger companies can earn more, depending on their skill, education, and other applicable talents (e.g., public relations). "Food production" workers (those more involved with hands-on ice cream production) earn between $15 and $22 per hour.

Prerequisites: A dairy science or food science degree is a good place to start; it's easier to evaluate ice cream if you know something about how the product is made. Beyond that, ample tongue training is key. Practice makes perfect.

Qualities employer is seeking: Sensitive, evaluative taste buds; an understanding of what ice cream should taste like, and what appeals to the general public; creativity and vision for helping out with product development; and a bright smile and ability to deal with the media.

Perks: Orgiastic portions of ice cream whenever you want it. (For a less sweet culinary job, see "Army Food Technologist," p. 224.)

Risks/drawbacks: The worst that could happen to John Harrison, official taste tester for Edy's/Dreyer's Grand Ice Cream, is that his taste buds cease to serve his company's purpose. Just in case, the company insures his tongue for $1 million, at an annual premium of about $5,000. "Since this is our only product," he explains, "the company saw my ability as an asset. It's like a key man insurance policy; it's someone holding the keys to our company."

Overview

For fans of ice cream, it's the ultimate job: get paid to eat ice cream. The job of an ice cream flavor developer/taster is more complicated than it sounds, though. John Harrison, probably the best known taster in the nation—and as much a spokesman as a master taster—performs his daily deeds drawing on ice cream expertise dating back to his childhood. "Ice cream is my expertise," says the seventeen-year veteran. "I could discern different flavor notes in wine, but I don't have the expertise. With ice cream, I know the product backward and forwards. I know every product, and I know its flavor." Harrison speaks obsessively about his taste buds; he knows his own tongue as a painter knows his oils. "I do not drink or smoke, and I stay away from onions or garlic. Friday night, I'll sometimes let my hair down and have a little pepper on my pizza." The $1 million insurance policy on his tongue seems extreme, and it may be partly for show. But Harrison can't imagine what he'd do without his buds:

"If I were to lose my ability to taste the top notes, it would be devastating. It happened eight years ago. I was traveling, and I got a cold. I was prescribed antibiotics that lopped off the top 15 to 20 percent of my taste. I couldn't work for quite a while."

"What if the strawberries have yeast and mold? What if you have a little spoil? It can get all the way up to putrefaction," says John Harrison, official taster for Grand Ice Cream.

Most ice cream flavor positions entail a combination of quality control, product development, training sales people on new flavors and products, and touring the country. "I buy back about $200 to $300 worth of our product," says Harrison. "I'm tasting the ice cream right at the grocery store, making sure the packaging, ingredients, and taste is the same quality."

Harrison works anywhere between forty and sixty hours per week. He spends about four to five hours each day eating ice cream. His average day starts early in the morning, at about 7 A.M. "I taste all of yesterday's ice cream flavors." Ice cream tasters rarely ingest the product; they only taste it, using all parts of the mouth. First, one checks the vanilla. Then, following a thorough palate cleansing with lukewarm water or an unsalted cracker, it's on to the fruitier products. Last, come the "bordeaux" flavors, the richer fudges and chocolates. You'd think he'd want to vomit at the slightest mention of ice cream by now, but he claims still to love the stuff.

As would any connoisseur of food or drink, an ice cream taster needs to wield a range of descriptive lingo to pinpoint just what's going on with the product. "We talk about bouquet, top notes, aroma, body, texture, appearance, that type of language. We all initially eat with our eyes, so color is very important; strawberry should be red. Number two is flavor, and there we look for balance, between dairy ingredient, sugar, and flavoring. Last, we look at body and texture. Cold, coarse, gummy, fluffy, sneezy, grumpy—that's what I'm looking for. All three are equally weighted. It's similar to wine-tasting, except when you start detecting defects."

Part of the challenge of flavor developing is combining flavors to offer new gustatory thrills, though not always through rigorous lab science. Consider how Harrison came up with Cookies & Cream: "I was in the parlor, eating my usual bowl of vanilla with some cookies on my plate," he reminisces. "Then I thought, why don't I save a step? I put the cookie in the ice cream. It was good. I gave it to marketing, but they filed it away, saying it was too much of a kids' flavor. That summer we were scheduled to make Perfectly Peach ice cream, but there was a freak hailstorm, ruining peach crops. So marketing pulled up the file, and now it's the fourth most popular flavor in the country."

Practical Information

The best way to find out about job openings in ice cream tasting is to contact companies directly. Harrison estimates there are approximately 500 ice cream companies in America, and so, presumably, at least 500 tasters. (As an example, Edy's/Dreyer's employs a number-one taster and back-up taster in each of its six plants.) Some companies enlist members of the public to comprise a nationwide focus group. Edy's/Dreyer's sometimes offers a contest to find tasters and flavor developers for its products. Check out the company's Web site at www.edys.com for more information.

Wedding Cake Chef

Job description: Bake and decorate wedding cakes. The job involves guiding the couple in their selection, from the planning stages to delivering the finished product on the day of the ceremony.

Compensation: The pay varies depending on whether one works in a commercial bakery or is a self-employed home baker. Bakers who are just starting out in the business will most likely make between $7 and $10 per hour. Individual home bakers tend to charge somewhere between $1.50 and $7 per slice, depending on the flavor of the cake and the intricacy of the decorations.

Prerequisites: Some formal training coupled with demonstrated hands-on experience. Many bakery owners administer on-site tests as part of the hiring procedure. "I usually say, 'Here are pictures of three different borders, do them,'" says Sandra Harrison of Cakes of Elegance, in Texas. "Someone who knows what they're doing will recognize the different borders—lattice, scrolls, swags, garlands—and will use the right icing bag and tip, apply the right pressure and know how quickly to move across the cake."

Qualities employer is seeking: An innate knowledge of cake fillings, frosting, and icing. Wedding cake chefs need to have "the nerves of an ER technician, the tact

of a therapist, and a bottomless affection for brides and grooms," writes *Seattle Times* reporter David Berger.

Perks: Constantly sharing in joyous family celebrations; churning out creations with names like "For the Love of Lemon" and "Tiers of Joy."

Risks/drawbacks: For most brides and grooms, the wedding cake is the centerpiece of the cherished and carefully orchestrated reception. Poor planning (resulting in no cake) or less-than-precise baking and cake construction (resulting in an ugly cake or one that falls apart) can be catastrophic.

Overview

The wedding cake chef's job begins with an initial consultation with the wedding participants. The first issue that's usually addressed is whether the cake will be an elaborate, colorful concoction or a more staid, traditional white cake with few frills. This discussion can lead quickly to consensus or disagreements that last for hours. According to Jeneva Remson, a wedding cake chef in Maryland, the dialogue between spouses at this consultation is almost eerily consistent. "It's real funny how it works," says Ms. Remson. "They'll look through all the books, and we'll put little markings on the ones that they both like, and she'll go, 'Which ones do you like?' and he'll go, 'Oh it doesn't matter it's your cake,' and she says, 'No no no, tell me which one you like,' and he shows her the one he likes and she goes, 'Ew, you like that one?' I mean almost always, and then he'll close the book and he'll go, 'I told you to pick it out, you pick out the one you like.' So it's real cute—sometimes the groom is in charge when he comes in, but usually it's her decision."

Most of the actual baking, such as creating the vanilla or chocolate circular sponge cakes that serve as the cores for most cakes, is usually done on the Thursday before the wedding. Friday is generally the day for decorating. This is where experience and artistic skills are paramount. Cake chefs have to know which of hundreds of different icing bag tips is appropriate for each kind of cake, as well as knowing when and how to use any of the following utensils: star cutters, hot-glue guns, green florist's tape, veining tools, and so on. The chef may also have to get appropriate small figurines, fresh flowers, or any other desired trinkets to serve as decorating flourishes.

Wedding cake chefs are frequently called upon to create nontraditional cakes for couples who want something more personalized—they may be asked to make a cake in the likeness of a cherished pet, a favorite automobile or boat, or any other sort of inanimate object (a haystack cake for farmers, say, or one in the shape of a hydrant for firefighters). Some of these original creations may be artistically challenging, and therefore, exciting; others may strike the chef as tacky and in poor taste. Steven Schultz, a baker in Maine, says he's happy to make any kind of cake, as long it's not pornographic or potentially insulting.

"One of the philosophical guidances of my business," says Schultz, "is whatever the bride wants is what the bride gets, no matter how hideously ugly I think it may be. It's not my wedding so I'm willing to do pretty much anything they want."

"Somebody knocked one over once," says Los Angeles pastry and wedding cake chef Donald Wressel. "I put the cake in the room. There were some waiters, and the band was warming up. One of the waiters said the saxophone player hit a high C and the cake fell over, but I thought he was pulling my leg. Fortunately, it was before the party entered the room, so I quickly got the cake and rebuilt it while they were in the cocktail reception. Then I just put it in when people were looking for their seats. And no one really knew that it had happened."

The most perilous part of the cake-making process is the actual delivery. Stories abound about cakes collapsing when the minivan bounced off the curb, or frosting melting due to improper cooling in sun-drenched vehicles. Even those cakes that are trucked in pieces and then assembled on the premises can be a challenge. All wedding cake chefs need to have a vast knowledge of how different kinds of cakes and cake support mechanisms (including wooden dowels and foam-core boards) behave under pressure. "A wedding cake must be very sturdy to stand throughout a long wedding without toppling when the happy couple finally cuts it," writes Colette Peters in her book *Colette's Wedding Cakes*. "A multilayered wedding cake is actually a magnificent piece of engineering."

Practical Information

There is no prescribed way to become a wedding cake chef. Some in the business may have a bushel of impressive certificates from baking and cake-making schools while others may have learned the ropes through trial and error or by spending time working as an assistant to an experienced baker. In general, most wedding cake chefs end up working in one of two capacities: the first is as an employee at a commercial baking establishment. Getting one of these jobs will frequently require proven skills and experience. The second is as a home baker, which may be an excellent choice for someone who wishes to have a moderate source of income while generally being able to stay at home, perhaps to spend more time with one's family.

Jeneva Remson suggests that would-be home bakers offer to make cakes for local events. This can be good practice

and can serve to promote one's work. "You usually have to start by just giving away cakes," says Ms. Remson. "You are invited to a baby shower, an office party, a going-away party and you say, 'Oh, can I bring the cake?' The next thing you know people are calling and asking if they can buy cakes from you." (Ms. Remson, who started her home business this way, eventually met a local caterer, and the two began working on weddings and special events together.)

One of the largest organizations in cake making and decorating is Wilton Industries, located in Woodridge, Illinois. Through a broad, national network of supermarkets and department stores (many of which carry Wilton's popular cake-making equipment), the company offers local courses in how to bake and properly decorate cakes. For more information on finding a course in a particular area, visit the company's Web site (www.wilton.com), which has a Wilton course search engine. The company also offers more in-depth courses at its site in Illinois. (The master course is two weeks long and costs $600; a course in advance gum paste lasts four days and costs $100; a course in lettering or rolled fondant takes one day and costs $70.)

There are a number of books and magazines on the subject of making cakes. *The Wedding Cake Book*, by Dede Wilson, has thirty recipes with detailed, step-by-step instructions and color photographs of each. *American Cake Magazine* is published six times per year, and has articles on many baking and cake decorating subjects. (Call 703-430-2356 or visit www.cakemag.com, which has an online order form—a subscription is $19—as well as reprints of recent pieces.)

Finally, one of the best ways to find work and to distinguish oneself is to become highly skilled in a particular niche of wedding cake baking or decoration—as with many professions, rare areas of expertise can command premiums. Mark St. Charles, a pastry chef in Wisconsin, for example, is an expert in liquefying chocolate and molding it into elaborate cake toppers. Steven Schultz shuns using inedible natural flowers and instead practices the craft—common in Europe although still relatively rare in the United States—of making realistic flowers with handmade sugar clay. "I try to reproduce the actually botany of the flowers," says Mr. Schultz, "as closely as possible to nature—with the various flower petals, stamens, sepals. It's painstaking work, but they are extremely beautiful once they are created." In addition to boosting his own traditional cake-making business because of his highly regarded flower-making skills, Schultz also ships these sugared creations to other bakers throughout the United States.

Army Food Technologist

Job description: Create, for soldiers' consumption, scientifically packaged meals and snacks that will remain unspoiled ("shelf-stable"), nutritious, and hopefully tasty, even after several years of storage at high temperatures

Compensation: The pay scale for army food technologists tends to mirror that of food scientists in general. Entry-level wages hover in the mid-twenties; technologists with master's degrees may earn in the high thirties; and experienced senior managers can earn salaries in the upper forties or lower fifties.

Prerequisites: Requirements vary with the position; most food technologists have degrees in food science, food nutrition, or in a related scientific field (chemistry, physics, microbiology, botany, or any other life science). Those who are interested in the field but don't have any suitable degrees can start out as food technicians and work their way up the ladder.

Qualities employer is seeking: A good culinary sense, as well as patience and attention to detail. Food technologists frequently conduct experiments to test and document the effect of minute changes in ingredients. For example, adding just enough salt to a shelf-stable bread to keep it from spoiling, without putting so much in that it kills the yeast, resulting in mush.

Perks: The small, patriotic rush that comes from knowing you're "doing your part" for the men and women in uniform. Getting to play with food.

Risks/drawbacks: After long periods of development, food items are tested by focus groups of field soldiers, who rate the product on a scale of one ("dislike extremely") to nine ("like extremely"). Low ratings can halt a project's development, make months and sometimes years of tests entirely moot, and generally be a real downer.

Overview

There are about one and a half million active-duty personnel in the U.S. Armed Forces. In the event of war or military action, all of them must still eat. Several dozen Army food technologists, located in a government-sponsored lab in Natick, Massachusetts, develop the rations for these soldiers. ("We do something for the warfighter every day" is the lab's motto.) Technically part of the Sustainability Directorate of the U.S. Army Soldier Systems Command, these workers use freezers, ovens, microwave freeze-driers, centrifuges, test tubes, and beer-barrel-sized pressure cookers to refine the so-called MREs, or "meals ready to eat," which became the predominant military food unit in the early 1980s.

These food pouches, which currently include meals ranging from beef teriyaki to Jamaican pork chops with noodles, must, according to military specifications, be able to last three years at eighty

degrees Fahrenheit. Researchers, however, routinely test new food ideas by subjecting them to an accelerated test of four weeks at 120 degrees—which quickly makes apparent any spoiling tendencies of the ingredients.

On almost a daily basis, different panels convene to taste test meals in development. The "consumer panel" consists of pretty much anyone who works at the Natick lab. "The consumer tests are the first gate that an item goes through in ensuring its acceptance in the field," says Dr. Cardello, who works in the Natick lab. The "technical panel" usually consists only of the food technologists themselves. In the most important final evaluation, the so-called "fail test," products are hauled out of the labs and brought out to field soldiers in real-life conditions.

Professional statisticians administer the fail tests, inquiring about a potential meal's odor, appearance, flavor, and texture. Among the entrées that recently made it up to the fail test stage only to receive low enough ratings to halt development are chicken à la king, tuna noodle casserole, and potatoes au gratin. Although the food technologists aren't criticized if their creations are deemed unacceptable, most naturally find it extremely satisfying when one of their projects is a success. Michelle Richardson, one of the lab's food technologists, has been working for several years on the development of shelf-stable sandwiches, like barbecue chicken, peanut butter and jelly, and grilled cheese. "The barbecue chicken is having its fail test this year, so I'm keeping my fingers crossed," says Richardson. "It feels bad when they don't like something, even though you know you can't please all the people all the time."

"People don't realize how we try to please the soldiers," says Agnes Russell, a food technician at the lab in Massachusetts. "They like Mom's home cooking. It's hard to get that in a pouch. We do the next best thing."

Most of the MREs are encased in trilaminate foil packaging that contains small, oxygen-absorbing iron packets to prevent rancid chemical reactions from taking place—moisture and oxygen, in particular, can wreak havoc on food in short periods of time. The foods are also thermostabilized—cooked at 250 degrees under pressure to kill bacteria so that no refrigeration is required. Even these highly refined techniques are not always flawless. Many foods lose their natural flavor and texture under such extreme conditions; others undergo extreme darkening (a phenomenon known as "nonenzymatic Maillard browning reaction"), which may not affect taste but may render a ration aesthetically unattractive, and therefore, not usable.

Perhaps the highest achievement an army food technologist can garner is when a menu idea becomes so successful that it migrates beyond the confines

of the military and eventually ends up as a commercially available food—freeze-dried coffee, granola bars, Tang, and noodles that can be cooked instantly in a cup were all first conceived in the Natick labs.

Practical Information

The section of the Natick lab that focuses on food and rations consists of about 100 employees, of which some are interns, some are food technologists, and some are food technicians; the latter position requires less prerequisite coursework or experience, but it commands a slightly lower starting salary. The labs run on a flex schedule, so employees work any eight hours between 6:30 A.M. and 6 P.M.. For those who want to pursue advanced degrees in food science, the department frequently foots part of the bill.

Over time, many of the Natick workers gravitate toward one specialty. Some may focus on developing more effective packaging or food sterilization techniques. Others concentrate on the food itself. "People specialize in such things as fat and oils, meat, fish, different fermentation activities, some will specialize in dairy products," says Dan Berkowitz, the recently retired senior food technologist who is frequently credited with dramatically increasing the acceptability of army food. (It was under Berkowitz's watch that a shelf-stable bread finally got the green light for production.) The atmosphere at Natick is highly team-oriented: A beef expert teaming up with a vegetable expert to focus on developing a stew or casserole is a routine kind of collaboration.

To inquire about positions available in the Natick labs, contact U.S. Army Soldier Systems Command; Research, Development, and Engineering Center; Kansas Street; Natick, MA 01760-5012 (508-233-4000). The organization also has an informative Web site (www.sscom.army.mil), replete with recent press releases and archived copies of the army-sponsored *Warrior* magazine. Another useful resource is the army's Civilian Personnel Online site (www.cpol.army.mil), which offers information for job-seekers, discussion groups, and an electronic resume-submittal option. (For a different kind of food development job—one that would certainly keep an army traveling on its stomach—see "Ice Cream Flavor Developer," p. 218.)

Brewmaster

Job description: Create recipes for, brew, ferment, and store beer; oversee production at brewing facilities; select brewing ingredients; set quality specifications; evaluate beer through taste, smell, and color; maintain and sanitize brewery equipment.

Compensation: Inexperienced brewers earn about $20,000. A typical head brewer in a midsized city microbrewery can earn $30,000 to $60,000. Brewers in large companies can earn as much as $80,000 to $130,000, but there are very few six-figure brewers out there. A side benefit for brewers in any tax bracket is access to free beer, the monetary value of which could range from a few hundred dollars annually up to perhaps $5,000 (although at this level, the ability to hold any job at all would be called into question).

Prerequisites: Brewing school is a big plus, though not absolutely necessary. (Fraternity membership in college does not count.) Knowledge of chemistry and engineering is a must.

Qualities employer is seeking: A brewer must be willing to do manual labor, especially in the small breweries where the brewmaster makes the beer and cleans the tanks. Mechanical skills are essential—if the equipment breaks down in a small brewery, there are no "repairmen." A brewmaster must have good PR skills and marketing savvy—responding to the needs of the market is just as important as the quality of the beer. A good brewer also has a creative flair for recipes. A passion for the drink goes without saying: "I haven't met a brewer who isn't curious full-time about beer," says David Grinnell, manager of brewery operations of Boston Beer Company, which brews Samuel Adams. That said, statements along the lines of "I can chug brewskies with the best of them" or "Dude, I live for beer and beer alone" are not likely to score points with a potential employer.

Perks: Free beer—see "Compensation." Great diversity within job—a day on the job can include going to farms and choosing grain, formulating recipes, tasting brews, fixing machinery, and cleaning out vats.

Risks/drawbacks: According to the Institute of Brewing Studies (IBS), the recent beer boom has leveled off, making jobs scarce and competitive. Working with alcohol can lead to an unhealthy or undecorous lifestyle featuring weight gain, unseemly belching, or even alcoholism. Driving home from work can be dangerous or illegal.

Overview

While it's doubtful that there has ever been a period in human history when beer was unpopular, craft brewing only began to boom in the United States in the last decade or so. Suddenly, the beer sections in liquor stores started offering a daunting variety of domestic craft

brews. Americans turned on to bocks, stouts, pale ales, hefeweizen, and even fruity lagers. Brewpubs opened everywhere, in cities and small towns. The sales of home brewing kits, which became legal in 1979, have hit all-time highs. By 1995 the craft brewing industry had become a $2 billion business. While that's only a fraction of the U.S.'s $50 billion beer industry, gaining even a small slice of this huge market has proved lucrative for new brewers.

"I really sometimes giggle my ass off when I'm walking around the brewery thinking about how much fun I'm having," says Eric Savage, brewmaster at Dock Street in Philadelphia, evidently taking full advantage of the nonmonetary perks of his job. "I really enjoy what I'm doing."

With the beer boom, more people became interested in making brewing a profession, and more opportunities arose to break into the business. The traditional path of brewing school is no longer a necessity. Aspiring brewers can now gain experience by homebrewing, apprenticing in microbreweries, or by working in brewpubs (a combination restaurant and bar that brews its own beer). Eric Savage, a former musician, started brewing as a hobby. "I really fell in love with it. I saw there was an industry in creating great beer. I started to beg the only local brewery for a job or an apprenticeship, and they said no. Finally I cornered the brewmaster here and said, 'I want to be a brewmaster, how do I do it?' And he said, 'We don't hire from off the street here, but if you want to bartend at the restaurant and work during the day for free, you can.'" Savage took him up on his offer, helping in the brewery part of the restaurant during his off-hours. He says it was an invaluable experience.

David Grinnell of Boston Beer Company didn't follow the straight and narrow career path to brewing, either. "I studied art history at Columbia, and was always interested in food and cooking and all the neat stuff that goes into putting flavors together." He took a summer job at the New Amsterdam Brewery, which was then in Manhattan. "It changed the direction of my life," he says. When that brewery closed, he snapped up an opportunity to help build the brewery up in Boston where he still works today.

While a day on the job may consist of sitting around and sampling beers, it's actually a small (albeit fun and also important) part of what a brewmaster does. A brewmaster chooses the grains, malts, hops, and yeast according to budget allowances. Then, after sanitizing the equipment—which is incredibly important to stave off bacteria that can ruin the beer—the brewing process begins.

Once a batch is finished, the brewmaster evaluates it. To do this, a brewer

must have an experienced, beer-honed palate. "If you're not ready to drink, you're not ready to brew," Savage says. Beer is evaluated according to taste (for flavor), touch (for body and feel in mouth), smell (first indication if a batch has gone bad), and appearance (color, clarity, head). While perfecting a recipe, a good brewmaster must always keep on the cutting edge of beer trends. "Every brewer I know is thinking about making the next beer, thinking about the next recipe," Grinnell says. "A lot of brewers are interested in beer history—there are a lot of extinct but interesting beer styles. There's been a creative frenzy for fifteen years of brewers investigating historical styles."

Both Savage and Grinnell note the growing competitiveness in the beer selling—and job—market. "Once you did business by virtue of being a microbrewery," Savage says. "Now lots of people have gotten into it and not everyone has produced great beers....There are too many of them and the quality has been diluted a little bit. Now you have to be good and aggressive to stay alive." While this is true, the IBS predicts the decline in boutique brewing will be a slow process that will eventually separate the chaff from quality quaff.

Practical Information

Aspiring brewers can volunteer to be apprentices, work in the restaurants of brewpubs while observing or helping out with brewing responsibilities, or attend a brewing school. The country's best schools include The Siebel Institute of Technology (773-279-0966; www.siebel institute.com), which has been teaching brewing practices for over 100 years and offers several programs for all different levels; and the American Brewers Guild (800-636-1331; www.abgbrew.com), which has an eleven-week craft brewer apprenticeship program. The Association of Brewers (303-447-0816; www.aob.org) has tons of information for both professionals and amateurs.

The New Brewer, which is published bimonthly by the Institute of Brewing Studies, a subsidiary of the Association of Brewers, can help you learn more about brewing. Other industry magazines include *Ale Street News* (www.alestreet news.com), which focuses primarily on microbreweries, brewpubs, and homebrewing, and *Beer: The Magazine,* which covers a broad spectrum of the whole industry, from choosing hops to marketing strategies. For books, check out *Beer for Dummies,* by Marty Nachel; *The New Complete Joy of Homebrewing,* by Charlie Papazian; and *A Textbook of Brewing,* by Jean De Clerck (which the Siebel Institute calls "the most relevant treatise available to the brewer").

To see the industry in action, crash the Great American Beer Festival, held each year in late September or early October in Boulder, Colorado, or the National Craftbrewers Conference and Trade Show, held each spring.

Restaurant Critic

Job description: Use your taste buds to influence the dining choices of the masses. Visit two to five restaurants a week, sample thirty to forty percent of the menu while remaining discreet about your objectives (no easy feat), and write critical reviews that evaluate food, service, decor, and value.

Compensation: The pay varies according to the size and location of the paper you're writing for—on average, from $25,000 to $75,000 per year. Most papers allow you to "expense" your "research" (read: free meals).

Prerequisites: A passion for food and a knowledge of culinary standards are needed. If you're the kind of person who thinks "Well, a burger is a burger, salad is salad, and shrimp is, well, shrimp," then you ought to look elsewhere; you need to be somewhat discriminating.

Qualities employer is seeking: Ability to eat, evaluate what you're eating, and write about it in a compelling manner within a given deadline.

Perks: The chance to write sentences like "The sea scallops were marvelously succulent, daringly served on a ribald bed of mashed bliss potatoes." Also, the chance to put on funny disguises to ensure that restaurants don't recognize you and pay special attention to you.

Risks/drawbacks: You can gain weight fast; having to wade through extravagant five-course meals when all you want is to cuddle up with some macaroni and cheese.

"I do a really good job of trying to keep (my appearance) under wraps," says Dennis Getto, restaurant critic for the *Milwaukee Journal Sentinel*. "I don't get into the big Hollywood stuff, but I will put a beard on."

Overview

"I had a respectable job. I was making real money. Every month my name appeared in print. I was even starting to write food articles for magazines in New York. Did this impress my parents? Not in the least. 'Food!' said my mother disdainfully, 'All you do is write about food,'" Ruth Reichl, the former restaurant critic of the *New York Times*, and now the editor of *Gourmet,* writes in her memoir. Writing about food eventually led Reichl to become the most famous restaurant critic in the United States; her whim could make or break a New York restaurant. "She's pretty much the word in New York," Bill Bruckman, a managing partner at Pietro's, told the *New York Observer*. When Reichl wrote that she ate "the single best steak I have had in New York" at that restaurant, the crowds poured in—and the restaurant ran out of beef.

How does one become a restaurant critic? Reichl spent years working with food in various capacities, as a waitress, chef, and caterer, when a loyal customer of her days cooking at a California collective called up and asked her: "Do you write as well as you cook?" Reichl had no idea, but she was certainly willing to give it a shot, and that's how she landed her first reviewing job with a San Francisco magazine.

Dennis Getto, restaurant critic for the *Milwaukee Journal Sentinel,* started out working five hours a week. "I got to go to one restaurant, with one other person, once, and then write a review," he says of his responsibilities at the time. But when the full-time critic moved to Oregon, "twelve of us applied, and they sent us all to the same restaurant.... In the restaurant, we were all bumping into each other." The paper chose three out of the twelve, and sent them out again. "They sent us to a Vietnamese place. I did a lot of research on Vietnamese food, wrote the review, and I got the job." Getto estimates that he owns 250 to 300 cookbooks, which he feels are essential for what he does. He's also taken classes from the likes of Julia Child, Jacques Pépin, and Hugh Carpenter. "It's important to me that I know how the food's made and what it should taste like. It's important that I be as authoritative as I can."

"I've always been involved in cooking," Getto continues. "My mother taught me to cook when I was six.... I was cooking for the family by nine. I grew up eating snails, squid, a lot of things that are part of a Calabrese diet. My friends didn't even know what these things were."

Patricia Mack, food editor at the *Bergen Record* newspaper in Hackensack, NJ, uses freelance reviewers in addition to reviewing herself. "Basically, you have to love eating and really enjoy food—that's primary. [Also key] is knowledge about what the standard is. You really need to understand what wonderful food is and have some measure to see where various restaurants fall. You need to understand the philosophy of food,

Credit: Dennis Getto

Like most restaurant critics, Dennis Getto, of the *Milwaukee Journal Sentinel,* dines incognito to avoid special treatment.

why the food is good, what goes with what, and why it works and what the logic behind it is. That takes not so much scholarship but eating a lot, and eating at a lot of good places."

While the job certainly has ample perks, there are a few drawbacks. Mack cited "evaluating someone's business" as the biggest downer. "Often people who truly believe they're doing a wonderful job are putting their heart and soul into [a restaurant], and here you are telling thousands of people that they just don't measure up. When you know you're giving someone a bad review, you bleed all over the page. We double-check when it's a really bad review, and we send out an independent reviewer to make sure that it just hasn't been a couple of bad nights."

Getto agrees. "As a restaurant critic, I really do want to see most restaurants succeed, especially with people who are putting out a lot of effort," he says. "If I'm going to be really hard on a restaurant, I'll try to go out of my way to give them every break I can, sometimes a third, fourth, and fifth visit. But that doesn't deter me from criticizing the place if it's not good." Then there are the threats. "I had one restaurant owner who [after a bad review] accused me of accepting $5,000 from another restaurateur. Another one went all the way to the chairman of the board to get me fired." Getto adds, "I haven't been beaten up but I've had three places who threatened to throw me out bodily if I ever showed up again." Getto adds "weight gain" as another side effect of the job. "Mimi Sheraton [former *New York Times* food critic] stormed out of the *New York Times,* eventually saying, 'I need to lose weight!' It's a manner of restraint. One of my mentors once told me I was starting to put on weight. He said to me, 'Look, you're a taster, eat one bite of everything.'"

Mack adds food poisoning to the list of job hazards. "I think I've had food poisoning," she says. "It's a technical call. You have to go to the hospital and be tested to know for sure, but I can almost bet that that's what came from those clams I ate in that restaurant."

And then there's the need to be discreet, so as not to tip off restaurant staff that you're a big shot reviewer; this is where the disguises come in. According

to the *New York Observer*, Ruth Reichl tries to be inconspicuous and "never complains about the food to a waiter. She makes someone else in her party order the wine. She tries not to look the staff in the eye." She avoids wearing flashy jewelry or even going to the bathroom. "It's just one more chance to be seen," she said. Despite discreetness, some restaurateurs obsess about sniffing a reviewer out. According to the *Observer*, "Most restaurant kitchens in Manhattan have posted on their walls a Xerox of a Xerox of an old photograph of Ms. Reichl." Reichl uses different aliases and has been known to don wigs to throw restaurants off her trail. "My picture is in the newspaper every week," Mack says, laughing, "but I don't look like that picture." She must not, because she claims she's only been recognized once. "It was at a little Italian restaurant. When the waiter was bringing back the bill with my credit card, I saw him look at the credit card and I saw him look at me. He said, 'You're that lady in the newspaper!' and he asked, 'How did I do?' Then he covered his face in horror and he said, 'Please, don't tell me!"

"I do a really good job of trying to keep [my appearance] under wraps," Getto boasts. "I don't get into big Hollywood stuff, but I will put a beard on or I will change the way I look in a lot of different ways. Or I'll go on a Saturday night so even if they do know who I am they won't be able to do anything special for me. Once my co-worker, who was drunk, stumbled into a restaurant and when he saw me screamed, 'Dennis Getto!' And I said, 'Where? Is he in here?' Three or four times people have recognized me. I don't do much to attract attention to myself."

Practical Information

"I often hear from people who say they would like to review restaurants," Mack says. "If they have good credentials and can present some samples of their writing, preferably published, I usually talk to them."

Dennis Getto advises: "Don't get discouraged. It is a very small group of people who are restaurant critics. Make sure you have a strong background in writing and never stop learning about food."

Culinary schools across the country, such as Johnson and Wales, 8 Abbot Park Place, Providence, RI 02903-3375, now offer food-writing courses.

There are numerous informative trade magazines: *Gourmet*, *Food and Wine*, and *Bon Appetit* can be found at your local newsstand and focus on cooking technique, food trends, cuisine styles, recipes, and restaurants around the world. Also, check out *Restaurants and Institutions* (847-635-8800; www.rimag.com); *Nations Restaurant News* (800-944-4676; www.nrn.com); and *Restaurant Business* (212-592-6264; www.restaurantbiz.com).

Founded by Julia Child, the James Beard Foundation perpetuates the art and education of fine cuisine. Contact them for a schedule of events, tastings,

lectures, and classes in your area. They also publish a magazine and newsletter that examines food trends, features interviews with chefs and critics, and lists required reading for food learning. Contact: James Beard Foundation, 167 West 12th Street, New York, NY 1001, (800-36-BEARD).

These books are recommended as required reading by Getto, Mack, and the James Beard Foundation:

Dining Out: Secrets from America's Leading Critics, Chefs, and Restaurateurs by Andrew Dornenberg and Karen Page

The Art of Dining: A History of Cooking and Eating by Sara Paston-Williams

Mastering the Art of French Cooking, vols. I and II, by Julia Child

The New Professional Chef by the Culinary Institute of America

The Art of Eating by M.F.K. Fisher

Beard on Food by James Beard

American Food by Evan Jones

James Beard's American Cookery by James Beard

Sommelier

Job description: Oversee and manage a restaurant's wine cellar and advise diners on choosing a wine to go with their meal.

Compensation: Full-time, experienced sommeliers make anything from $40,000 to $90,000 a year. At exclusive, top-of-the-line restaurants, particularly in New York, salaries can go as high as $120,000. Sommeliers find numerous opportunities to supplement their income, too, by writing for wine magazines, consulting with retailers (i.e., sampling new wines and advising them what to buy), and hosting wine-tasting dinners.

Prerequisites: Sommeliers need to be very familiar with the restaurant business, ideally with four to six years of experience. Many are, in fact, graduates of culinary schools. It is also common for sommeliers to begin their careers as waiters, before making the switch to the wine cellar. In any case, as Stephen Fisher, sommelier/cellarmaster at the Ritz-Carlton in Boston points out, "You couldn't just leave college and be a sommelier."

Qualities employer is seeking: First, a candidate for a sommelier position needs to know wines, a subject that can take years to master. An excellent sense of taste is also essential (for another job for refined taste buds, see "Ice Cream Flavor Developer," p. 218). While the old rule of thumb—red wine for red meats, and

white wine for chicken and fish—applies in some cases, wine selections (as any sommelier will tell you) are much more complicated than that. The appropriate wine depends, in large part, on the preparation, sauces, and flavorings of the meal it is to accompany. Although people commonly associate wine expertise with snobbery, a good sommelier needs tact and flexibility to work well with the public. Restaurant patrons are often intimidated by a large wine list, or they are simply unsure what kind of wine they want with their meal.

Perks: On the one hand, sommeliers sample extraordinary wines on a daily basis—and get paid to do this. On the other, they can't get drunk, which arguably defeats the purpose of all that drinking. Indeed, intoxication on the job is a firing offense, and wine tasting requires discipline. Sommeliers travel frequently (sometimes at their own expense) to wine regions in California and France to visit winemakers and sample new vintages. Wine companies sponsor frequent wine-tasting events, and sommeliers may attend as many as four or five a week.

Risks/drawbacks: One drawback of the job is the late hours, which can be tough on social and family life; sommeliers also frequently work on weekends and holidays, when restaurants can be at their busiest.

Overview

Sommelier (pronounced saw-muh-LYAY) is a French word meaning "wine steward." Historically, a sommelier worked in a royal or noble household as the keeper of the master's wine cellars. Nowadays, they can be found only at first-rate restaurants that feature extensive wine lists. Sommeliers must continually keep abreast of new wines, vintages, and a whole assortment of regions, vineyards, and grape varieties. "I'm constantly searching for wines. I've got to be on top of the new wines coming to market, and knowledgeable about all of them," says Fisher. The mark of a good sommelier is the ability to recognize specific wines in blind tests. Fisher recalls that "a colleague and I would test each other with blindfolds every Tuesday afternoon" at the Ritz-Carlton, usually to the amazement of the other staff and passing guests.

"One of the most satisfying things about being a sommelier is having people come to find you when they've finished their meal and are ready to leave, to thank you for the wine you selected for them," says Phil Pratt, sommelier at New York's high-profile "21" Club.

Depending on the restaurant, the sommelier's duties may include purchasing wines, selecting the house wine—usually an affordable wine that can be bought in large quantities—and keeping the cellar stocked. Working with the public presents its own challenges, particularly when dealing with "cowboys." A cowboy, according to sommelier Phil Pratt, is "someone in a high-powered situation who likes to show he's got a lot of money," and who picks a bottle based on its impressively high price rather than for the wine itself. Ideally, though, a sommelier is there to ensure that the diners enjoy a wine best suited to their palate, their meal, and their budget. "The greatest advantage to a guest, even for someone who doesn't know wine, is to come in and get much more out of their meal than they expected. You want to recommend the best kind of wine they will like and can afford," says Fisher.

Practical Information

Sommeliers are a rare breed in a day when fast service and casual dining are becoming the norm. Phil Pratt estimates that in all of the restaurants in New York City, there may only be twenty-five or thirty full-time sommeliers. Frequently, the job of advising diners on selecting a wine falls to a waiter, or even the manager, neither of whom may know what to recommend, or who may try to push customers into picking bottles that are beyond their price range. Although the wine industry has plenty of female vintners, magazine writers, sales reps, and marketers, it's still rare to see a female sommelier. There are, however, indications that the gender imbalance is changing.

Jobs don't open up very often, so aspiring sommeliers often start out waiting tables, working for wine wholesalers, or getting jobs as assistant cellarmasters, sometimes called "cellar rats." Cellar rats are responsible for organizing and maintaining the wine cellar and for keeping the sommelier supplied with bottles, ice, decanters, and other equipment during mealtimes.

If you're serious about becoming a sommelier, Phil Pratt advises that you should "read everything you can find about wines and taste everything you can find. Open yourself up to every kind of food and wine experience you can come across." Acquaint yourself with popular magazines such as *Wine Spectator* and *Wine Enthusiast*, as well as trade magazines, like *The Wine Advocate* and *The Vine*, to establish a working knowledge of popular vintages and what experts look for in a wine. The few people who make it to the level of sommelier find it very satisfying: Not many other careers require you to sample a variety of the world's finest wines. Says Stephen Fisher, "I feel like I've been blessed by God."

Professor at Hamburger University

Job description: There are twenty-seven professors at McDonald's center for management training, Hamburger University (HU), in Oak Brook, Illinois. Despite the name, Hamburger University faculty members do not teach anything about cooking hamburgers. They leave such matters to "field" courses, concentrating instead on the more theoretical aspects of McDonald's business.

Compensation: Professors make "high five-figure packages," according to Rafik Mankarious, dean of the University.

Prerequisites: Real-world experience is what counts at HU, the kind of knowledge that comes from spending at least fifteen years working at and managing McDonald's franchises. The usual scholarly credentials for university professors—Ph.D.s, published research, a formal teaching background—have their place, but not at Hamburger U.

Qualities employer is seeking: A clear lecturing style that can be translated easily into as many as twenty-six languages is necessary. Teaching at Hamburger can resemble giving a speech to the UN General Assembly. With a remarkably diverse student body from all over the world—students who don't necessarily speak fluent English—lectures are simultaneously translated using state-of-the-art electronic translating equipment. The school employs 100 freelance interpreters.

Perks: Prestige from being a professor at what has been called the "Harvard of the fast-food business." There is the ever-popular Hot Hamburgers quiz game, but unfortunately not much else by way of typical collegiate distractions. There are, alas, no athletic rivalries with the rival school, Dunkin' Donuts University (located in Braintree, Massachusetts).

Risks/drawbacks: Burnout. Unlike other universities, Hamburger's classes continue year-round. "We're in the real world over here," says the former dean, Hal Theis.

Overview

Professors at Hamburger spend about five hours a day teaching. The eighty-acre manicured campus in Oak Brook sees about 6,000 students a year, put up at the nearby "lodge," a Hyatt-run hotel. The students are restaurant managers and middle managers who are eligible for further training. There is no tuition for the classes, and the local franchisees usually pay for the expenses of their students. Some classes are accredited, providing students thirty-two hours of course credit that can be applied towards non-Hamburger-oriented schools.

No prior teaching or research experience is necessary. Indeed, few of the professors make lateral shifts from other teaching institutions. Professors come from the ranks of McDonald's franchise managers. Hamburger offers their professorial recruits comprehensive training in presentation and teaching skills.

"Hamburger University is to our staff what the arches are to our customers," according to Rafik Mankarious, dean of HU.

This is not your staid ivory tower teaching post. The profs at Hamburger have a reputation as a social bunch. For the professors, on a two- to three-year hiatus from their fieldwork at McDonald's restaurants, their stint at HU is a networking dream and can lead to new professional opportunities.

As at other large universities, the faculty at Hamburger combines teaching with ongoing research. HU professors are involved in formulating McDonald's corporate strategy and pioneering new theories of fast-food restaurant management.

Practical Information

The job market for McDonald's professors is tight, but it's still better than elsewhere in academia; there are no tenured positions and the faculty churn rate is high. Of the twenty-seven professorships at the main Oak Brook campus, about ten open up every year. Interested applicants should send a cover letter and resume to the Office of the Dean, Hamburger University, 1000 McDonald's Drive, Oak Brook, IL 40432.

People without credentials to be HU professors can still be involved in McDonald's vast educational system. Hamburger University offers other employment positions worth exploring: teaching assistants, "instructional designers" (academics in charge of creating the curriculum), and in operations and administration. There are also teaching opportunities abroad. McDonald's runs satellite HU campuses in Germany, Japan, Malaysia, Singapore, Hong Kong, Mexico, Brazil, Canada, England, Scotland, and Australia. And while they may not have the same panache as Hamburger University, McDonald's "training centers" all over the world offer opportunities to teach. Contact the McDonald's recruitment department at 630-623-3000.

For more information, visit HU's Web site at www.mcdonalds.com/careers/hambuniv/index.html.

14 Let's Get Physical

Harlem Globetrotter Opponent

(American) Football Player in Europe

Armwrestler

Yoga Instructor

Harlem Globetrotter's Opponent

Job description: Travel the country and the world, training every day and playing to win—yet, consistently losing—against the interminably happy Harlem Globetrotters.

Compensation: "Players do very well, but nobody gets really rich here. There are no millionaires," says Red Klotz, owner and coach of the New York Nationals and preceding Globetrotter opponent teams.

Prerequisites: Near-NBA-caliber basketball skills.

Qualities employer is seeking: A sense of humor, a love of travel, and constant pluck are a must. Not only do the New York Nationals spend six or seven months out of the year on the road, they're being beaten and out-pranked all the while. Even when the team isn't traveling, they're still playing, so the schedule can be grueling. Coach Klotz also concentrates on finding players who don't harbor racial biases. Klotz is serious about making sure his players are in it for the love of the game.

Perks: It doesn't feel quite as bad to lose when no one expects you to win. And those rare wins feel better than anything you've ever experienced. Then, of course, there's traveling the world and being paid to play basketball.

Risks/drawbacks: Insanity, terminal depression: If losing every night for months on end isn't bad enough, just imagine losing every night to guys who do their own halftime show.

Overview

Brought together by coach Red Klotz, a former member of the NBA champion 1947–48 Baltimore Bullets and a longtime organizer of opposition teams for the Harlem Globetrotters, players for the Nationals hail from top college basketball programs all over the country. Before the Nationals, these players shared the court with college teammates who went on to the NBA, and many of them hope to continue their careers, as other Globetrotter opposition players have, by moving on to coaching, playing for the Globetrotters, or even joining the NBA. As coach Klotz says, when asked about where his players come from and why, "There just isn't enough room (in the NBA) for everybody "

"I've never told my players to do anything but play the best game of basketball possible," assures New York Nationals coach Red Klotz.

Touring with the Nationals allows players to stay in the game, playing at a highly competitive level for over 300 games a year. Unlike NBA players, these guys never rest. The annual Globetrotters tour begins with training at Disney World, starting on Christmas Day. Within a month, the teams depart for a jaunt around the United States that lasts until April. The summer schedule for opposition teams varies from year to year, though most often the team joins a summer league. During 1998, the Nationals' first year as a team, there was a fall European tour with the Globetrotters, where they spent nights accepting challenges from local teams in stops around the world. All in all, not too much time is spent at the team headquarters in Margate City, New Jersey.

When asked about the caliber of play between his team and the Globetrotters, Klotz seems slightly defensive. Most likely with good reason—there are only so many ways to ask, "Do you throw the games?" Klotz defends his team steadfastly: "The whole trick is for us to try to beat them. If we didn't try, they would get lax. This way, the audience gets a good game of basketball, plus all of the tricks and shots." Klotz also adamantly opposes the notion that his players feel oppressed by working so hard just to get secondary status on the programs and a win/loss record even the Denver Nuggets would scoff at. "They don't feel like they're beneath the Globetrotters," says Klotz. "They're not playing second fiddle. They play because they love to play basketball."

Klotz also reminds suspicious onookers that the current Globetrotters are the same team who beat the Kareem Abdul-Jabbar traveling team, as well as the College All-Stars. Klotz is rightfully pleased that his young group has gotten within three or four points of beating the Globetrotters on numerous occasions. With practice, they may even win someday; the Washington Generals, the last regular opposition team coached by Klotz, triumphed over the Globetrotters on a few occasions before they disbanded two years ago.

Credit: Red Klotz

It's not whether you win or lose, because you always lose. The overmatched New York Nationals team consists of talented former college hoopsters.

Practical Information

A scout handles recruiting, with occasional input from Klotz and recommendations from alumni players. You don't need to worry about your location; players come from all over the country. Instead, worry about keeping your jump shots clean and learning to dunk. If you're not yet in college, drink plenty of milk, and work on getting yourself into a school with a good basketball program where the coaches and the other players are going to be good enough to challenge you. And remember that there's more out there than just the NBA.

If you'd like more information about the team, you can write to Coach Red Klotz at the Red Klotz Sports Center, 114 S. Osborne Avenue, Margate City, NJ 08412.

(American) Football Player in Europe

Job description: Get paid to play American football on European club teams, often coaching as well.

Compensation: Players are paid between $1,000 and $3,000 a month for about nine months. A free car and apartment is not unusual, and sometimes there's a meal arrangement as well.

Prerequisites: College football experience is necessary. "It doesn't matter if you played Division III or if you almost got drafted into the NFL," says former Vienna Viking Mark Bianchi, "but you have to have some experience."

Qualities employer is seeking: Patience, patience, patience. Bianchi, who also coached in Moscow, recalls the first day of practice: "We had to show them how to put their helmets on." It doesn't hurt to speak a second language, although most Europeans speak enough English that the language barrier isn't a huge problem. It's easier to say "first down and ten" than to translate it into intelligible French.

Perks: As an American, you're the star of the team for two reasons. First, because you've had some real football experience, you'll beat the pants off almost any

European. Second, you're an American, and contrary to commonly held misconceptions of Continental disdain, many Europeans love American culture. As for other perks, you get to see Europe and be completely immersed in some fascinating cultures—in exchange for playing a game that you might otherwise be playing for free in your backyard.

Risks/drawbacks: It's difficult to get a position. Almost all of the jobs are handed down or advertised through word of mouth. And once you've gotten the job, it's not as if you're going to be making a lot of money. There's the ever-present risk of physical injury, and a tenuous sort of job security. Contracts are usually made on a handshake, not in writing, and you can be fired if your team doesn't perform well.

Overview

American football is to Europe what soccer is to America: It's an increasingly popular sport, but it is still overshadowed by a more firmly established national pastime. American football fanatics in Europe are a small but enthusiastic group. Club football teams have cropped up around the continent and are most popular in England, Germany, and Italy. These teams are intense, for nonprofessional sports teams. They practice around fifteen hours a week, court big corporate sponsors, and have the money to pay Americans to beef up their ranks. Games can attract thousands of fans. (Soccer matches, on the other hand, can attract tens of thousands.) The level of playing tends to improve the farther west you go; players are more experienced and have more money in, say, Frankfurt than in Kiev.

Mark Bianchi, former Vienna Viking, arrived at his first practice in Moscow to discover that "most of them couldn't throw a football. These were professional athletes who just weren't trained as football players. All they wanted to do was throw the long bomb, like they saw on TV. They threw like they were throwing lefty."

Bianchi, for example, was the defensive coach for a team in Moscow that had only twenty-two sets of pads. "Every time we sent in a sub, they had to swap pads." Substitutes of unusual size were left looking ridiculous and risking injury in pads that didn't fit. The solution: "We subbed as little as possible." For players who are used to the resources of American universities with solid football programs, the transition can be difficult. On the other hand, the job requires a manageable time commitment ("maybe thirty hours a week") and affords the leisure time to enjoy European culture.

Practical Information

Doing the job isn't the hard part; getting it is. While you can try working through an agent or job placement agency, your best bet by far is to try talking to former players or coaches. It also doesn't hurt to have played a position that Europeans recognize and appreciate: quarterback, receiver, running back. Defensive linemen are far less likely to get the job than somebody on offense, because offense players have the romantic positions that everybody watches. The European idea of football is all about the long throw, the sixty-yard sprint, the big touchdown—not defense and teamwork.

Playing football in Europe would seem to be an ideal arrangement: Europeans are grateful to have a competent player in their midst, Americans are happy to see Europe and spend their time playing a game they love. While it's virtually impossible to make a career out of it, it's a great way to spend a few years.

Armwrestler

Job description: Armwrestle in competitions officially sanctioned by United States Arm Sports on a local, national, or international level.

Compensation: Earnings vary by tournament and prize. Most local competitions have a first-prize range of $100 to $500, and some of the larger international meets offer first prizes up to $2,000. It is possible to compete in both right- and left-handed categories, and in all weight classes higher than your own, and people over forty can also compete in a "masters" category. Although the prize money can add up, income from armwrestling must be supplemented by a steady job, if you want to make a living. (Looking for portable part-time work to support your armwrestling? Try working as a crossword puzzle writer, p.149.)

Prerequisites: Well-developed triceps and biceps.

Qualities employer is seeking: A passion for the sport and the resourcefulness to gain enough financial support to travel the world and compete.

Perks: In addition to the lump sums of money awarded to winners, armwrestlers enjoy a camaraderie that, in most cases, transcends the expected antipathy between competitors at the table. They travel the world, on their own or in regional or national teams, as ambassadors of American goodwill and sportsmanship.

Risks/drawbacks: Unfortunately for regular competitors, and even for the many world champions, armwrestling is not a lucrative venture. The thrill of victory often has to suffice, as prize money typically goes toward the cost of travel. Then again, there is the possibility of losing, lumping the frustration of defeat on top of the investment.

"Desire is the most important thing on the table," says Bill Cox, president of the International Armwrestling Federation. "Guys try to break each other's arms, then hug each other."

Overview

Arm sports are perhaps best represented in American popular culture by the much-lambasted Sylvester Stallone vehicle *Over the Top*. The movie, a father-son reconciliation story set in the underbelly of roadhouse armwrestling, suffers from lamentable writing and acting, but also captures on film the bygone wild days of arm sports in the late 1980s. Every wrestler in the movie besides Stallone was a professional (cheaper by half than Hollywood extras), and some are still on the armwrestling circuit today. However, their world of sleazy roadhouses and saloons, of personal vendettas and underhanded scare tactics, is as much a relic as Sly himself. United States Arm Sports and the organizations for which it serves as an umbrella have "cleaned up" the sport over the past ten years, making it accessible to the wives and children of wrestlers and moving organized meets from the traditional sports bars and roadhouses to lounges at Holiday Inns.

Armwrestling styles and attitudes come in as many varieties as there are personalities. One of the featured wrestlers in *Over the Top* psyches his opponents out onscreen and off by swallowing a lit cigar—a definite vestige of armwrestling's rowdier days. Jim Fitzsimmons, one of the top contenders in the world championships in Ontario 1998, has a more subtle but equally effective approach: an overconfident swagger, a killer stare, a firm grip, a slight sneer, and most important, victory after pounding victory.

The right attitude and a soupçon of luck can land you a steady job, too. Stallone offered to employ old-guarder Jim Norman as his personal trainer (Jim turned him down), and one current three-time world champ served as personal trainer to the New Kids on the Block (whom no one, apparently, could turn down).

The recent cleanup of arm sports in the United States means that women can officially join in the competition. Not only do women compete with each other in several weight classes, but a few get so good that they wrestle men. Graceann Swift, 133 to 154 pound, right-hand champion, routinely defeats men 100 pounds heavier than she is. Armwrestling has yet to gain the international legitimacy of boxing or

wrestling; it has yet to become an Olympic sport, and the United States still does not sponsor a national team. Its popularity as a backyard barbecue diversion and its new official association with family values, however, means that anyone with the will to train can participate. All you need is a set of weights and the desire to win.

Practical Information

Anyone who dishes out a $10 to $15 registration fee can enter a tournament, but it's not that easy to win. Many armwrestlers have been in the game a long time, and their ability to compete does not decrease with age; many of the masters champions also hold titles won by defeating men half their age. At least one of the more famous young champions has been known to resort to subtle cheating tactics that referees cannot detect, but it is not necessary to fight dirty to win. Gerry Cadorette, two-time world champion, says that winning depends 45 percent on strength and 65 percent on technique, the most important aspect of which is a firm, insurmountable grip. When training, work the triceps first and the biceps second—and practice early and often to develop your technique and your 'tude.

Once a wrestler is a regular in the armwrestling community, he or she can serve a number of functions outside competition. Bill Cox, president of the International Armwrestling Federation wrestled in the seventies and is now a nationwide organizer and promoter. At meets, it's hard to tell the coaches from the wrestlers (many do both) and many competitors fraternize with the referees, who obviously came from their ranks.

The best source for armwrestling opportunities and events is the expansive and well-managed Web site of United States Arm Sports (www.armwrestling.com), an authoritative armwrestling resource, as well as an interesting browse.

Yoga Instructor

Job description: Instruct students in hatha yoga breathing, postures (*asanas*), and spirituality.

Compensation: Instructors charge $50 to $100 for a private class, which typically lasts about seventy-five to ninety minutes. Gyms pay instructors $40 to $50 per class. Yoga centers pay $20 to $25 as a base, and $2 for every person beyond the first ten who attend the class. Venerated teachers can earn six figures a year. Incipient instructors are fortunate if they take in $400 dollars a week. Most yoga instructors have a second source of income. (See "Radio Contest Winner" for a good sideline, especially if you listen to pop radio while you meditate, p. 211.)

Prerequisites: Many instructors have experience in some form of physical training before turning to yoga. Many yoga centers offer yoga certification programs that can be as short as two weeks. Most potential instructors only enroll in these courses after spending several years practicing as a layperson. Says instructor Sara Melson, "I don't believe just anyone can do it. You have to have an understanding of how the body works, and you have to be able to communicate it in a clear and calm way."

Qualities employer is seeking: Certification isn't required by all employers, in part because there is no standard for certificates. The very concept of imposing standards and certificates is anathema for some. Says Sara Ivanhoe, instructor at Yoga Works in L.A. and star of the newly released *Joy of Yoga* instructional video: "Yoga is thousands of years old. There are many different schools and different styles. Who are we to come up with some sort of criteria [for teaching]?" Employers seek instructors with experience, and they're looking for somebody that can connect with the students, inspire the students, and bring them back again and again.

Perks: Excellent physical and spiritual health is the greatest reward that many instructors achieve. Some earn additional benefits: "I just got back from spending a month teaching in the Caribbean. They've invited me to come back twice a year," says Ivanhoe. Sara Melson, who has instructed yoga for two years, had this to say: "Any experience with yoga is very feeding. It's a spiritual practice. It's extremely therapeutic to teach it. By the end of an hour you yourself are relaxed." Ivanhoe points to the progress of her students as a rewarding experience: "I get immediate feedback that what I'm doing improves their lives. I see lawyers telling me they deal with stress better, older people who are standing up better, parents who tell me they have more patience with their kids. And I played a part in it."

Risks/drawbacks: "You're freelance. If I get hurt, I'm out of business. How do I make a living?" Ivanhoe asks. (As a body part model, perhaps? See p. 110.)

Overview

There are many types of yoga. Hatha yoga revolves around the asanas, or postures, of which there are several thousand. "It started out with meditation—people sitting in the lotus position [seated, legs crossed]. When you sit in meditation for a really long time, your hips and back get tight. So they started doing exercises to strengthen and stretch so they could sit for a long time. That's how the asanas got started," explains celebrity instructor Ivanhoe. Almost all the postures are named after different things in nature—lion pose or tree pose or scorpion pose. The word yoga itself translates to mean "union."

Credit: Sara Ivanhoe

Can you bring your ankles behind your head? If so, you may have what it takes to be a yoga instructor, among other jobs.

In practicing hatha yoga, the practitioner attempts to achieve union with nature (or the divine, depending on your perspective).

Hatha yoga was passed from guru to disciple for generations on end. Iyengar was the first person to teach yoga in a class, as well as the individual responsible for bringing hatha yoga to the West, where it has grown in popularity for nearly thirty years.

Westernization of hatha yoga often means stripping it of its spiritual Hindu heritage. "A lot of people don't want to feel like they're doing a religion," says Ivanhoe, "and there's a lot to doing yoga postures just for your health. It improves posture, increases lung capacity, improves circulation, and makes you strong, flexible, graceful, and balanced." Some instructors take issue with the separation of spirituality from physicality. Says Melson, "If you're really doing yoga, it is a prayer. There is no difference."

Iyengar techniques, which focus on physical alignment within each pose, present one form of hatha yoga. A second technique, taught by Shri K. Pattabhi Jois, embraces a specific series of poses (called *astanga*), and presents a more rigorous physical treatment for the practitioner. In the last decade, the mainstreaming of Jois's rigorous form of practice has combined with the spiritual stripping of Iyengar's teaching to create a sort of power yoga that can be practiced in gyms in lieu of aerobics and traditional Western stretches.

"After the first month, I just loved it and I walked up to the instructor and said, 'How do I become an instructor?' I want to give other people the benefit of what I've learned, and to be able to learn more myself. I think it can really benefit people's lives," states Ziv Termeforoosh, an instructor at Yoga Garden in Santa Monica, California.

The popularity of power yoga classes has grown to phenomenal proportions on the coasts, particularly in Los Angeles, New York, and San Francisco. And with celebrities like Madonna pushing the values of astanga on Oprah Winfrey, the practice of yoga is likely to run rampant across the United States in the next few years. Serious practitioners like Ivanhoe and Melson view the present celebrity fad as both ironic and useful. Says an instructor, "I think of Madonna as a fairly materialistic and self-centered person. I think it's funny that she has this pretense of being spiritualistic. But basically, she got into it 'cause she heard it was a cool physical practice, and now she's really into it. And because she's such a public figure, people in Kansas are getting into yoga. You shouldn't be chanting mantras and making money off of it, but to me, she's getting people to do it, and that's what is important."

Practical Information

Yoga instructors spend at least an hour every day practicing the craft. The number of asanas is so great that few living individuals know how to perform all of them correctly. The study of hatha yoga can be a lifetime commitment.

The explosion of interest in hatha yoga not only means an increasing number of students, but an abundance of potential instructors. As acquiring work becomes more and more competitive, the best recourse to becoming a yoga instructor is a rigorous two to three years of instruction that focuses on the history, the asanas, an understanding of physiology, the spirituality of yoga, and on communication skills. Several of the larger and more established yoga centers in America now offer these types of programs. The Web site www.yogafinder.com can help you find classes near you.

You can also find more information in *Yoga Journal* magazine, or at *Yoga Journal's* Web site, www.yogajournal.com. Another good Internet resource is www.yogasite.com.

15 On the Move

NATIONAL GEOGRAPHIC Photographer

Publishers Clearing House Prize Patrol Member

Circus Roustabout

Bicycle Messenger

Club Med GO

White House Advance Person

NATIONAL GEOGRAPHIC Photographer

Job description: Travel everywhere to take the pictures that fill one of the most esteemed and popular magazines in the world.

Compensation: Staff photographers earn about $500 per day; one says he earns $100,000 a year from magazine assignments and the sale of photos the magazine doesn't use.

Prerequisites: Sam Abell, a *National Geographic* staff photographer for more than thirty years, may have lost perspective on what it takes to land his job: "You need a liberal education, with a specialty in languages, sociology, and anthropology," he says. "You also need extensive experience working for publications on deadline, typically through newspaper work." Sound too easy? Kent Kobersteen, director of photography at *National Geographic*, injects a bit more realism while detailing the job's prerequisites. "Photography is an extremely competitive business. There are far fewer jobs or freelance assignments than photographers. Because of our magazine's circulation, the number of resources we have, and the place photography plays in our publication, we're at the top of the heap when it comes to photography. We're kind of like the Chicago Bulls of publications when it comes to photography. It sounds arrogant, but it's fact."

Qualities employer is seeking: Photographers must be extremely willing to travel—and must be durable. Kobersteen admits that a solid education helps. "Our photographers are extremely intelligent. They're fine journalists, they're driven, they have great natural eyes. Any pro can handle almost any assignment for a day or a week, but if it's going to be eight months, they'd better care about their subject." A large part of landing a *National Geographic* job entails understanding the idea behind the magazine's award-winning photography. As Kobersteen explains, "If you think about a picture in a newspaper, it's often a very literal picture of a person or an event. Then if you think about photography in a museum, it's more stylistic, very interpretive. On that spectrum, we're certainly towards the literal, but we try to be more interpretive, to show the emotion of a situation." And as a final tip to scoring a job, network. "It's an incestuous business. We all talk. If you do work that's published, people see it. If you're great, people find out about you. By the same token, if you screw up, that word goes through the community, too."

Perks: *National Geographic* photographers capture every nook and cranny of the globe, from towering mountains to tiny microbes. They travel to ultra-exotic locales, witness remarkable events, and are reassigned subjects frequently enough to take away the tedium.

Risks/drawbacks: The job of a world-wandering voyeur obviously presents a number of dangers. Just ask Flip Nicklin, a renowned photographer of whales, who was nearly pushed out to sea by an especially affectionate specimen after he massaged the whale's eyeball. "It was like a giant door driving you through the water," Nicklin told the *Los Angeles Times*. "He was like a giant puppy run amok." Another photographer once kept watch in a tree for twenty-one straight days in hopes of catching gorillas at a watering hole. Another complained of being once covered in insects and worms that attached to his feet and buttocks. Another has had malaria twelve times. In addition to the physical danger, the constant travel that the job requires tends to wreak havoc on relationships at home.

Overview

In some ways, Sam Abell's job sounds like hell. He travels constantly, about six to eight months out of the year, leaving him little time to spend with his wife. He starts each day's work before dawn, and he toils well into the night. Yet Abell's job as staff photographer for *National Geographic* magazine is probably one of the most coveted in the world, both within and outside his field. During the thirty years he's worked for the magazine, Abell has snapped everything from Shinto ceremonies in Japan to a Shaker village in Kentucky. He even met his wife on the job, in a situation evocative of the best-selling book and hit movie *The Bridges of Madison County*; Abell was working on a book about the Pacific Crest Trail: "My wife was a thru-hiker, which means she walked the whole way," Abell recalls. "I greatly admired that achievement. We met in 1974, and we were married in '77."

"You get a nonstop, in-depth education on the road. That's priceless. And if you believe that you were born to take pictures, and you believe in the expressive power of photography, then this is the best job in the world," says Sam Abell, *National Geographic* staff photographer.

"But most say the job can actually ruin a good romance," Abell says. "The job can take a big toll on your home life. I'm married, and most of the photographers are married. And many have families. But you're on the road a lot."

"It's tough to have a personal life if you're gone eight months out of the year," Kobersteen admits. "It's sometimes difficult to keep a marriage together, or even have boyfriends or girlfriends. On occasion, the partner goes along, but the job's tough enough without distractions. Is that unfair? Yes. But if there are two photographers, and one has a distraction, guess who's going to do the best job and get the next assignment?"

Practical Information

National Geographic magazine employs only five staff photographers, each of whom usually undertakes between one and three assignments per year. Abell says he gets "good, typical benefits," and he's allowed to freelance. He uses a 35-millimeter camera and generally takes 250 to 300 rolls of film (about 10,000 shots) for each assignment; on average, about thirty photos make it into a publication. One photographer, Jim Blair, says he travels with as many as fifteen bags packed with clothes for two months, 300 to 400 rolls of film, and up to six cameras. The photographers generally shoot early in the morning and at dusk, to capture the best light; they deal with travel and other logistics during midday. Unlike the magazine's writers, who spend a portion of their time working at home, the photographer's job is done entirely in the field.

For one assignment, Nicklin says, he racked up 150,000 air miles, spending $200,000 and reading more than 100 books. Kobersteen says a photographer's fee and expenses run between $60,000 and $250,000. "But if we have $200,000 invested in a set of pictures and the editor decides he doesn't want to publish it, we won't," he says. For anyone just starting out, Kobersteen admits, *National Geographic* can't offer much. "Frankly, the likelihood is pretty slim that someone would just walk through the door with the caliber I need." He says his department only offers one internship each year, provides a fellowship to university faculty for the sake of education, and sometimes budgets to sponsor a young photographer who shows promise for working with the magazine. "But because we put so much of our resources into coverage," he says, "and because what we're looking for is so different and demands that a photographer be rounded, sophisticated, well-seasoned, and have a well-defined style, there's not that much opportunity for someone just starting out." The real key, however—a secret that holds for landing any job—is a combination of talent and raw desire. "Picture taking, being able to express yourself visually, is a gift," Abell explains. "Although I didn't have many gifts given to me, being able to see things and to record them photographically seems to be a gift that I was given."

Publishers Clearing House Prize Patrol Member

Job description: Travel around bestowing oversized novelty checks, balloons, flowers, and champagne to the winners of the Publishers Clearing House Sweepstakes.

Compensation: Everyone on the Prize Patrol also has a non-Prize Patrol job at Publishers Clearing House, usually in the advertising, PR, or contest departments. Salary for the members of the Prize Patrol depends on their desk jobs. Of the six current members, salaries range from $30,000 into the six figures.

Prerequisites: Since nobody wants to get handed a big check, flowers, and balloons by a sullen or laconic messenger, a winning smile, an energetic disposition, and an enthusiastic spirit should help you convince Dave Sayer, the head of the Prize Patrol, to let you join his team. First, however, you'll need to get a marketing job at Publishers Clearing House, for which you should have a college degree and a background in advertising, direct-mail marketing, or public relations.

Qualities employer is seeking: Patrol members must be able to sneak up on a winner's house without attracting undue attention, despite being tailed around by a television news crew. One former member of the Prize Patrol was not careful and was picked up by the police while casing a house to see if the winner was home.

Perks: Satisfaction of giving away millions of dollars. Appear on national television after the Super Bowl.

Risks/drawbacks: No tips (company policy). You and your family are not eligible to win the sweepstakes. Friends complain when you show up at their house carrying only a bottle of wine.

Overview

Bulk-mailed letters sent out to millions of households include a description of what will happen when the Prize Patrol van turns up your driveway ("provided you have and return the winning entry"): "All of a sudden there will be a knock on the door, you'll open it and find the PCH Prize Patrol there with flowers, balloons and the big $1,000,000.00 check with [your name] on it. If your winning moment is like the ones I've been a part of in the past, there will probably be screams of delight, congratulatory hugs and maybe even some tears of joy."

This is indeed how it happens, according to Sayer, who, as the head of the Prize Patrol, has been hand-delivering checks since the Prize Patrol started in 1988. The popular gimmick, which recalls the 1950s TV show, *The Millionaire* (in which an unidentified benefactor bestowed checks on unsuspecting recipients each week), was conceived by Todd Sloan, a young advertising executive at PCH who argued that the company's standard procedure of flying prize recipients to New York for a staged award ceremony was dull. The winners, he said, "looked like bad actors." They experimented with surprising winners at their homes while Sloan videotaped their responses. They quickly discovered that the winners' unrehearsed reactions made for compelling television.

In the beginning, people were suspect. "Once we were trying to convince this lady that she had won some money from us and she just refused to believe us," said Sloan. "Her kids came to the door and the lady went back in her house and kept doing her laundry. Her kids finally said, 'Mom, I think they're for real.' We went into her house. She kept doing her laundry the whole time."

Now, the problem is reversed: The Prize Patrol is easily spotted, jeopardizing the surprise. In 1995, on a cold day in Minnesota, someone identified the prize van while it was en route to delivering a $10 million prize. The recipient was not home, so they had to wait. "It became the biggest media event in St. Cloud, Minnesota, ever," said Sloan. "A radio station was doing updates every half-hour, tracking where we were. 'Well, they're eating dinner now.' I was in my hotel, and the three local affiliates were all doing stand-ups from outside the front of the hotel, 'In this hotel tonight is the Prize Patrol. They haven't found their winner yet.' It was like being the Beatles."

A lot of craftiness is involved in pulling off a good, clean hit. Like burglars, the team cases out the neighborhood in a dark, unmarked van that they rent at the airport. They will call the winner's home, pretending to be looking for someone else or to have a flower delivery, in order to determine when the person is likely to be home. Then they'll stop at a florist and supermarket to buy flowers, balloons, and champagne. Once they've confirmed the address (there have been embarrassing mistakes in which the Prize Patrol has descended

Credit: Jamie Rosen

Prize Patrolers need to act like burglars, showing up unexpectedly at people's homes. In the unlikely event the recipient is not there, the Prize Patrol team leaves their calling card. (Bounty hunters, p.29, tend to be a bit more subtle.)

upon the wrong house, profoundly disappointing the resident there) and believe the recipient is home, the team is ready to spring into action. When Sayer gives the sign, they put on their signature blue blazers with PCH patches, hang a big "Publishers Clearing House Prize Patrol" sign on the van, and splinter out, each person attending to his prearranged station: one to flowers, one to balloons, one to champagne, and Dave to the check (Dave always gets the check).

"You get to be part of an unforgettable moment in someone's life," said Dave Sayer, head of the Prize Patrol. "It's a lot like being a Santa Claus, except without the hassle of dealing with chimneys."

Then there is the annual Super Bowl appearance, where the Prize Patrol delivers one of their "superprizes" in a live thirty-second spot that airs during the first commercial break after the game. These high-pressure events, in front of the largest television audience of the year, leave no room for error. While adding to the authenticity of the Prize Patrol's mission, these prize attacks have resulted in some less-than-ideal footage. In 1998, for example, the winner was not home, and the team stood around staring at a closed door for thirty seconds.

While it has never happened in a live spot, there is always the risk of someone appearing in an unprepared state, such as the so-called "Towel Girl Incident," when an attractive young woman came to the door from the shower, thinking that her brother had forgotten his keys. "She opened the door and saw all of us there. We said, 'Come on out.' And she came out in her towel and we showed her the check and she started trembling. I thought she might drop the towel," said Sloan. "Didn't happen." The girl ran inside and changed, but the team had to convince her to put the towel back on for the rest of the taping, so the tape didn't seem suspiciously disjointed to the television audience.

Practical Information

The team is "on prize patrol" for fifty to sixty days a year, delivering prizes totaling tens of millions of dollars (every prize of $10,000 and up is hand-delivered by the Prize Patrol). There is not much turnover, as positions only open up once every two or three years. Given the fringe benefits of traveling and appearing on television, competition is steep.

Candidates should send a cover letter and resume to Publishers Clearing House, Inc., 382 Channel Drive, Port Washington, NY 11050, Attn: Dave Sayer.

Circus Roustabout

Job description: *Roustabout* is a generic term for circus crewmembers. The tent crew is in charge of setting up the tent. The house crew sets up the seating. Grooms take care of the horses. Electrics take care of the lighting and sound. Members of any category may be asked to do whatever work is necessary. House and tent crew drive the trucks. Everyone, including the elephants (who pull the stakes out), pitches in to strike the circus.

Compensation: The more skilled or strenuous the work, the better the pay. In many circuses, all moneys tendered are considered travel reimbursements. Pay ranges from $300 to $600 a week, varying from circus to circus. Given that roustabouts work six days a week for as many as eighteen hours a day, this may seem like slave wages. But the circus puts you up and feeds you three meals a day, so most roustabouts can put away a good chunk of their earnings.

Prerequisites: Willingness to work long hours, travel, and live among clowns in circus conditions, plus a strong back are necessities for circus workers. Endurance is necessary for the long hours. (Striking the circus tent is frequently done at night, and most positions involve starting at 7 A.M. and working until after the evening show closes at 10 P.M.) Given the physical and emotional output necessary, most roustabouts are fairly young (i.e., between eighteen and forty-five).

Qualities employer is seeking: Some references are useful. Experience is a bonus, but since crew members often leave the circus without much notice, the determinant factor is whether a position is available when you apply; getting a job crewing is largely dependent on timing. Some circuses have requirements regarding personal appearance (e.g., no long hair or earrings on men, and, unless you're the tattooed man, no visible tattoos).

Perks: Some roustabouts run away with the circus, swept up with the romance of the job. Travel is a big incentive, though working six days a week means you don't do a whole lot of sightseeing. A groom for the Big Apple Circus ranked the bonds she forged with the other workers and the animals as the greatest reward of her job, seconded by the opportunity to meet the strange people who hang around the circus. Roustabout Lisa Austin found the audiences' responses to be a great reward. "It truly is amazing. You see a little of people's spirits spark up, watching the show. Everybody leaves with a huge smile on their face."

Risks/drawbacks: Individuals who work for the circus for a number of years sometimes have trouble acclimating to sedentary life.

"They have a little school for the families that stay on. The circus is a little town on wheels, complete with small town gossip and everybody knowing you. But it isn't one big happy family. The performers have thirty-two-foot Winnebagos, full-on luxury on wheels, and then there's us who have shit," says roustabout Lisa Austin, commenting on social injustice within the circus.

Overview

The circus is a European invention of the late eighteenth century, when riding masters such as Phillip Astley began performing horse tricks for the public. Horses have always been a central feature to the circus, and pundits today question whether a horseless circus is really a circus at all. The late nineteenth century saw the golden age of the circus, when new acts were a matter of public wonder, and trapeze artists could become household names. Modern distractions like vaudeville and the birth of cinema helped to diminish interest in the circus over the first half of this century, but circus enthusiasm revived in the 1960s, as street performers catapulted circus acts from tents right onto city streets. Some modern circuses have done away with the animals altogether (e.g. , Cirque du Soleil, the New Pickle Circus, Circus Oz). Some of the more successful old-school circuses today include Ringling Brothers Barnum and Bailey Circus, Billy Martin's Circus, the Clyde Beatty-Cole Brothers Circus, Circus Vargas, Circus Knei, the UniverSoul Big Top Circus, and the Big Apple Circus.

Circuses vary enormously. Billy Martin's circus is a "mud show," performed on dirt with minimal trappings, and frequently moving locations after just a day or two. The Ringling Brothers have two American units and one European unit that do three-ring shows inside large stadiums. Circus Knei was started by an equestrian family and specializes in horse stunts. The UniverSoul Big Top Circus

offers performers of primarily African-American descent.

The individual nature of the circus will determine what your life is like as a roustabout. Cirque du Soleil is renowned for having excellent chefs. A perk of working for Ringling Brothers is traveling by train. For the most part, expect to share a bedroom and to tipple a few: "Drinking in local bars was the main activity besides work for most of the crew," says Austin.

Practical Information

Like Porta Pottis? Crave travel? Don't mind freaks sharing your quarters? Working for the circus is more of a lifestyle choice than a career move. Meals are communal. Living quarters are often communal. Most of the crew members are single, and romantic somersaults among the troupe are common (though both sexes should be forewarned that in many crews the men outnumber the women four or five to one).

If it is for you, send a resume to the home office of circuses that appeal to you. Visit the production team of every circus that comes to town. They'll probably ask you to send a resume to their home office, but some may know of positions open with other circuses; job opportunities are often spread through word of mouth. And check the classifieds of your local paper. Circuses with midseason openings will advertise in advance of their arrival, hoping to pick up fresh recruits quickly.

Bicycle Messenger

Job description: Deliver packages, letters, and other time-sensitive documents, preferably faster than the automotive competition.

Compensation: In a good week, a bike messenger with a big-city delivery company might take home $500 before taxes. Many messengers work as "independent contractors," so their employers don't have to provide medical insurance, equipment compensation, overtime pay, vacation time, or sick leave. In other words, if you get hurt on the job, you're out of luck, unless your boss is unusually progressive.

Prerequisites: In the city, agility, quick-wittedness, and "a really powerful survival instinct" are more important than brute strength, says Shawn Bega, president of Bega Services Cycle Messengers and a twelve-year veteran of the Washington, D.C. bike messenger scene. The swiftness of a delivery is not limited by RPMs but by the ability to slip through the two-foot gaps between cars. Even in smaller towns, where the roads tend to be safer and the pace more civilized, riders still need endurance, bike repair skills, a good mental map, and a high tolerance for exhaust fumes.

Qualities employer is seeking: Employers want riders who know the city, will ride in all weather with heavy packages, and are polite to customers.

Perks: The degree of job satisfaction among bicycle messengers is exceptional. "I absolutely love it," says Bega. "I get paid to ride my bike all day. I'm outside. The hours are flexible. I can wear whatever I want. This is the life." Bike messengers are proud to work hard, live free, and enjoy moral superiority over motorists—"mean and green," they call themselves.

Risks/drawbacks: Estimates vary, but about five bicycle messengers are killed on the job each year in the United States. City councils blame the messengers, whom they accuse of recklessness, and messengers blame the drivers, whom they accuse of carelessness. Crashing and getting hurt is part of being a rookie; veterans rarely crash, and when they do, they crash softly.

Overview

The typical bicycle messenger makes thirty or forty runs per day, covering twenty to sixty miles. "You don't have to be Marco Pantani when you start, but sure, it helps," says Bega. Many messengers smoke cigarettes and drink with enthusiasm (and the messenger patois contains at least a dozen words for marijuana), but they can't help but get fit on the job.

Despite the air of postapocalyptic chaos cultivated by urban bicycle messengers, there's a strong social order to the culture. For one thing, messengers are fiercely loyal to each other regardless of company affiliation. "If you're out there and you see a guy with a flat, you'll absolutely stop and lend him a pump." And if a messenger is hassled by a driver, all available comrades will rally, forming a wall of angry spandex the offending motorist will never forget.

In contrast to the warm fraternity of the road, a more confrontational relationship exists between riders and their bosses. Wages stay low because employers can always dip into the steady stream of rookies and college students, many of whom are in it for fun and don't demand a lot of money. Messengers are talking of unionizing, and the Teamsters have offered to help them organize. In the meantime, though, hundreds of riders are joining large messenger associations that will help cover medical expenses, find lawyers if members get into accidents, negotiate with hostile security guards who won't let messengers use the front doors, and generally try to raise the riders' standard of living.

The legislative politics of messengering are contentious all over the country, and several cities are cracking down hard on gonzo bikers. The trade literature tells the story of a messenger in Boston who knocked down a pedestrian on a sidewalk, prompting the city to push for a strict licensing system and a law requiring bike messengers to carry more liability insurance than drivers. But in San Francisco, when an unlicensed driver hit and killed a bike messenger, the driver didn't even get a ticket. An

editorialist for *Auto Free Times* writes, "The contrast between these two incidents brings into stark relief a double-standard that bicycle messengers the world over have known for some time: while cyclists maintain a vastly superior safety record, the carnage wrought by drivers carries a special sort of immunity."

And a note on gender politics: While bike messengering is still a male-dominated profession, serious female riders get a lot of respect from the corps. Vet-eran "courier chicks" often choose to lift more, work in worse weather, and ride harder than many of their male colleagues in order to prove themselves, and among the rank-and-file, the extra effort pays off. Women may, however, still have a harder time getting equal treatment from certain bosses and dispatchers, who sometimes would rather not risk a lucrative delivery on a rider they suspect to be weak or slow.

"I wouldn't want your job on a day like today. And I wouldn't want your job on any day no matter what the weather. Hey, just sign the damned waybill!"

—Steven Davey, "Handy Bike-Courier Answers to Stupid Questions," *Now Magazine*, Spring 1998

Practical Information

As much as veterans deride rookies and dilettantes, bike messengering can be a great day job for students, artists, and musicians. The hours are often flexible, and a messenger's intimate relationship with the city can be food for his or her soul. Bega's advice to aspiring messengers is to get to know the city, make friends in messenger bars, check newspapers for job openings, and then, once you're working, rely on word-of-mouth to lead you to openings at the best companies. Because the urban messenger world works by the rule of honor, a rookie will get work if his or her reputation with veteran messengers is good. Messengers lose jobs over disagreements with bosses or dispatchers; firing offenses include skimming checks, losing packages, or "pissing off clients," says Bega.

Employment opportunities may be best in a small city where the economy is strong and the messenger market isn't glutted. That's what Seth Elliot found when he moved from Eugene, Oregon (where he worked for the Center for Appropriate Transport), to Chapel Hill, North Carolina, designed a bike that can haul 200 pounds in its low-slung cargo hold, and started his own company, Pedalers Express. In his natty red-and-black uniform, Elliot garners more respect than some of his green-haired city cousins, and he gets to proselytize freely on the virtues of bicycling. "Bikes are better; they don't pollute, and they liven up the city," he says. "If you're on a bike, you can make eye contact with people

and say hi. You don't need continued road development—you don't need to be part of that whole system. The vast majority of auto deliveries within a city are under 10 pounds, and I can carry 200 pounds on my bike and not pollute at all." With copy shops, film processors, university offices, banks, and attorneys sending him on fifteen to twenty runs a day, business is so good that Seth has hired a friend to help out part time. Even so, he still has time for a decent burrito at lunchtime and the freedom to take weekends off.

Some jargon for the aspiring messenger: *gravy*, a high-paying delivery; *gristle*, the opposite; *copsicle*, police officer on a bike; *urban food log*, burrito; *10-9*, "Would you say that again, please?" (October ninth, 10-9, is International Bicycle Messenger Appreciation Day.)

The International Federation of Bike Messenger Associations maintains a Web site with industry news, links to chat groups, competition results, back issues of courier zines, and messenger-related articles from the mainstream media. The address is www.messengers.org. (Interested in moving at a bicycle's pace all day with no pedaling? How about becoming a blimp pilot? See p. 40.)

Club Med GO

Job description: Every GO (short for *gentil organisateur*, which means "congenial host" in French) has a simple mission: Make Club Med so great that guests (aka, GMs or *gentils membres*) will remember it for a lifetime. This may mean working as a tennis instructor, rock climbing instructor, animator (a full-time comedian, like a Club Med street performer), circus instructor, or perhaps the quintessential Club Med position, silk painting instructor. But first and foremost, all GOs are dedicated to maintaining the famous Club Med atmosphere twenty-four hours a day, seven days a week.

Compensation: A new GO earns $530 per month, plus room, board, and one round-trip ticket to Club Med.

Prerequisites: Language skills are helpful but not necessary. (Club Med, short for *Club Méditerranée*, is a French company, so French is always useful. In the Americas, where many of the resorts are in Latin locales, Club Med also likes to hire Spanish speakers.) Applicants must be at least nineteen years old, or for child care positions, twenty-one years old. However, there is no upper age limit. One Florida yoga instructor is in his seventies.

Qualities employer is seeking: Above all, GOs need enthusiasm—the kind of enthusiasm that flows in an unending stream from the core of your personality

(or if not, the ability to fake it). This enthusiasm should make itself manifest for guests in the form of superior customer service, and in being enthusiastic about the entire Club Med experience. Each "village"—Club Med is a community, not just a hotel or a resort—is staffed by around 100 live-in GOs, housed in rooms of two, with very little time off. The result is an atmosphere akin to summer camp, and the people who stick with it are the ones who like being away from home at the center of a party for six months at a time. Good GOs also overcome the repetitive nature of the job by finding creative, new ways to teach their basket-weaving and silk-painting groups.

Perks: Being paid to live in a resort is a good start. Free trips to other countries, a fabulous tan, and the opportunity to learn flying trapeze are other often-heard perks among Club Med employees. Then, there's the infamous romance of Club Med–GOs have many opportunities to make *liaisons amoureuses* (French for "hook-ups") of the employee/employee or employee/guest variety. For many visitors, their chance for romance is a large part of the Club Med vacation experience. The company neither encourages nor discourages GOs from getting involved with guests or each other; it merely acknowledges that flings happen. "We don't ask our employees to have romances with the guests," said one Club Med exec.

Risks/drawbacks: The potential for losing touch with reality can be considered a job hazard or a perk. Employers outside of the village may have trouble understanding the value of the six years you spent at Club Med.

Overview

Club Med virtually invented the all-encompassing vacation resort concept nearly fifty years ago on the French Mediterranean (hence, the name). The company is huge, with 104 villages on six continents, one floating village aboard the *Club Med II*, and about 8,000 GOs working at any time. After a couple of years of declining popularity and revenues, the company has recently come under the direction of Philippe Bourguignon, the man who made EuroDisney something even the French could tolerate. Bourguignon's plan to refocus the resorts toward a model of "pure service" may affect the substance of the GO position in the years to come.

Currently, the quality of a GO's Club Med experience depends largely on the management at the village where he or she works. Because an on-site general manager, known as the *chef de village*, sets the tone for each village, the level of organization in each location varies. GOs receive minimal training for their jobs, and with a *chef* who takes a hands-off approach to the business of running the club, this can lead to a feeling of being thrown in at the deep end of the lagoon.

Most GO positions last for six months, although some require as little as a four-month commitment. After one

six-month tour of duty in the Americas (there are five Club Meds in Mexico, three in the Bahamas, and many more throughout Florida and the Caribbean), North American GOs are eligible to work in villages in South America, Asia, South Africa, and Europe. Most GOs are offered subsequent employment and remain on the job for a year or two. While being a GO is, in many ways, an ideal job, it is rarely a career.

"I had a successful career as an attorney, but I needed a complete change of life. Working as a GO offered an interlude," says Catherine Ferguson, a former GO and current member of the Club Med corporate management.

A GO's employment is not always steady over his or her time with Club Med, however, and not by choice. Because more Club Med villages are open in winter than in summer, not all GOs can work year-round. Conveniently, there are a large number of Quebecois GOs who choose to work only in winter and help to meet the seasonal demand for additional GOs. Shorter-term seasonal work is possible around Christmas and Easter, and au pairs are hired on an as-needed basis for short assignments in exchange for room and board.

Practical Information

Some skills are in greater demand than others, and not every Club Med village offers every activity. However, what company, resort or otherwise, will refuse to hire a trapeze artist? Club Med is no different; they're always looking for trapezists and others with cool carnival skills; water-ski instructors and in-line skate teachers are a dime a dozen.

Thanks to the short and intense nature of the job, approximately 3,500 new GOs are hired each year. Working hours vary by position and time of year. GOs work seven days a week, with occasional one-day breaks, but most GOs feel on-duty any time they're in the village. It's almost impossible to be a convincing customer-service machine if you guard your private time by turning a cold shoulder when the classes are over. Office and extracurricular job holders work shift hours.

Club Med's employment Web site, www.cooljobs.com/clubmed, has excellent information on the job and the application process.

White House Advance Person

Job description: Travel around the United States and abroad orchestrating trips for the president, vice president, and/or their spouses.

Compensation: The White House uses part-time volunteers who make $30 per diem stipends for domestic trips, $100 for overseas trips. Campaigns, however, use paid, full-time advance people, generally paying $75 to $125 a day, plus a $30 per diem stipend. Depending on the budget of the campaign, this can either be lower (sometimes unpaid) to several hundred dollars a day for some flush campaigns. Rumor was that Ross Perot's campaign paid $1,000 a day for lead advance people (leads are more experienced and coordinate the rest of the team), prompting defectors from both the Clinton and Bush camps.

Prerequisites: Experience is required for the plum jobs, like advancing a POTUS trip to Paris (*POTUS* is advance shorthand for the president of the United States; there's also *VPOTUS*, the vice president; *FLOTUS*, the first lady; and *SLOTUS*, the second lady; see "Jargon," sidebar). However, given that much of this work is unpaid and politicians are always on the go, it is easy to get started by volunteering for trips in your local area. National campaigns also host "advance schools" where they indoctrinate hundreds of novices in the art of advance work.

Qualities employer is seeking: Ability to remain calm when, amidst a whirlwind of Secret Servicemen whispering into their sleeves, a mob of press photographers pressing up against a barricade, and protesters screaming in the distance, the president of the United States strides by and suddenly leans over to you and asks for the nearest men's room.

Perks: Everyone takes your call when you say you're with the White House advance team. You get to bypass traffic as you breeze from the airport to downtown in record time, escorted by a formidable police motorcade. WHCA (White House Communications Administration) issues you a walkie-talkie with a microphone that clips onto your sleeve and a speaker that attaches to your ear, just like the ones used by the Secret Service.

Risks/drawbacks: Taking an errant assassination bullet.

Overview

It is not uncommon to see advance people still working in their fifties or sixties—some of whom have been coordinating trips and events for U.S. presidents dating back to Kennedy. This is a cool job, which you can continue to do, on and off, as long as you want. Given the short institutional memory of campaigns and presidential administrations, there is always a need for experienced advance people to

coordinate the sensitive details surrounding White House trips. Once you're in, it's a great gig. You get to go drinking with Secret Service agents. You travel in style all over the world, arrange meetings with heads of state, gain access to places you would never see as a tourist, and get treated like royalty everywhere you go.

The main point of advance is to spend a week of intense work, behind the scenes, to craft an event that conveys a desired visual message on television. "With advance work today, each night you're producing a thirty-second campaign commercial. What you do appears on the nightly news. The way that event goes could affect the outcome of the election," says advance man Paul Giorgio. "If you want to send a message that your candidate is strong on defense, you do an event at a defense plant. If you want to show concern about the elderly, you do an event at a nursing home. You're creating a picture and hoping that the picture ends up on television that night.

This means working with the "principal," as the candidate is called, and understanding how to manipulate the press for the campaign's ends. Wherever Dukakis went on the campaign, for example, his advance people put a six-inch riser (known throughout the campaign as the "runt ramp") behind the podium to compensate for the governor's diminutive stature. The famous

Credit: AP/Worldwide

A picture is worth a few million votes. This famous image of diminutive presidential hopeful Michael Dukakis was widely ridiculed and did irreparable damage to his campaign.

picture of the nerdy-looking Dukakis in a tank is a classic example of bad advance, and contributed to his landslide defeat. "That's the lasting image of that campaign. They still talk about that picture," says Giorgio.

As an advance person, you become privy to the amazing world that exists behind the scenes whenever the president or vice president goes anywhere outside Washington. Starting a week or so prior to an event, hundreds of people are mobilized to coordinate even the shortest trips: At every stop, there are Secret Service people with bomb-sniffing dogs, WHCA technicians with an eighteen-wheel rig containing satellite dishes and communications equipment sufficient to launch a nuclear war, batteries of press and aides, not to mention the politicians and officials of the organizations involved in hosting their special guest. When Al Gore's daughter, Karenna, graduated from Harvard college, for example, the Veep's bare-bones traveling entourage occupied thirty hotel rooms.

There are lots of exciting perks in this line of work, but foreign trips are the pinnacle. "If you're a tourist in Moscow, everything is in Russian. It can be sort of a dreary experience," explains Ron Goldstein, who has advanced dozens of politicians. "But when we landed, we were part of the White House entourage. What that means is that you don't have to deal with cabs. You don't have to deal with street signs. You don't have to deal with anything." Whenever you travel, you have at your disposal all the resources of the richest country in the world. You'll get issued a special State Department passport during the trip. You'll get an interpreter assigned to you. And as a representative of the White House, you'll get red carpet treatment everywhere. "In Moscow, they open up the Kremlin for you and give you a private tour. I got a private tour of the King's Palace in Morocco when I was there. I was a private guest of King Hussein in Jordan," says Goldstein. "Between our government and their government, they just throw everything open for you."

Practical Information

The catch-22 is that the White House, as well as major campaigns, does not want to entrust the details of high-profile trips to inexperienced advance people. Starting out, the best approach is to get hooked up as a volunteer with an advance team working in your area. You can do this by contacting your local branch of the Democratic National Committee or Republican National Committee, or local campaign offices. Inquire with these organizations about upcoming trips and events. Often this will mean volunteering as an unpaid driver for an auxiliary vehicle shuttling press or aides from the airport to the event. On these trips, try to get involved in the meat of the advance work by piggybacking onto the projects of the main team members.

Advance teams are broken down by function, and you should pick a specialty. Start with the easiest, least competitive functions, like "motorcade." Ron Goldstein, a veteran advance person explains:

Interview with Ron Goldstein, White House advance veteran

Ron Goldstein is an advance expert, currently making his living doing private-sector advance for corporate clients (he is now working for the steel industry).

On getting slotted for foreign trips: "You have to pay your dues. You have to work the tank towns, not just the San Francisco, the New York, and the L.A. gigs. If you work in the middle of the country and a lot of other places—the mill towns, real America—and pay your dues for the president and the vice president, and then they'll reward you with a foreign trip. I was asked to go on my first foreign trip and it was very addictive. It has a lot to do with campaigning for it, too. You have to call the [White House Scheduling and Advance] office and use the office just right. You can't call them too much and you can't call them too little either."

His experience at Nelson Mandela's inauguration: "I was hanging out with Ron Brown and Jesse Jackson, and we were just gawking at the room we were in. If you turned to your left there was Boutros Boutros-Ghali, on your right was Prince Philip, in front of you was Fidel Castro and Yasir Arafat. All the world leaders were collected in this one room. I had my camera and I couldn't stop taking pictures. Ron Brown was even taking pictures. Jesse Jackson and I kept looking at each other and saying, 'My God, isn't this incredible?' Even though Jesse Jackson may be the highest civil rights leader in the United States, he was just so humbled, almost on an even par with someone like me, an advance person."

On "rolling": "There's a lot of jockeying going on with all this planning for politicians. Rolling is when one party suddenly throws a curveball into the schedule. For instance, if the host on the ground is a congressman, the congressman may not tell you that he's gonna grab the vice president's hand and lead him into a room full of his friends and supporters. This helps him but not you. If he's savvy, he won't tell you because he knows you'll say, 'No dice, no time, we're not doin' that.' So at the last second, the congressman may just do it anyway. Next thing you know, the vice president is stuck in a room being friendly to these people, and he can't get out. Meanwhile, there are people waiting somewhere else to meet him. So you have to be prepared and resourceful. We have a saying, 'Those who roll last, roll best.' You make sure that when someone rolls you, you roll them back, and you're the last one to do the rolling."

"In the pecking order, you have 'lead,' you have 'site,' you have 'press,' and you have motorcade. Motorcade is the lowest rung. It's the people who are newest. They don't trust them to do the site and the press. They trust them to do the cars." Once you do a competent job and learn the routine, and know whose ass to kiss for future trips, it's relatively easy to migrate to other positions.

Getting assigned to foreign trips is a separate challenge. According to an official in the White House Advance Office, foreign trips are a treat for people who pay their dues. "This is a little reward for the people who do the shitty trips to Cleveland, Garfield Heights, and Fresno," he said. "After people have been doing these for awhile, we'll send them to Japan or something like that."

Keeping on the active roster of advance—and getting slotted for the intensely competitive foreign trips—requires a certain amount of jockeying, especially inside the Beltway.

"You've never been rolled until you've been rolled by the Vatican," said Paul Giorgio, who has been advancing politicians since 1972. (For what it means to get rolled, see the sidebar on jargon.)

The power can get a little heady, but it's vital to remember that you're just an expendable foot soldier. If you're really lucky, you might get a chance to exchange a few words of small talk with the president or vice president, but they're not going to ask your opinion on what to do at the next G-7 summit. This reality is lost on many advance people, who mistake proximity to power with power itself.

Start by sending a resume to the Office of Scheduling and Advance for the White House. For the president: 202-456-1606. For the vice president: 202-456-2461.

Advance Jargon

Blue Goose: The podium that the president and vice president speak from; several exist and are shipped around the country in special metal boxes, along with the White House seals.

Bubble: The secure space the Secret Service maintains around the president or vice president. This often creates a conflict between the president's protectors and his handlers. "Their job is to have him in a bubble. Our job is to let him have access," says Goldstein.

Burn bag: Bag used for keeping sensitive papers, which are shredded daily during a trip.

Football: The suitcase-like apparatus with the controls for launching nuclear weapons, handcuffed to a military aide and always kept near the president (and vice president).

Getting rolled: When the host of an event the president or vice president is attending makes sudden, undesirable changes to the schedule.

Secure package: The core of the president or vice president's motorcade consisting of his bullet-proof limousine and several heavily-armed Chevy Suburbans, which can be detached from the rest of the motorcade in an emergency.

POTUS: President of the United States. Also VPOTUS, FLOTUS, and SLOTUS (vice president, first lady, second lady).

Wheels down: When *Air Force I* or *Air Force II* touches down; the beginning of a trip.

Wheels up party: Celebration among staff and security members once their duties are complete, after *AF I* or *AF II* is "wheels up."

NOTES

p. 4: "I've been stung...": *Bangor Daily News,* July 27, 1998.

p. 5: Bees increase food output: *Bangor Daily News,* July 27, 1998.

p. 7: "These animals are athletes...": Jan Golash as quoted in the *New York Times,* February 25, 1998.

p. 7: "I thought it was...": Dave Blasko as quoted in the *San Francisco Chronicle,* June 6, 1997.

p. 7: "Many of my clients...": Dr. Allen Schoen as quoted in the *New York Times,* February 25, 1996.

p. 8: "anything that works...": Carvel Tiekert as quoted in the *New York Times,* April 12, 1998.

p. 8: "Clients come here...": Dr. Allen Shoen as quoted in the *New York Times,* February 25, 1996.

p. 22: "I stepped to turn...": Kirk Guy as quoted in the *Las Vegas Review-Journal,* August 8, 1998.

p. 22: "One time, this bull...": Frank McIlvain as quoted in the *Dallas Morning News,* April 3, 1998.

p. 26: "Executive Outcomes is a business...": Bert Sachse as quoted in *Harper's,* February 1997.

p. 26: "consensus among government officials...": Defense Intelligence Agency as quoted in *The Nation,* July 28, 1997.

p. 26: "we also have principals...": an EO official as quoted in *Harper's,* February 1997.

p. 27: "We are not mercenaries...": a Vinnell employee as quoted in *The Progressive,* April 1996.

p. 28: "We're not going to get involved...": Eeben Barlow as quoted in *MacLean's,* November 6, 1995.

p. 30: Bounty hunters resembling SWAT teams: *CBS Sixty Minutes* report by Steve Croft, aired January 5, 1997.

p. 31: Information about NIBE: NIBE Website, www.bounty-hunter.net.

p. 32: Eleonora Florance's experience: "Earning It; Swallowing Bitter Pills for Pay: The Trials of Guinea Pigs," *New York Times,* September 29, 1996.

p. 32 "OK, if it comes back up again...": Mike Yeager as quoted by Ulysses Torassa in *The Plain Dealer,* May 10, 1998.

p. 32 "Doing these studies...": John Sanchez as quoted by David J. Morrow in "Earning It; Swallowing Bitter Pills for Pay: The Trials of Guinea Pigs," *New York Times,* September 29, 1996.

p. 33: "This is not something...": Christopher Hendy as quoted by Torsten Ove in "When Life's a Test of Pills: Medical Study Subjects Can Make More Cash Than by Flinging Fries...," *Pittsburgh Post-Gazette,* February 8, 1998.

p. 34–35: Death of student Hoi Yan: interview with Robert Helms, posted at http://members.aol.com/dirtzine/pig.htm.

p. 35: Selling kidneys: posted at http://transweb.org/qa/asktw/answers/answers9505/Sellingkidneysisillegal.html

p. 38: "Such places...": Jack Kerouac, journal entry at Desolation Peak, as quoted in *The Independent,* October 20, 1996.

p. 40: "I'm a very lucky...": John Crayton as quoted by Deborah Belgum in "Enormously Enjoyable Aviation," *Los Angeles Times,* May 19, 1996.

p. 41: "We fly low and slow...": Dominique Maniere as quoted by James V. O'Conner in "The Blimp That Calls Westchester Home," *New York Times,* October 22, 1995.

p. 41: Goodyear Blimp information: Goodyear's Website, http://www.goodyear.com/blimp/controls.html; http://www.goodyear.com/blimp/personnel.html

p. 41: Bigfoot Crash: Robert McFadden, "Blimp Crash-Lands on Roof of a Building in Manhattan," *New York Times,* July 5, 1993.

p. 44: "I'm lucky...": Al Verly as quoted by Gary Massaro, "Voice of Copter Takes Listeners to Scene," *Rocky Mountain News,* November 16 1994.

p. 50: urinating passenger: WRAL-TV online, July 14, 1998, search.wral-tv.com/features/5onyourside.1998/0714-skyrage/

p. 50: "People just love to drink...": Studs Terkel, *Working* (Avon Books, 1972).

p. 52 "Airshow performers are pilots...": "Aerobatic Arizona," *Arizona Flyways,* January-February 1997.

p. 56: "It gets to where...": Circuit City employee as quoted by Allan Richter in "Uncovering Store Problems Using Undercover Shoppers," *Computer Retail Week,* July 24, 1995.

p. 56: "retailers need some way to evaluate...": Bruce Van Kleek as quoted by Jennifer Steinhauer, "The Undercover Shoppers," *New York Times,* February 4, 1998.

p. 56: "We try to evaluate...": Lea Kubas as quoted by Rosemary Frei, "Over the Counter, Undercover," *Canadian Business,* May 1997.

p. 57: "He ever so carefully hid...": Jim Jolly as quoted by Jennifer Steinhauer, The Undercover Shoppers," *New York Times,* February 4, 1998.

p. 57: "These people have stopwatches...": Carl Braunlich as quoted in "Mystery Guests Haunt Hotels," *Information Access Company,* May 1995.

p. 57: "I'm always afraid...": Candace Radar, as quoted in "Service with a Smile, or Else," *Baltimore Sun* August 21, 1997.

p. 68: "You get away with murder...": interview with Hedda Lettuce, hedda.com/interview.html

p. 70: "You're born naked...": Catherine Chermayeff, Jonathon David; Nan Richardson, *Drag Diaries* (San Francisco: Chronicle Books, 1995).

p. 70: Definition of drag: Catherine Chermayeff, Jonathon David; Nan Richardson, *Drag Diaries* (San Francisco: Chronicle Books, 1995).

p. 70: "just a way to give...": interview with Divine, blueperiod.com/Dreamland/DivineInterview.html

p. 70: "Drag queens are not...": "Drag Queen as Messiah," hedda.com/messiah.html

p. 70: "Keep on reinventing...": interview with Charlene Unger, October 6, 1998.

p. 72: "In this business...": Ellis Henican, "The Public Side of a Private Eye," *Newsday,* November 14, 1997.

p. 73: "He looked like death...": Tony Passanisi as quoted by Ken Garcia in "Sleuth Techs Sam Spades," *San Francisco Chronicle,* June 27, 1998.

p. 73: "Almost all companies...": Tom Wagner as quoted by John Rondy in "Do You Know Who You're Hiring?" *Small Business Times,* June, 1997.

p. 76: Joke and other information: John H. Richardson, "Stalkerazzi; Celebrity Photography," *Esquire,* January, 1998.

p. 82: "Ask to have your name...": Dennis E. Hensley, "Four Points in Ghostwriting Contracts," *Writer's Digest,* February 1998.

p. 82: "On any given week...": Jack Hitt, "The Writer Is Dead: But His Ghost is Thriving, *New York Times,* March 25, 1997.

p. 87: Male gay perfomers' earnings: interview with Phineas Narco, rame.net, 1997.

p. 88: "Girls make much more money...": "The Adult Movie FAQ," Usenet rec.arts.movies.erotica, http://www.rame.net/faq/ascii.

p. 88: "men are just props.": *Ottawa Citizen,* May 31, 1998.

p. 89: "Working in porn...": Reuters, May 5, 1998.

p. 89: "It has more to do...": "The Money Shot," *The New Yorker,* October 1995.

p. 103: Florida compensation for executioners: Michael Daly, "Executioner? Hey, a Job's a Job," *New York Daily News,* March 7, 1995.

p. 103: Nebraska compensation for executioners: Leslie Boellstorff, "Penal Chief Protects Executioner Identity," *Omaha World Herald,* August 31, 1994."

p. 103: New Jersey's compensation for execution technicians: Michael Norman, "Site of Executions Ready in Trenton," *New York Times,* August 21, 1983.

p. 103: Don Cabana reference: Jim Dwyer, "The Executioner's Burden: Job Scars the Soul, Says Former Warden," *New York Daily News,* June 14, 1997.

p. 104: Connecticut focusing on details: Lynne Tuohy, "Execution: Months of Planning for Final Minutes," *The Hartford Courant,* July 24, 1996.

p. 105: "They are not known...": Peter Matos as quoted by Lynne Tuohy in "Execution: Months of Planning for Final Minutes," *The Hartford Courant.*

p. 105: "We had some fringe...": Vernon Bradford as quoted in "Executioner Hired Through Newspaper Ad," U.P.I., January 26, 1984.

p. 111: "Satan sneaks up...": "Master Class," *Jane,* April 1998.

p. 111: "Stay out of the sun...": "Well in Hand; New Hand-Care Products," *Town & Country Monthly,* May 1997.

p. 111: "I start wearing...": "Winning Hands Need Care, Nothing Special," *The Plain Dealer,* February 13, 1997.

p. 112: "People are always...": "Well in Hand; New Hand-Care Products," *Town & Country Monthly,* May 1997.

p. 112: "You can take as many...": "Winning Hands Need Care, Nothing Special," *The Plain Dealer,* February 13, 1997.

p. 117: "Right now...": Beth Daley, "Infectious Chic," *Boston Globe,* March 2, 1997.

p. 117 :"Members of the young...": Paul Galloway, "Fat Joe and His Illustrated Pals," *Chicago Tribune,* April 1, 1997.

p. 117: "When I started...": Daniel Wattenberg, "A Parent's Guide to Body Piercing," *Forbes,* September 23, 1996.

p. 123: "If you do bad taxidermy...": Gary Lowry as quoted by Don Fraser in "Mounting a New Career: Ex-clerk Turns Taxidermy Hobby into Full-Time Dream Job," *Ottawa Citizen,* March 19, 1998.

p. 121: "Most people think...": Kory Kamps as quoted by Kris Radish in "Stuffing Hunters Full of Dreams; Taxidermist Isn't Alone on Store's Day," *Milwaukee Journal Sentinel,* March 30 1998.

p. 122: "a Texas deer...": Chris Streetman as quoted by Russel Tinsley in *Taxidermy Guide (*Stoeger Publishing Company, 1990).

p. 122: "I grew up in east New Orleans...": Kevin Haynes as quoted by Richard Boyd in *Duck Aficionado* Turns to Taxidermy," *Times-Picayune,* May 21, 1998.

p. 125: "Whenever I walk out..." Noella Charest-Papagno as quoted in *Techniques Magazine,* January 1998.

p. 142: "Has there ever been...": Joseph P. Kahn, "Summer's Hero: The Ice-cream Man Has Become an Icon of Summertime America," *Boston Globe,* August 11, 1992.

p. 143: "Over the years...": Omar Sillah as quoted by Jacqueline Salmon, "Serving up Good Humor," *Washington Post,* July 6, 1998.

p. 151: "Crosswords are...": Associated Press, October 31, 1998.

p. 153: "There is a famous...": John Mercer as quoted by Helen Jones in "Brand Specialists Laughing All the Way to the Bank," *Glasgow Herald,* January 3, 1998.

p. 154: "You can come up with fabulous names...": Art Medici as quoted by Dana S. Calvo in "It May Be the Name Game, but They're All Business," *New York Times.*

p. 154: "Finding the right name...": Bridgett Ruffel as quoted in "Brand Specialists Laughing All the Way to the Bank," *Glasgow Herald,* January 3, 1998.

p. 174, 176: Roy Rivenburg, "The Iceman Goeth," *Los Angeles Times,* March 2, 1994.

p. 176: "It's weird because,": Mrs. Epstein as quoted in *New York Observer.*

p. 190: "Cutting metal from high...": Doug Iseler, "Tales from the Front," *Water Engineering and Management,* April 1, 1997.

p. 196: Quotations of Ted Giannoulas and Matt Marlowe: Wayne McKnight, "Workout Comes with the Job," *Tampa Tribune,* June 12, 1998.

p. 196: Tommy Lasorda versus The Chicken: John Henderson: "The Chicken Is a Different Bird," *Denver Post,* August 31, 1998.

p. 197: Matt Marlow's story: Wayne McKnight, "You Can Call Him Ray...," *Tampa Tribune,* June 12, 1998.

p. 197-198: Mascot Mania, Inc.: Mark Hermann, "The Windup: This School Has a Liberal Dress Code," *New York Newsday,* October 12, 1997.

p. 212: "I love to hear my name...": Bob Gross as quoted in the *Chicago Tribune,* January 22, 1986.

p. 214: "To compete in this arena...": Beau Weaver, www.spokenword.com

p. 216: "On a demo tape...": Barbara Rosenblatt, *Back Stage,* July 17, 1998.

p. 220: "the nerves of a ER...": Dave Berger, "Hollyhock Bakery Matches Up the Delicious with the Beautiful," *Seattle Times,* July 14, 1998.

p. 222: "Somebody knocked...": Donald Wressel, as quoted by Pamela Parseghian in "Donald Wressell: Baking His Cakes and Eating Them Too," *Nations' Restaurant News,* January 20, 1997.

p. 225: "People don't realize...": Dena Kleiman, "Helping the Army March on Its Stomach Without Bicarb Breaks," *New York Times,* July 24, 1991.

p. 261: "The contrast...": Editorial, "Don't Kill the Messenger," *Auto Free Times,* September, 1998.

p. 262: Bike messenger patois: Michael Finkel, "Naked City," *Bicycling Magazine,* March 1997.

p. 262: Bike messenger slang: Editorial, "Don't Kill the Messenger," *Auto Free Times,* September, 1998.

INDEX